Rick Riolo, Trent McConaghy and Ekaterina Vladislavleva (Eds.)

Genetic Programming Theory and Practice VIII

Genetic and Evolutionary Computation

Series Editors

John R. Koza
Consulting Editor
Medical Informatics
Stanford University
Stanford, CA 94305-5479 USA
Email: john@johnkoza.com

For other titles published in this series, go to http://www.springer.com/series/6016

Rick Riolo • Trent McConaghy
Ekaterina Vladislavleva
Editors

Genetic Programming
Theory and Practice VIII

Foreword by Nic McPhee

 Springer

Editors
Dr. Rick Riolo
University of Michigan
Center for the Study of Complex
Systems
323 West Hall
Ann Arbor Michigan 48109
USA
rlriolo@umich.edu

Dr. Ekaterina Vladislavleva
University of Antwerp
Dept. Mathematics & Computer Science
Campus Middelheim
G.103
2020 Antwerpen
Belgium
katyavladislavleva@me.com

Dr. Trent McConaghy
Solido Design Automation, Inc.
102-116 Research Drive
S7N 3R3 Saskatoon
Saskatchewan
Canada
trent_mcconaghy@yahoo.com

ISSN 1566-7863
ISBN 978-1-4614-2719-3   ISBN 978-1-4419-7747-2 (eBook)
DOI 10.1007/978-1-4419-7747-2
Springer New York Dordrecht Heidelberg London

© Springer Science+Business Media, LLC 2011
Softcover reprint of the hardcover 1st edition 2011
All rights reserved. This work may not be translated or copied in whole or in part without the written
permission of the publisher (Springer Science+Business Media, LLC, 233 Spring Street, New York, NY
10013, USA), except for brief excerpts in connection with reviews or scholarly analysis. Use in connection with any form of information storage and retrieval, electronic adaptation, computer software, or by
similar or dissimilar methodology now known or hereafter developed is forbidden.
The use in this publication of trade names, trademarks, service marks, and similar terms, even if they are
not identified as such, is not to be taken as an expression of opinion as to whether or not they are subject
to proprietary rights.

Printed on acid-free paper

Springer is part of Springer Science+Business Media (www.springer.com)

Contents

Contributing Authors

Claus Aranha is a graduate student at the Graduate School of Frontier Sciences in the University of Tokyo, Japan (caranha@iba.t.u-tokyo.ac.jp).

Wolfgang Banzhaf is a professor at the Department of Computer Science at Memorial University of Newfoundland, St. John's, NL, Canada (banzhaf@mun.ca).

Steven Bergen is a graduate student in the Department of Computer Science, Brock University, St. Catharines, Ontario, Canada (sb04qv@brocku.ca).

Tom Caldwell is a database developer and member of the Computational Genetics Laboratory at Dartmouth College (tom.caldwell@dartmouth.edu).

Flor Castillo is a Lead Research Specialist in the Polyglycols, Surfactants, and Fluids group within Performance Products R&D organization of The Dow Chemical Company (facastillo@dow.com).

Brian Dyre is an Associate Professor of Experimental Psychology (Human Factors), a member of the Neuroscience Program, and the director of the Idaho Visual Performance Laboratory (IVPL) at the University of Idaho, USA (bdyre@uidaho.edu).

Jonathan Fisher is a computer programmer and member of the Computational Genetics Laboratory at Dartmouth College (jonathan.m.fisher@dartmouth.edu).

Simon Harding is a postdoctoral research fellow at the Department of Computer Science at Memorial University of Newfoundland, St. John's, NL, Canada (simonh@cs.mun.ca).

Robert B. Heckendorn is an Associate Professor of Computer Science and a member of the Bioinformatics and Computational Biology Program at the University of Idaho, USA (heckendo@uidaho.edu).

Malcolm Heywood is a Professor of Computer Science at Dalhousie University, Halifax, NS, Canada (mheywood@cs.dal.ca).

Douglas Hill is a computer programmer and member of the Computational Genetics Laboratory at Dartmouth College (Douglas.P.Hill@Dartmouth.edu).

Hitoshi Iba is a professor of Computer Science at the Graduate School of Engineering in the University of Tokyo, Japan (iba@iba.t.u-tokyo.ac.jp).

Arthur K. Kordon is a Data Mining and Modeling Leader in the Advanced Analytics Group within the Dow Business Services of The Dow Chemical Company (akordon@dow.com).

Michael F. Korns is Chief Technology Officer at Freeman Investment Management, Henderson, Nevada, USA (mkorns@korns.com).

Mark E. Kotanchek is Chief Technology Officer of Evolved Analytics, a data modeling consulting and systems company, USA/China (mark@evolved-analytics.com).

Roger Lew is a graduate student in the Neuroscience Program at the University of Idaho, USA (rogerlew@vandals.uidaho.edu).

Peter Lichodzijewski is a graduate student in the Faculty of Computer Science at Dalhousie University, Halifax, Nova Scotia, Canada (piotr@cs.dal.ca).

Hod Lipson is an Associate Professor in the school of Mechanical and Aerospace Engineering and the school of Computing and Information Science at Cornell University, Ithaca, NY, USA (hod.lipson@cornell.edu).

Trent McConaghy is co-founder and Chief Scientific Officer of Solido Design Automation Inc., which makes variation-aware IC design software for top-tier semiconductor firms. He is based in Vancouver, Canada. (trent_mcconaghy@yahoo.com).

Julian F. Miller is a lecturer in the Department of Electronics at the University of York, UK (jfm7@ohm.york.ac.uk).

Jason H. Moore is the Frank Lane Research Scholar in Computational Genetics and Associate Professor of Genetics at Dartmouth Medical School, USA (Jason.H.Moore@Dartmouth.edu).

Michael Orlov is a graduate student in Computer Science at Ben-Gurion University, Israel (orlovm@cs.bgu.ac.il).

Kristine Pattin is a Molecular and Cellular Biology graduate student and member of the Computational Genetics Laboratory at Dartmouth College (Kristine.A.Pattin@Dartmouth.edu).

Joshua L. Payne is a postdoctoral research fellow in the computational genetics laboratory at Dartmouth College (jpayne@uvm.edu).

Riccardo Poli is a Professor of Computer Science in the School of Computer Science and Electronic Engineering at the University of Essex, UK (rpoli@essex.ac.uk).

Rick Riolo is Director of the Computer Lab and Associate Research Scientist in the Center for the Study of Complex Systems at the University of Michigan, USA (rlriolo@umich.edu).

Brian J. Ross is a Professor of Computer Science at Brock University, St. Catharines, ON, Canada (bross@brocku.ca).

Michael Schmidt is a graduate student in computational biology at Cornell University, Ithaca, NY, USA (mds47@cornell.edu).

Moshe Sipper is a Professor of Computer Science at Ben-Gurion University, Israel (sipper@cs.bgu.ac.il).

Guido F. Smits is a Research and Development Leader in the New Products Group within the Core R&D Organization of the Dow Chemical Company, Belgium (gfsmits@dow.com).

Terence Soule is an Associate Professor of Computer Science, a member of the Bioinformatics and Computational Biology Program, and Director of the Neuroscience Program at the University of Idaho, USA (tsoule@cs.uidaho.edu).

Lee Spector is a Professor of Computer Science in the School of Cognitive Science at Hampshire College, Amherst, MA, USA (lspector@hampshire.edu).

Carlos Villa is a Senior Research Specialist in Polyurethanes Process Research within Performance Products R&D organization of The Dow Chemical Company (Cmvilla@dow.com).

Ekaterina Vladislavleva is a Lecturer in the Department of Mathematics and Computer Science at the University of Antwerp, Belgium (katya@vanillamodeling.com).

Preface

The work described in this book was first presented at the Eighth Workshop on Genetic Programming, Theory and Practice, organized by the Center for the Study of Complex Systems at the University of Michigan, Ann Arbor, May 20-22, 2010. The goal of this workshop series is to promote the exchange of research results and ideas between those who focus on Genetic Programming (GP) theory and those who focus on the application of GP to various real-world problems. In order to facilitate these interactions, the number of talks and participants was small and the time for discussion was large. Further, participants were asked to review each other's chapters *before* the workshop. Those reviewer comments, as well as discussion at the workshop, are reflected in the chapters presented in this book. Additional information about the workshop, addendums to chapters, and a site for continuing discussions by participants and by others can be found at http://cscs.umich.edu/gptp-workshops/ .

We thank all the workshop participants for making the workshop an exciting and productive three days. In particular we thank the authors, without whose hard work and creative talents, neither the workshop nor the book would be possible. We also thank our keynote speaker Jürgen Schmidhuber, Director of the Swiss Artificial Intelligence Lab IDSIA, Professor of Artificial Intelligence at the University of Lugano, Switzerland, Head of the CogBotLab at TU Munich, Germany, and Professor SUPSI, Switzerland. Jürgen's talk inspired a great deal of discussion among the participants throughout the workshop.

The workshop received support from these sources:

- The Center for the Study of Complex Systems (CSCS);

- John Koza, Third Millennium Venture Capital Limited;

- Michael Korns, Freeman Investment Management;

- Ying Becker, State Street Global Advisors, Boston, MA;

- Mark Kotanchek, Evolved Analytics;

- Jason Moore, Computational Genetics Laboratory at Dartmouth College;

- Conor Ryan, Biocomputing and Developmental Systems Group, Computer Science and Information Systems, University of Limerick; and

- William and Barbara Tozier, Vague Innovation LLC.

We thank all of our sponsors for their kind and generous support for the workshop and GP research in general.

A number of people made key contributions to running the workshop and assisting the attendees while they were in Ann Arbor. Foremost among them was Howard Oishi, who makes GPTP workshops run smoothly with his diligent efforts before, during and after the workshop itself. After the workshop, many people provided invaluable assistance in producing this book. Special thanks go to Philipp Cannnons who did a wonderful job working with the authors, editors and publishers to get the book completed very quickly. Jennifer Maurer and Melissa Fearon provided invaluable editorial efforts, from the initial plans for the book through its final publication. Thanks also to Springer for helping with various technical publishing issues.

RICK RIOLO, TRENT MCCONAGHY AND
EKATERINA (KATYA) VLADISLAVLEVA

Foreword

If politics is the art of the possible, research is surely the art of the soluble. Both are immensely practical-minded affairs. — Peter Medawar[1]

The annual Genetic Programming Theory and Practice (GPTP) is an important cross-fertilization event, bringing practitioners and theoreticians together in a small, focussed setting for several days. At larger conferences, parallel sessions force one to miss the great majority of the presentations, and it's not uncommon for a theoretician and a practitioner to have little more contact than a brief conversation at a coffee break. GPTP blows away any stereotypes suggesting that theoreticians neither care about nor understand the challenges practitioners face, or that practitioners are indifferent to theoretical work, considering it an ivory tower exercise of no real consequence. The mutual respect around the table is manifest, and many participants have made substantial contributions to both theory and practice over the years. As a result, the discussions and debate are open, inclusive, lively, rigorous, and often intense.

Despite the "Genetic Programming" in the title, GPTP has always been a showcase for problem solving techniques, without standing too much on the ceremony of names and labels. Many of the techniques and systems discussed this year have moved considerable distances from the standard s-expression GP of the early 90's, and more and more hybrid systems are bringing together powerful tools from across evolutionary computation, machine learning, and statistics, often incorporating sophisticated domain knowledge as well.

The creativity of our community, however, creates a plethora of challenges for those who wish to provide a theoretical understanding of these techniques and their dynamics, and evolutionary computation and GP work have long been dogged by a gap between the racing front of practical exploration and the rather more stately pace of theoretical understanding. Given that mismatch, events like GPTP become even more important, providing valuable opportunities for the community to take stock of the current state-of-play, identifying gaps, opportunities, and connections that have the potential to shape and inform work for years to come.

This year's papers continue to press many of the Hard Problems of the field. A number explore multi-objective evolutionary systems, co-evolution, and various types of modularity, hierarchy, and population structure, all with the goal of finding solutions to complex, structured, and often epistatic, problems. A

---

[1] Review of Arthur Koestler's *The Act of Creation*, in the New Statesman, 19 June 1964.

constant challenge is finding effective representations, and many of the representations here don't look much like a traditional tree-based GP. Similarly, configuration and parameter settings are a consistent burr, and this year's work includes approaches that evolve this information, and approaches that dynamically set these values as a deterministic function of the current state. Application domains range widely through areas such as finance, industrial systems modeling, biology and medicine, games, art, and music; many, however, could still be described as forms of regression or classification, a vein that I suspect people will continue to mine successfully for years to come. A thread running through almost all the applications, in some cases more explicitly than others, is the importance of identifying and incorporating important domain knowledge, and it seems clear that few folks are tackling really tough problems without including the best domain knowledge they can lay their hands on. Another important trend is the continued conversion of GP into an increasingly off-the-shelf tool, what Rick Riolo and Bill Tozier might call the transition from an art to a craft. Several participants are building systems with the express goal of making high quality GP tools available to non-programmers, people with problems to solve but who aren't interested in (or able to) implement a state-of-the-art evolutionary algorithm themselves.

One of the great values in participating in this sort of workshop is the conversation and discussion, both during the presentations and in the halls. Perhaps the biggest "buzz" this year was about the increased computation power being made available through cluster and cloud computing, multiple cores, and the massive parallelism of graphic processing units (GPUs). This topic came up in several papers, and was discussed with both excitement and skepticism throughout the workshop. EC, along with most machine learning and artificial intelligence work, is a processor hungry business and one that parallelizes and distributes in fairly natural ways. This makes the increasing availability of large number of low-cost processing units, whether through physical devices or out on the Internet, very exciting. It wasn't that long ago when population sizes were often 100 or less. These would now be considered small in many contexts, with population sizes routinely being several orders of magnitude larger. GPUs and cloud computing, however, make it possible to reasonably process populations of millions of individuals today, and no doubt many more in the next few years.

This has enormous potential impact for both practice and theory in the field. People often comment on the fact that in the next few decades we'll likely have computers (or clusters of computers) with computational power comparable to that of the human brain. This also gives us the ability run much more complex evolutionary systems, effectively simulating much richer evolutionary processes in more complex environments. Many have commented over the years that to see the true potential of evolutionary algorithms we need to place them in more complex environments, and this came up again in this year's GPTP discussions. If we only present our systems with simple problems, or problems with easily discovered local optima, we shouldn't be surprised if their behaviors are often disappointingly simple. One of the reasons for this simplicity has all too often been the limit on available computing power. The continued growth in computing capacity make it possible to run much richer systems and tackle more challenging problems, shedding light in exciting new places.

These changes may have strong implications on the theory side as well. Many theoretical results (such as those from schema theory and many statistical techniques) require infinite population assumptions, for example. While many of the predictions of these theories have been shown to hold for finite populations, sampling effects have often led to significant variances especially for small populations, and many researchers have been skeptical of the practical value of results built on infinite population assumptions. If we reach a point where we're routinely using population sizes in the millions, then while there will surely be issues of sampling, these will likely be profoundly different than those seen with populations of hundreds.

More generally, as population sizes grow, it will become increasingly important to develop and extend theoretical techniques that process individuals in aggregate. Even if we could theoretically characterize each individual in a population of millions, to do so would likely be useless as we would drown in the data. We will instead need ways to characterize the broader properties of the population, probably using tools like statistical distributions and coarse graining.

Another subject of considerable discussion throughout the workshop was that of "selling" GP in particular and evolutionary systems in general. Despite the substantial and growing evidence of GP's ability as a powerful problem solving tool, many remain skeptical. Sometimes this is because people are naturally nervous about the unknown, but caution is certainly warranted when there is a great deal at stake, such as people's lives or millions of dollars. One traditional way to address this is to try to focus on the evolution of "understandable" solutions so one can offer the ideas embedded in a comprehensible solution instead of trying to pitch a black box that no one understands. Several of this year's participants were avoiding the difficulty of selling GP by simply sidestepping it. They bundle GP as part of a complex set of tools that collectively address the customer's problem, and find that in that setting the customer is often less concerned with the technical details of each component.

I'm in a privileged position in that I rarely have to "sell" my work and so don't have to face these issues, which I understand are very real. I must say, however, that I found it somewhat disheartening to hear so many people talk about obscuring the evolutionary component of their systems. Evolution is an incredibly powerful concept, but one that is all too little understood by the general public (especially in the United States). As an educator and evolutionary enthusiast, I see evolutionary computation as a great opportunity to help people understand that evolution is real, an idea that not only led to the amazing diversity of life on Earth, but which can also be harnessed in silico to solve tough problems and explore important new areas. To veil its use and successes seems, to me, to be a lost opportunity on many levels. Not surprisingly, however, there are no simple answers, and the conversations on all of these ideas and issues will continue well into the future, fueled and re-energized by events such as GPTP.

None of this would be possible, of course, without the hard work of the folks at the University of Michigan Center for the Study of Complex Systems (CSCS), who organize and host the gathering each year. Particular thanks go to CSCS's Howard Oishi for his administrative organization and support, and to the organizing committee and editors of this volume: Rick Riolo (CSCS), Trent McConaghy (Solido Design Automation), and Katya Vladislavleva (University of Antwerp). Like all such events, GPTP costs money and we greatly appreciate the generous contributions of Third Millennium; State Street Global Advisors (SSgA); Michael Korns, Investment Science Corporation (ISC); the Computational Genetics Laboratory at Dartmouth College; Evolved Analytics; the Biocomputing and Developmental Systems Group, CSIS, the University of Limerick; and William and Barbara Tozier of Vague Innovation LLC.

All that work and those donations made it possible for a group of bright, enthusiastic folks to get together to share and push and stretch. This volume contains one form of their collective effort, and it's a valuable one. Read on, and be prepared to take a few notes along the way.

Nic McPhee, Professor
Division of Science and Mathematics
University of Minnesota, Morris
Morris, MN, USA
July, 2010

Genetic Programming Theory and Practice 2010: An Introduction

Trent McConaghy[1], Ekaterina Vladislavleva[2], and Rick Riolo[3]

[1]*Solido Design Automation Inc., Canada;* [2]*Department of Mathematics and Computer Science, University of Antwerp, Antwerp, Belgium;* [3]*Center for Study of Complex Systems, University of Michigan.*

Abstract   The toy problems are long gone, real applications are standard, and the systems have arrived. Genetic programming (GP) researchers have been designing and exploiting advances in theory, algorithm design, and computing power to the point where (traditionally) hard problems are the norm. As GP is being deployed in more real-world and hard problems, GP research goals are evolving to a higher level, to *systems* in which GP algorithms play a key role. The key goals in GP algorithm design are reasonable resource usage, high-quality results, and reliable convergence. To these GP algorithm goals, we add GP system goals: ease of system integration, end-user friendliness, and user control of the problem and interactivity. In this book, expert GP researchers demonstrate how they have been achieving and improving upon the key GP algorithm *and* system aims, to realize them on real-world / hard problems. This work was presented at the GP Theory and Practice (GPTP) 2010 worshop. This introductory chapter summarizes how these experts' work is driving the frontiers of GP algorithms and GP systems in their application to ever-harder application domains.

Keywords: genetic programming, evolutionary computation

1.   The Workshop

In May 2010 the Center of Studies of Complex Systems at the University of Michigan – with deep historical roots in evolutionary computation tracing back to Holland's seminal work – opened its doors for the invitees of the workshop on Genetic Programming in Theory and Practice 2010. Over twenty experienced and internationally distinguished GP researchers gathered in Ann Arbor to close themselves in one room for two and a half days, present their newest (and often controversial) work to the critical attention of their peers, discuss the challenges of genetic programming, search for common traits in the field's development, get a better understanding of the global state-of-the-art and share the vision on the "next big things" in GP theory and practice.

The atmosphere at the workshop has always been enjoyable, with every participant trying to get a deep understanding of presented work, provide constructive comments on it, suggest links to the relevant topics in the broad field of computing, and question generality, scalability of the approach. The workshop fosters a friendly atmosphere wherein inquiring minds are genuinely trying to understand not only what they collectively know or can do with GP, but also what they collectively do not yet know or cannot yet do with GP. The latter understanding is a major driving force for further developments that we have observed in all workshops.

We are grateful to all sponsors and acknowledge the importance of their contributions to such an intellectually productive and regular event. The workshop is generously founded and sponsored by the University of Michigan Center for the Study of Complex Systems (CSCS) and receives further funding from the following people and or organizations: Michael Korns of Freeman Investment Management, State Street Global Advisors, Third Millenium, Bill and Barbara Tozier of Vague Innovation, Evolved Analytics, the Computational Genetics Laboratory of Dartmouth College and the Biocomputing and Developmental Systems Group of the University of Limerick.

We also thank Jürgen Schmidhuber for an enlightening and provocative keynote speech, which covered his thoughts on what makes a scientific field mature, a review of his work in solving difficult real-world problems in pragmatic ways, and his theoretical work in GP- and non-GP-based program induction.

2.   Summary of Progress

Last year, GPTP 2009 marked a transition wherein the aims of GP algorithms – reasonable *resource* usage, high *results* quality, and *reliable* convergence – were being consistently realized on an impressive variety of "real-world" *applications* by skilled practitioners in the field. This year, for GPTP 2010, researchers have begun to aim for the next level: for *systems* where GP algorithms play a key role. This was evident by the record number of GPTP demos, and by a renewed emphasis on system usability and user control. Also reflecting this transition, discsussions had a marked unity and depth of questions on the philosophy and future of GP, on the need to re-think the algorithms and re-design systems to solve conceptually harder problems.

This chapter is organized accordingly. After a brief introduction to GP, Section 4 describes goals for design of GP algorithms and systems. Then the contributions of this volume (from the workshop) are summarized from two complementary perspectives: section 5 describes the "best practice" techniques that GP practitioners have invented and deployed to achieve the GP algorithm and system aims (including the improvements of GPTP 2010), and section 6 describes the application domains in which success through best practices has been reported. We conclude with a discussion of observations that emerged from the workshop, challenges that remain and potential avenues of future work.

To make the results of the workshop useful to even a relative novice in the field of GP, we first provide a brief overview of GP.

3.   A Brief Introduction to Genetic Programming[2]

Genetic programming is a search and optimization technique for executable expressions that is modeled on natural evolution. Natural evolution is a powerful process that can be described by a few central, general mechanisms; for an introduction, see (Futuyma, 2009). A population is composed of organisms which can be distinguished in terms of how fit they are with respect to their environment. Over time, members of the population breed in frequency proportional to their fitness. The new offspring inherit the combined genetic material of their parents with some random variation, and may replace existing members of the population. The entire process is iterative, adaptive and open ended. GP and other evolutionary algorithms typically realize this central description of evolution, albeit in somewhat abstract forms. GP is a set of algorithms that mimic of survival of the fittest, genetic inheritance and variation, and that iterate over a "parent" population, selectively "breeding" them and replacing them with offspring.

Though in general evolution does not have a problem solving goal, GP is nonetheless used to solve problems arising in diverse domains ranging from engineering to art. This is accomplished by casting the organism in the population as a candidate program-like solution to the chosen problem. The organism is represented as a computationally executable expression (aka structure), which is considered its genome. When the expression is executed on some supplied set of inputs, it generates an output (and possibly some intermediate results). This execution behavior is akin to the natural phenotype. By comparing the expression's output to target outputs, a measure of the solution's quality is obtained. This is used as the "fitness" of an expression. The fact that the candidate solutions are computationally executable structures (expressions), not binary or continuous coded values which are elements of a solution, is what distinguishes GP from other evolutionary algorithms (O'Reilly and Angeline, 1997).

GP expressions include LISP functions (Koza, 1992; Wu and Banzhaf, 1998), stack or register based programs (Kantschik and Banzhaf, 2002; Spector and Robinson, 2002a), graphs (Miller and Harding, 2008; Mattiussi and Floreano, 2007; Poli, 1997), programs derived from grammars (Gruau, 1993; Whigham, 1995; O'Neill and Ryan, 2003), and generative representations which evolve the grammar itself (Hemberg, 2001; Hornby and Pollack, 2002; O'Reilly and Hemberg, 2007). Key steps in applying GP to a specific problem collectively define its search space: the problem's candidate solutions are designed by choosing a representation; variation operators (mutation and crossover) are selected (or specialized); and a fitness function (objectives and

---

[2] Adapted from (O'Reilly et al., 2009).

constraints) which expresses the relative merits of partial and complete solutions is formulated.

For a more detailed overview we refer the reader to the book (Poli et al., 2008), which is available for free online.

4.   GP Challenges and Goals

In the early days of GP, the challenge was simply to "make it work" on small problems. As the field of GP research has matured, to be able to solve challenging real-world problems GP experts have strived to improve GP *algorithms* in terms of efficient computational *resource* usage, ensuring better quality *results*, and attaining more *reliable* convergence. With the maturation of "best practice" approaches, researchers are starting to create whole *systems* using GP which present its own challenges: ease of system integration, end-user friendliness, user control of the problem (perhaps interactively). This section elaborates on these GP algorithm and system goals and challenges.

GP Algorithm Goals and Challenges

A successful GP algorithm has at least the following attributes.

Efficent Use of Computational Resources includes shorter runtime, reduced usage of processor(s), and reduced memory and disk usage, for a given result. Achieving efficent use of computer resources has traditionally been a major issue for GP. A key reason is that GP search spaces are astronomically large, multi-modal, epistatic (e.g., variable interactions), have poor locality[3], and other nonlinearities. To handle such challenging search spaces, significant exploration is needed (e.g. large population sizes). This entails intensive processing and memory needs. Exacerbating the problem, fitness evaluations (objectives and constraints) of real-world problems tend to be expensive. Finally, because GP expressions have variable length, there is a tendency for them to "bloat"— to grow rapidly without a corresponding increase in performance (*cf.* Poli's Chapter 5 in this book). Bloat can be a significant drain on available memory and CPU resources.

Ensuring Quality Results. The key question is: "can a GP result *be used* in the target application?" This may be more difficult to attain than evident at first glance because the result may need to be human-interpretable, trustworthy, or predictive on dramatically different inputs— attaining such qualities can be

---

[3] Poor locality means that a small change in the individual's genotype often leads to large changes in the fitness and introducing additional difficulty into the search effort. For example, the GP "crossover" operation of swapping the subtrees of two parents might change the comparison of two elements from a "less than" relationship to an "equal to" relationship. This usually gives dramatically different behavior and fitness.

challenging. Ensuring quality results has always been perceived as an issue, but the goal is becoming more prominent as GP is being applied to more real world problems. Practitioners, not GP, are responsible for deploying a GP result in their application domain. This means that the practitioner (and potentially their client) must trust the result sufficiently to be comfortable using it. Human-interpretability (readability) of the result is a key factor in trust. This can be an issue when deployment of the result is expensive or risky, when customers' understanding of the solution is crucial; when the result must be inspected or approved; or to gain acceptance of GP methodology.

Reliable convergence means that the GP run can be trusted to return reasonable, useful results, without the practitioner having to worry about premature convergence or whether algorithm parameters like population size were set correctly. GP can fail to capably identify sub-solutions or partially correct solutions and successfully promote, combine and reuse them to generate good solutions with effective structure. The default approach has been to use the largest population size possible, subject to time and resource constraints. This invariably implies high resource usage, and still gives no guarantee of hitting useful results even if such results exist. Alternative approaches to increase the number of iterations with smaller population sizes still lack robust scenarios for computing resource allocation.

Goals for GP Incorporated in larger Systems

These are necessary attributes of GP for successful "GP systems," i.e., systems in which GP plays a key role[4]. A successful GP system must no doubt have many other attributes particular to the context in which it is deployed, but each of the following factors certainly have high impact on the system's success.

Ease of system integration is how easy the GP algorithm is to deploy as part of the entire system, by the person or a team building the system. Even if a GP algorithm does well on the algorithm challenges, its may be hard for system integrators (or other researchers) to deploy because of high complexity or many parameters. Simple algorithms with few parameters are worth striving for; and if this is not possible, then readily available software with simple application programming interfaces and good documentation is a reasonable solution.

End-user friendliness is the end-user's perspective of how easy the system is to use when solving the problem at hand, when GP is only a subcomponent of the overall system. The user wants to solve a problem economically, with

---

[4]GP may not even be the centerpiece of the system—that's fine!

quality results, reliably. The user task should be smooth and efficient, not tedious and time consuming.

User (Interactive) Control of the Problem. The system (and its subsystems) should not be solving a problem any harder than it needs to be, especially when it makes a qualitative difference to resource usage, result quality, or convergence. To meet this goal, users should be able to specify problems to be solved with as much resolution as appropriate. In some cases, this also means interactivity with results so far, to further guide exploration according to the user's needs, intuitions or subjective tastes. And it specifically does *not* mean user-level control of the GP algorithm itself: the end-user should not have to be a GP expert to use GP to solve a problem, just as GP experts do not have to be experts on electronics in order to use computers.

For more book-length texts on applying GP to industrial problems, we refer the reader to recent books on the subject – by GPTP participants themselves: (Kordon, 2009), (Iba et al., 2010), and (McConaghy et al., 2009).

5.   GP Best Practices

First, we describe general best practices that GP practitioners use to achieve GP algorithm goals. Then, we review advances made at GPTP 2010 toward attaining those GP algorithm goals, followed a review of GPTP 2010 work that addresses GP system goals.

In general, GP computational resource use has been made more efficient by improved algorithm design, improved design of representation and operators in specific domains. The importance of high demands of GP for computational resources has been lessened by Moore's Law and increasing availability of parallel computational approaches, meaning that computational resources become exponentially cheaper over time. Results quality has improved for the same reasons. It is also due to a new emphasis by GP practitioners on getting interpretable or trustworthy results. Reliability has been enhanced via algorithm techniques that support continuous evolutionary improvement through a systematic or structured fashion, so that the practitioner no longer has to "hope" that the algorithm isn't stuck. Implicit or explicit diversity maintenance also helps. Finally, thoughtful design of expression representation and genetic operators, for general and specific problem domains, has led to GP systems achieving human-competitive performance. Techniques along these lines include evolvability, self-adaptiveness, modularity and bloat control.

At GPTP 2010, the following papers demonstrated advances in GP algorithm aims (efficient computational resource usage, results quality, or reliable convergence):

- Poli (Chapter 5) draws on recently developed theory to construct a very simple technique that manages bloat.

- Harding *et al.* (Chapter 6) and Spector (Chapter 2) illuminate the state of the art in using self-modifying individuals to achieve highly scalable GP.

- Pattin, Moore *et al.* (Chapter 12) also uses self-adaptation and demonstrates how to incorporate expert knowledge in novel ways, for highly scalable GP.

- Lichodzijewski and Heywood (Chapter 3) and Soule *et al.* (Chapter 4) make further advances in GP scalability through evolution of teams.

- Orlov and Sipper (Chapter 1) is an excellent example of best-practice operator design to maintain evolvability in a highly constrained space.

- Smits *et al.* (Chapter 9) points towards evolution in the "compute cloud," by exploring massively parallel evolution.

- Iba and Aranha (Chapter 13) exploits the structure of the resource-allocation problem in operator and algorithm design to improve GP scalability and results quality.

- Bergen and Ross (Chapter 14) explores how to handle problems with ≫2 objectives yet maintain convergence.

- Korns (Chapter 7) and McConaghy (Chapter 10) aggressively transform and simplify their respective problems for GP as much as possible, to greatly reduce GP resource needs.

At GPTP 2010, the following papers demonstrated advances in GP system goals (system-integrator usability, user-level usability, or user control of the problem and interactivity).

For system integrator usability: Schmidt and Lipson (Chapter 8) shows an approach that achieves the reliable convergence of the popular ALPS algorithm (Hornby, 2006), but with a simpler algorithm having fewer parameters. Harding *et al.* and Spector (Chapter 2) are also examples of relatively simple algorithms, algorithms that have been simplified over the years as their designers gained experience with them. In his keynote address, Jürgen Schmidhuber described the achievement of best-in-class results using simple backpropagation neural networks but with modern computational resources.

For user-level usability: Castillo *et al.* (Chapter 11) prescribes a flow for industrial modeling people where they can use GP as part of their overall *manual* flow in developing trustworthy industrial models. In the special demos session, many researchers presented highly usable GP systems, including Kotanchek's DataModeler (symbolic regression and data analysis package for Mathematica), Schmidt and Lipson's Eureqa (symbolic regression), Bergen and Ross's Jnetic Textures (art), and Iba and Aranha's CACIE (music).

For user control of the problem / interactivity: Korns (Chapter 7) describes an SQL-style language to specify symbolic regression problems, so that function search only changes subsections of the overall expression. Bergen and Ross (Chapter 14) and Iba and Aranha (Chapter 13) describe systems that emphasize usability in interactive design of art and music, respectively.

What is equally significant in these papers is that which is not mentioned or barely mentioned: GP algorithm goals that have already been solved sufficiently for particular problem domains, allowing researchers to focus their work on the more challenging issues. For example, there are several papers that do some form of symbolic regression (SR), which historically has had major issues with interpretability or bloat. Yet in these pages, the SR papers barely discuss interpretability or bloat, because best practices avoid the issue in one or more ways, most notably: pareto optimization using an extra objective of minimizing complexity, templated functional forms like McConaghy's CAFFEINE or Korns' abstract expressions or simply using the GP system to generate promising subexpressions in a manual modeling flow. Other off-the-shelf techniques that solve specific problems well have been around for years and are being increasingly adopted by the GPTP community. These include grammars to restrict program evolution (Whigham, 1995; O'Neill and Ryan, 2003), competent algorithms to handle multiple objectives and/or constraints e.g. (Deb et al., 2002), and meta-algorithms providing diversity and continuous improvement like ALPS (Hornby, 2006). Finally, significant compute resources are available to most: in an informal survey at the workshop, we found that most groups use a compute cluster, and two groups are already using "the compute cloud."

6.   Application Successes Via Best Practices

One of the fascinating aspects of GP research is that GP is so general, i.e. "search through a space of (program or structure) entities," that it can be used to attack an enormous variety of problems, including many problems that are currently unapproachable by any other technique. This year's batch of applications is no exception. This section briefly reviews the applications.

One of the long-standing aims of AI, and GP, has been evolution of software in the most general sense possible. GPTP this year was fortunate to have three groups present work directly on this. Orlov and Sipper (Chapter 1) present FINCH, a system to evolve Java bytecode, an evolutionary substrate that has evolvability close to machine code, yet returns interpretable Java code thanks to industry-standard bytecode decompilers. Spector (Chapter 2) presents an autoconstructive version of PUSH, a GP system which evolves stack-based programs. Finally, Harding *et al.* (Chapter 6) presents a self-modifying Cartesian GP which evolves graphs that can be interpreted as software, circuits, equations, and more.

Two chapters introduce wholly new problems for GP. McConaghy (Chapter 10) introduces the problem of building density models at a distribution's tails (and dusts off the general problem of symbolic density modeling), for the application of SRAM memory circuit analysis. Lichodzijewski and Heywood

(Chapter 3) introduce the problem of solving a Rubik's cube with GP, taking the perspective of temporal sequence learning.

GP continues to help the artistic types. Bergen and Ross (Chapter 14) describe a sophisticated interactive system for interactive evolutionary art, and Iba and Aranha (Chapter 13) describe an advanced system for interactive evolutionary music. Both systems have been already used extensively by artists and musicians.

In a biology application, Pattin, Moore *et al.* (Chapter 12) describe the use of GP for disease susceptibility modeling.

GP remains popular in financial applications. Korns (Chapter 7) ups the ante on a set of symbolic regression and classification problems that are representative of financial modeling problems to aid stock-trading decisionmaking. Iba and Aranha (Chapter 13) describes a system for portfolio allocation.

For the problem of industrial modeling (e.g. of inferential sensors at Dow), Castillo *et al.* (Chapter 11) focuses on a structured approach to exploit GP results within industrial modelers' model development flows. Undoubtedly, the symbolic regression approach in Smits *et al.* (Chapter 9) will find end usage in Dow's industrial modeling environment as well.

Other approaches used standard problems in (symbolic) classification or regression as their test suites, though the emphasis was not the application. This includes work by Soule *et al.* (Chapter 4), Poli (Chapter 4), and Schmidt and Lipson (Chapter 8).

7. Themes, Summary and Looking Forward

The toy problems are gone; the GP systems have arrived. No doubt there will continue to be qualitative improvements to GP algorithms and GP systems for years to come. But is there more? We posit there is.

Despite these achievements, GP's computer-based evolution does not demonstrate the potential associated with natural evolution, nor does it always satisfactorily solve important problems we might hope to use it on. Even when using best practice approaches to manage challenges in resources, results, and reliability, the computational load may still be too excessive and the final results may still be inadequate. To achieve success in a difficult problem domain takes a great deal of human effort toward thoughtful design of representations and operators.

Many questions and challenges remain:

- What does it take to make GP a science? (Is this even a realistic question?) How can work on applications facilitate the continued development of a GP theory?

- What does it take to make GP a technology? (Is this even a realistic question?) What fundamental contributions will allow GP to be adopted into broader use beyond that of expert practitioners? For example, how can GP be scoped so that it becomes another standard, off-the-shelf method in the "toolboxes" of scientists and engineers around the world? Can GP follow in the same vein of linear programming? Can it follow the example of support vector machines and convex optimization methods? One challenge is in formulating the algorithm so that it provides more ease in laying out a problem. Another is determining how, by default – without parameter tuning, GP can efficiently exploit specified resources to return results reliably.

- How do we get 1 million people using GP? 1 billion? (Should they even know they're using GP?)

- Success with GP often requires extensive human effort in capturing and embedding the domain knowledge. How can this up-front human effort be reduced while still achieving excellent results? Are there additional automatic ways to capture domain knowledge for input to GP systems?

- Scalability is always relative. GP has attacked fairly large problems, but how can GP be improved to solve problems that are 10x, 100x, 1,000,000x harder?

- What opportunities await GP due to new computing architectures and substrates, with potentially vastly richer processing resources? This includes massively multicore processors, GPUs, and cloud computing; but it also includes digital microfluidics, modern programmable logic, and more.

- What opportunities await GP due to massive memory and storage capacity, coupled with giant databases? For example, this has already profoundly affected machine learning applied to speech recognition, not to mention web search. Massive and freely available databases are coming online, especially from biology.

- What "uncrackable" problems await a creative GP approach? The future has many challenges in energy, health care, defence, and more. For many fields, there are lists of "holy grail" problems, unsolved problems, even problems with prize money attached.

These questions and their answers will provide the fodder for future GPTP workshops. We wish you many hours of stimulating reading of this volume's contributions.

References

Deb, Kalyanmoy, Pratap, Amrit, Agarwal, Sameer, and Meyarivan, T. (2002). A fast and elitist multiobjective genetic algorithm: Nsga-ii. *IEEE Transactions on Evolutionary Computation*, 6:182–197.

Futuyma, Douglas (2009). *Evolution, Second Edition*. Sinauer Associates Inc.

Gruau, Frederic (1993). Cellular encoding as a graph grammar. *IEE Colloquium on Grammatical Inference: Theory, Applications and Alternatives*, (Digest No.092):17/1–10.

Hemberg, Martin (2001). GENR8 - A design tool for surface generation. Master's thesis, Department of Physical Resource Theory, Chalmers University, Sweden.

Hornby, Gregory S. (2006). ALPS: the age-layered population structure for reducing the problem of premature convergence. In Keijzer, Maarten, Cattolico, Mike, Arnold, Dirk, Babovic, Vladan, Blum, Christian, Bosman, Peter, Butz, Martin V., Coello Coello, Carlos, Dasgupta, Dipankar, Ficici, Sevan G., Foster, James, Hernandez-Aguirre, Arturo, Hornby, Greg, Lipson, Hod, McMinn, Phil, Moore, Jason, Raidl, Guenther, Rothlauf, Franz, Ryan, Conor, and Thierens, Dirk, editors, *GECCO 2006: Proceedings of the 8th annual conference on Genetic and evolutionary computation*, volume 1, pages 815–822, Seattle, Washington, USA. ACM Press.

Hornby, Gregory S. and Pollack, Jordan B. (2002). Creating high-level components with a generative representation for body-brain evolution. *Artificial Life*, 8(3):223–246.

Iba, Hitoshi, Paul, Topon Kumar, and Hasegawa, Yoshihiko (2010). *Applied Genetic Programming and Machine Learning*. CRC Press.

Kantschik, Wolfgang and Banzhaf, Wolfgang (2002). Linear-graph GP—A new GP structure. In Foster, James A., Lutton, Evelyne, Miller, Julian, Ryan, Conor, and Tettamanzi, Andrea G. B., editors, *Genetic Programming, Proceedings of the 5th European Conference, EuroGP 2002*, volume 2278 of *LNCS*, pages 83–92, Kinsale, Ireland. Springer-Verlag.

Kordon, Arthur (2009). *Applying Computational Intelligence: How to Create Value*. Springer.

Koza, John R. (1992). *Genetic Programming: On the Programming of Computers by Means of Natural Selection*. MIT Press, Cambridge, MA, USA.

Mattiussi, Claudio and Floreano, Dario (2007). Analog genetic encoding for the evolution of circuits and networks. *IEEE Transactions on Evolutionary Computation*, 11(5):596–607.

McConaghy, Trent, Palmers, Pieter, Gao, Peng, Steyaert, Michiel, and Gielen, Georges G.E. (2009). *Variation-Aware Analog Structural Synthesis: A Computational Intelligence Approach*. Springer.

Miller, Julian Francis and Harding, Simon L. (2008). Cartesian genetic programming. In Ebner, Marc, Cattolico, Mike, van Hemert, Jano, Gustafson, Steven, Merkle, Laurence D., Moore, Frank W., Congdon, Clare Bates, Clack, Christopher D., Moore, Frank W., Rand, William, Ficici, Sevan G., Riolo, Rick, Bacardit, Jaume, Bernado-Mansilla, Ester, Butz, Martin V., Smith, Stephen L., Cagnoni, Stefano, Hauschild, Mark, Pelikan, Martin, and Sastry,

Kumara, editors, *GECCO-2008 tutorials*, pages 2701–2726, Atlanta, GA, USA. ACM.

O'Neill, Michael and Ryan, Conor (2003). *Grammatical Evolution: Evolutionary Automatic Programming in a Arbitrary Language*, volume 4 of *Genetic programming*. Kluwer Academic Publishers.

O'Reilly, Una-May and Angeline, Peter J. (1997). Trends in evolutionary methods for program induction. *Evolutionary Computation*, 5(2):v–ix.

O'Reilly, Una-May and Hemberg, Martin (2007). Integrating generative growth and evolutionary computation for form exploration. *Genetic Programming and Evolvable Machines*, 8(2):163–186. Special issue on developmental systems.

O'Reilly, Una-May, McConaghy, Trent, and Riolo, Rick (2009). GPTP 2009: An example of evolvability. In Riolo, Rick L., O'Reilly, Una-May, and McConaghy, Trent, editors, *Genetic Programming Theory and Practice VII*, Genetic and Evolutionary Computation, chapter 1, pages 1–18. Springer, Ann Arbor.

Poli, Riccardo (1997). Evolution of graph-like programs with parallel distributed genetic programming. In Back, Thomas, editor, *Genetic Algorithms: Proceedings of the Seventh International Conference*, pages 346–353, Michigan State University, East Lansing, MI, USA. Morgan Kaufmann.

Poli, Riccardo, Langdon, William B., and McPhee, Nicholas Freitag (2008). *A field guide to genetic programming*. Published via http://lulu.com and freely available at http://www.gp-field-guide.org.uk. (With contributions by J. R. Koza).

Spector, Lee and Robinson, Alan (2002). Genetic programming and autoconstructive evolution with the push programming language. *Genetic Programming and Evolvable Machines*, 3(1):7–40.

Whigham, P. A. (1995). Grammatically-based genetic programming. In Rosca, Justinian P., editor, *Proceedings of the Workshop on Genetic Programming: From Theory to Real-World Applications*, pages 33–41, Tahoe City, California, USA.

Wu, Annie S. and Banzhaf, Wolfgang (1998). Introduction to the special issue: Variable-length representation and noncoding segments for evolutionary algorithms. *Evolutionary Computation*, 6(4):iii–vi.

Chapter 1

FINCH: A SYSTEM FOR EVOLVING JAVA (BYTECODE)

Michael Orlov and Moshe Sipper

Department of Computer Science, Ben-Gurion University, Beer-Sheva 84105, Israel.

Abstract   The established approach in genetic programming (GP) involves the definition of
functions and terminals appropriate to the problem at hand, after which evolution
of expressions using these definitions takes place. We have recently developed
a system, dubbed FINCH (Fertile Darwinian Bytecode Harvester), to evolutionarily improve actual, *extant* software, which was *not intentionally written* for
the purpose of serving as a GP representation in particular, nor for evolution in
general. This is in contrast to existing work that uses restricted subsets of the
Java bytecode instruction set as a representation language for individuals in genetic programming. The ability to evolve Java programs will hopefully lead to a
valuable new tool in the software engineer's toolkit.

Keywords: Java bytecode, automatic programming, software evolution, genetic programming.

1.   Introduction

The established approach in genetic programming (GP) involves the definition of functions and terminals appropriate to the problem at hand, after which
evolution of expressions using these definitions takes place (Koza, 1992; Poli
et al., 2008). Poli et al. recently noted that:

> While it is common to describe GP as evolving *programs*, GP is not typically used
> to evolve programs in the familiar Turing-complete languages humans normally
> use for software development. It is instead more common to evolve programs
> (or expressions or formulae) in a more constrained and often domain-specific
> language. (Poli et al., 2008, ch. 3.1; emphasis in original)

The above statement is (arguably) true not only where "traditional" tree-
based GP is concerned, but also for other forms of GP, such as linear GP and
grammatical evolution (Poli et al., 2008).

```
class F {                        0  iconst_1
int fact(int n) {                1  istore_2
    // offsets 0-1               2  iload_1
    int ans = 1;                 3  ifle 16
                                 6  iload_1
    // offsets 2-3               7  aload_0
    if (n > 0)                   8  iload_1
        // offsets 6-15          9  iconst_1
        ans = n *                10 isub
            fact(n-1);           11 invokevirtual #2
                                 14 imul
    // offsets 16-17             15 istore_2
    return ans;                  16 iload_2
}}                               17 ireturn

(a)                              (b)
```

Figure 1-1. A recursive factorial function in Java (a) and its corresponding bytecode (b). The argument to the virtual method invocation (`invokevirtual`) references the `int F.fact(int)` method via the constant pool.

We have recently developed a system, dubbed FINCH (Fertile Darwinian Bytecode Harvester), to evolutionarily improve actual, *extant* software, which was *not intentionally written* for the purpose of serving as a GP representation in particular, nor for evolution in general. The only requirement is that the software source code be either written in Java or can be compiled to Java bytecode. The following chapter provides an overview of our system, ending with a précis of results. Additional information can be found in (Orlov and Sipper, 2009; Orlov and Sipper, 2010).

Java compilers typically do not produce machine code directly, but instead compile source-code files to platform-independent *bytecode*, to be interpreted in software or, rarely, to be executed in hardware by a Java Virtual Machine (JVM) (Lindholm and Yellin, 1999). The JVM is free to apply its own optimization techniques, such as Just-in-Time (JIT) on-demand compilation to native machine code—a process that is transparent to the user. The JVM implements a stack-based architecture with high-level language features such as object management and garbage collection, virtual function calls, and strong typing. The bytecode language itself is a well-designed assembly-like language with a limited yet powerful instruction set (Engel, 1999; Lindholm and Yellin, 1999). Figure 1-1 shows a recursive Java program for computing the factorial of a number, and its corresponding bytecode.

The JVM architecture is successful enough that several programming languages compile directly to Java bytecode (e.g., Scala, Groovy, Jython, Kawa, JavaFX Script, and Clojure). Moreover, Java *decompilers* are available, which facilitate restoration of the Java source code from compiled bytecode. Since the design of the JVM is closely tied to the design of the Java programming language, such decompilation often produces code that is very similar to the original source code (Miecznikowski and Hendren, 2002).

We chose to automatically improve extant Java programs by evolving the respective compiled bytecode versions. This allows us to leverage the power of a well-defined, cross-platform, intermediate machine language at just the right level of abstraction: We do not need to define a special evolutionary language, thus necessitating an elaborate two-way transformation between Java and our language; nor do we evolve at the Java level, with its encumbering syntactic constraints, which render the genetic operators of crossover and mutation arduous to implement.

Note that we do not wish to invent a language to improve upon some aspect or other of GP (efficiency, terseness, readability, etc.), as has been amply done. Nor do we wish to extend standard GP to become Turing complete, an issue which has also been addressed (Woodward, 2003). Rather, conversely, our point of departure is an *extant*, highly popular, general-purpose language, with our aim being to render it evolvable. The ability to evolve Java programs will hopefully lead to a valuable new tool in the software engineer's toolkit.

The motivation behind evolving Java bytecode is detailed in Section 2. The principles of bytecode evolution are described in Section 3. Section 4 describes compatible bytecode crossover—the main evolutionary operator driving the FINCH system. Alternative ways of evolving software are considered in Section 5. Program halting and compiler optimization issues are dealt with in Sections 6 and 7. Current experimental results are summarized in Section 8, and the concluding remarks are in Section 9.

2.   Why Target Bytecode for Evolution?

Bytecode is the intermediate, platform-independent representation of Java programs, created by a Java compiler. Figure 1-2 depicts the process by which Java source code is *compiled* to bytecode and subsequently *loaded* by the JVM, which *verifies* it and (if the bytecode passes verification) decides whether to *interpret* the bytecode directly, or to *compile* and *optimize* it—thereupon executing the resultant native code. The decision regarding interpretation or further compilation (and optimization) depends upon the frequency at which a particular method is executed, its size, and other parameters.

Our decision to evolve bytecode instead of the more high-level Java source code is guided in part by the desire to avoid altogether the possibility of producing non-compilable source code. The purpose of source code is to be easy for human programmers to create and to modify, a purpose which conflicts with the ability to automatically modify such code. We note in passing that we do not seek an evolvable programming language—a problem tackled, e.g., by

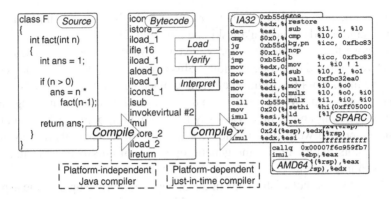

Figure 1-2. Java source code is first compiled to *platform-independent* bytecode by a Java compiler. The JVM only loads the bytecode, which it verifies for correctness, and raises an exception in case the verification fails. After that, the JVM typically interprets the bytecode until it detects that it would be advantageous to compile it, with optimizations, to native, *platform-dependent* code. The native code is then executed by the CPU as any other program. Note that no optimization is performed when Java source code is compiled to bytecode. Optimization only takes place during compilation from bytecode to native code.

(Spector and Robinson, 2002)—but rather aim to handle the Java programming language in particular.

Evolving bytecode instead of source code alleviates the issue of producing non-compilable programs to some extent—but not completely. Java bytecode must be *correct* with respect to dealing with stack and local variables (cf. Figure 1-3). Values that are read and written should be type-compatible, and stack underflow must not occur. The JVM performs bytecode verification and raises an exception in case of any such incompatibility.

We wish not merely to evolve bytecode, but indeed to evolve *correct* bytecode. This task is hard, because our purpose is to evolve given, unrestricted code, and not simply to leverage the capabilities of the JVM to perform GP. Therefore, basic evolutionary operations, such as bytecode crossover and mutation, should produce correct individuals.

3.   Bytecode Evolution Principles

We define a *good* crossover of two parents as one where the offspring is a *correct* bytecode program, meaning one that passes verification with no errors; conversely, a *bad* crossover of two parents is one where the offspring is an *incorrect* bytecode program, meaning one whose verification produces errors. While it is easy to define a trivial slice-and-swap crossover operator on two programs, it is far more arduous to define a *good* crossover operator. This latter is necessary in order to preserve variability during the evolutionary process, because incorrect programs cannot be run, and therefore cannot be ascribed a

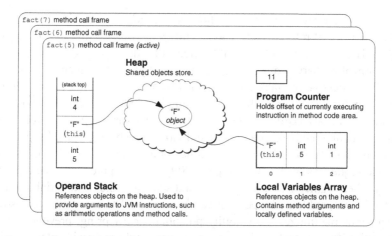

Figure 1-3. Call frames in the architecture of the Java Virtual Machine, during execution of the recursive factorial function code shown in Figure 1-1, with parameter $n = 7$. The top call frame is in a state preceding execution of invokevirtual. This instruction will pop a parameter and an object reference from the operand stack, invoke the method fact of class F, and open a new frame for the fact(4) call. When that frame closes, the returned value will be pushed onto the operand stack.

fitness value—or, alternatively, must be assigned the worst possible value. Too many bad crossovers will hence produce a population with little variability.

Note that we use the term *good* crossover to refer to an operator that produces a viable offspring (i.e., one that passes the JVM verification) given two parents; *compatible* crossover, defined below, is one mechanism by which good crossover can be implemented.

The Java Virtual Machine is a stack-based architecture for executing Java bytecode. The JVM holds a stack for each execution thread, and creates a frame on this stack for each method invocation. The frame contains a code array, an operand stack, a local variables array, and a reference to the constant pool of the current class (Engel, 1999). The code array contains the bytecode to be executed by the JVM. The local variables array holds all method (or function) parameters, including a reference to the class instance in which the current method executes. In addition, the variables array also holds local-scope variables. The operand stack is used by stack-based instructions, and for arguments when calling other methods. A method call moves parameters from the caller's operand stack to the callee's variables array; a return moves the top value from the callee's stack to the caller's stack, and disposes of the callee's frame. Both the operand stack and the variables array contain typed items, and instructions always act on a specific type. The relevant bytecode instructions are prefixed accordingly: 'a' for an object or array reference, 'i' and 'l' for integral types **int** and **long**, and 'f' and 'd' for floating-point types **float** and **double**.[1] Finally, the constant pool is an array of references to classes, methods, fields, and other unvarying entities. The JVM architecture is illustrated in Figure 1-3.

In our evolutionary setup, the individuals are bytecode sequences annotated with all the necessary stack and variables information. This information is gathered in one pass over the bytecode, using the ASM bytecode manipulation and analysis library (Bruneton et al., 2002). Afterwards, similar information for any sequential code segment in the individual can be aggregated separately. This preprocessing step allows us to define compatible two-point crossover on bytecode sequences (Orlov and Sipper, 2009). Code segments can be replaced only by other segments that use the operand stack and the local variables array in a depth-compatible and type-compatible manner. The compatible crossover operator thus maximizes the viability potential for offspring, preventing type incompatibility and stack underflow errors that would otherwise plague indiscriminating bytecode crossover. Note that the crossover operation is *unidirectional*, or asymmetric—the code segment compatibility criterion as described here is not a symmetric relation. An ability to replace segment α in individual A with segment β in individual B does not imply an ability to replace segment β in B with segment α.

As an example of compatible crossover, consider two identical programs with the same bytecode as in Figure 1-1, which are reproduced as parents A and B in Figure 1-4. We replace bytecode instructions at offsets 7–11 in parent A with the single iload_2 instruction at offset 16 from parent B. Offsets 7–11 correspond to the fact(n-1) call that leaves an integer value on the stack, whereas offset 16 corresponds to pushing the local variable ans on the stack. This crossover, the result of which is shown as offspring x in Figure 1-4, is *good*, because the operand stack is used in a compatible manner by the source segment, and although this segment reads the variable ans that is not read in the destination segment, that variable is guaranteed to have been written previously, at offset 1.

Alternatively, consider replacing the imul instruction in the newly formed offspring x with the single invokevirtual instruction from parent B. This crossover is *bad*, as illustrated by incorrect offspring y in Figure 1-4. Although both invokevirtual and imul pop two values from the stack and then push one value, invokevirtual expects the topmost value to be of reference type F, whereas imul expects an integer. Another negative example is an attempt to replace bytecode offsets 0–1 in parent B (that correspond to the int ans=1 statement) with an empty segment. In this case, illustrated by incorrect offspring z in Figure 1-4, variable ans is no longer guaranteed to be initialized

---

[1] The types **boolean**, **byte**, **char** and **short** are treated as the computational type **int** by the Java Virtual Machine, except for array accesses and explicit conversions (Lindholm and Yellin, 1999).

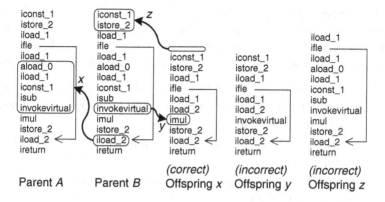

iconst_1	iconst_1			iload_1
istore_2	istore_2			ifle
iload_1	iload_1			iload_1
ifle	ifle			aload_0
iload_1	iload_1	iconst_1	iconst_1	iload_1
aload_0	aload_0	istore_2	istore_2	iconst_1
iload_1	iload_1	iload_1	iload_1	isub
iconst_1	iconst_1	ifle	ifle	invokevirtual
isub	isub	iload_1	iload_1	imul
invokevirtual	invokevirtual	iload_2	iload_2	istore_2
imul	imul	imul	invokevirtual	iload_2
istore_2	istore_2	istore_2	istore_2	ireturn
iload_2	iload_2	iload_2	iload_2	
ireturn	ireturn	ireturn	ireturn	

| | | (correct) | (incorrect) | (incorrect) |
| Parent *A* | Parent *B* | Offspring *x* | Offspring *y* | Offspring *z* |

Figure 1-4. An example of good and bad crossovers. The two identical individuals *A* and *B* represent a recursive factorial function (see Figure 1-1; here we use an arrow instead of branch offset). In parent *A*, the bytecode sequence that corresponds to the fact(n-1) call that leaves an integer value on the stack, is replaced with the single instruction in *B* that corresponds to pushing the local variable ans on the stack. The resulting correct offspring *x* and the original parent *B* are then considered as two new parents. We see that either replacing the first two instructions in *B* with an empty section, or replacing the imul instruction in *x* with the invokevirtual instruction from *B*, result in incorrect bytecode, shown as offspring *y* and *z*—see main text for full explanation.

when it is read immediately prior to the function's return, and the resulting bytecode is therefore incorrect.

A mutation operator employs the same constraints as compatible crossover, but the constraints are applied to variations of the same individual. The requirements for correct bytecode mutation are thus derived from those of compatible crossover. To date, we did not use this type of mutation as it proved unnecessary, and instead implemented a restricted form of constants-only point mutation, where each constant in a new individual is modified with a given probability.

4.   Compatible Bytecode Crossover

As discussed above, compatible bytecode crossover is a fundamental building block for effective evolution of correct bytecode. In order to describe the formal requirements for compatible crossover, we need to define the meaning of variable accesses for a segment of code. That is, a section of code (that is not necessary linear, since there are branching instructions) can be viewed as reading and writing some local variables, or as an aggregation of reads and writes by individual bytecode instructions. However, when a variable is written before being read, the write "shadows" the read, in the sense that the code executing prior to the given section does not have to provide a value of the correct type in the variable.

Variables Access Sets.   We define variables access sets, to be used ahead by the compatible crossover operator, as follows: Let a and b be two locations in the same bytecode sequence. For a set of instructions $\delta_{a,b}$ that could potentially be executed starting at a and ending at b, we define the following access sets.

$\delta_{a,b}^r$: set of local variables such that for each variable v, there exists a *potential* execution path (i.e., one not necessarily taken) between a and b, in which v is read before any write to it.

$\delta_{a,b}^w$: set of local variables that are written to through at least one potential execution path.

$\delta_{a,b}^{w!}$: set of local variables that are guaranteed to be written to, no matter which execution path is taken.

These sets of local variables are incrementally computed by analyzing the data flow between locations a and b. For a single instruction c, the three access sets for δ_c are given by the Java bytecode definition. Consider a set of (normally non-consecutive) instructions $\{b_i\}$ that branch to instruction c or have c as their immediate subsequent instruction. The variables accessed between a and c are computed as follows:

$\delta_{a,c}^r$ is the union of all reads δ_{a,b_i}^r, with the addition of variables read by instruction c—unless these variables are guaranteed to be written before c. Formally, $\delta_{a,c}^r = \left(\bigcup_i \delta_{a,b_i}^r \right) \cup \left(\delta_c^r \setminus \bigcap_i \delta_{a,b_i}^{w!} \right)$.

$\delta_{a,c}^w$ is the union of all writes δ_{a,b_i}^w, with the addition of variables written by instruction c: $\delta_{a,c}^w = \left(\bigcup_i \delta_{a,b_i}^w \right) \cup \delta_c^w$.

$\delta_{a,c}^{w!}$ is the set of variables guaranteed to be written before c, with the addition of variables written by instruction c: $\delta_{a,c}^{w!} = \left(\bigcap_i \delta_{a,b_i}^{w!} \right) \cup \delta_c^{w!}$ (note that $\delta_c^{w!} = \delta_c^w$). When $\delta_{a,c}^{w!}$ has already been computed, its previous value needs to be a part of the intersection as well.

We therefore traverse the data-flow graph starting at a, and updating the variables access sets as above, until they stabilize—i.e., stop changing.[2] During the traversal, necessary stack depths are also updated. The requirements for compatible bytecode crossover can now be specified.

Bytecode Constraints on Crossover.   In order to attain viable offspring, several conditions must hold when performing crossover of two bytecode programs. Let A and B be functions in Java, represented as bytecode sequences. Consider segments α and β in A and B, respectively, and let p_α and p_β be the necessary depth of stack for these segments—i.e., the minimal number of

---

[2]The data-flow traversal process is similar to the data-flow analyzer's loop in (Lindholm and Yellin, 1999).

elements in the stack required to avoid underflow. Segment α can be replaced with β if the following conditions hold.

- Operand stack: (1) it is possible to ensure that $p_\beta \leqslant p_\alpha$ by prefixing stack pops and pushes of α with some frames from the stack state at the beginning of α; (2) α and β have compatible stack frames up to depth p_β: stack pops of α have identical or narrower types as stack pops of β, and stack pushes of β have identical or narrower types as stack pushes of α; (3) α has compatible stack frames deeper than p_β: stack pops of α have identical or narrower types as corresponding stack pushes of α.

- Local variables: (1) local variables written by β (β^w) have identical or narrower types as corresponding variables that are read after α (*post-α^r*); (2) local variables read after α (*post-α^r*) and not necessarily written by β ($\beta^{w!}$) must be written before α (*pre-$\alpha^{w!}$*), or provided as arguments for call to A, as identical or narrower types; (3) local variables read by β (β^r) must be written before α (*pre-$\alpha^{w!}$*), or provided as arguments for call to A, as identical or narrower types.

- Control flow: (1) no branch instruction outside of α has branch destination in α, and no branch instruction in β has branch destination outside of β; (2) code before α has transition to the first instruction of α, and code in β has transition to the first instruction after β; (3) last instruction in α implies transition to the first instruction after α.

Detailed examples of the above conditions can be found in (Orlov and Sipper, 2009).

Compatible bytecode crossover prevents verification errors in offspring, in other words, all offspring *compile* sans error. As with any other evolutionary method, however, it does not prevent production of non-viable offspring—in our case, those with runtime errors. An exception or a timeout can still occur during an individual's evaluation, and the fitness of the individual should be reset accordingly.

We chose bytecode segments randomly before checking them for crossover compatibility as follows: For a given method, a segment size is selected using a given probability distribution among all bytecode segments that are branch-consistent under the first control-flow requirement; then a segment with the chosen size is uniformly selected. Whenever the chosen segments result in *bad* crossover, bytecode segments are chosen again (up to some limit of retries). Note that this selection process is very fast (despite the retries), as it involves fast operations—and, most importantly, we ensure that crossover *always* produces a viable offspring.

```
float x;  int y = 7;              int x = 7;  float y;
if (y >= 0)                       if (y >= 0) {
    x = y;                            y = x;
else                                  x = y;
    x = -y;                       }
System.out.println(x);            System.out.println(z);

(a)                               (b)
```

Figure 1-5. Two Java snippets that comply with the context-free grammar rules of the programming language. However, only snippet (a) is legal once the full Java Language Specification (Gosling et al., 2005) is considered. Snippet (b), though Java-compliant syntactically, is revealed to be ill-formed when semantics are thrown into play.

5.   The Grammar Alternative

One might ask whether it is really necessary to evolve bytecode in order to support the evolution of unrestricted Java software. After all, Java is a programming language with strict, formal rules, which are precisely defined in Backus-Naur form (BNF). One could make an argument for the possibility of providing this BNF description to a grammar evolutionary system (O'Neill and Ryan, 2003) and evolving away.

We disagree with such an argument. The apparent ease with which one might apply the BNF rules of a real-world programming language in an evolutionary system (either grammatical or tree-based) is an illusion stemming from the blurred boundary between *syntactic* and *semantic* constraints (Poli et al., 2008, ch. 6.2.4). Java's formal (BNF) rules are purely syntactic, in no way capturing the language's type system, variable visibility and accessibility, and other semantic constraints. Correct handling of these constraints in order to ensure the production of viable individuals would essentially necessitate the programming of a full-scale Java compiler—a highly demanding task, not to be taken lightly. This is not to claim that such a task is completely insurmountable—e.g., an extension to context-free grammars (CFGs), such as logic grammars, can be taken advantage of in order to represent the necessary contextual constraints (Wong and Leung, 2000). But we have yet to see such a GP implementation in practice, addressing real-world programming problems.

We cannot emphasize the distinction between syntax and semantics strongly enough. Consider, for example, the Java program segment shown in Figure 1-5(a). It is a seemingly simple syntactic structure, which belies, however, a host of semantic constraints, including: type compatibility in variable assignment, variable initialization before read access, and variable visibility. The similar (and CFG-conforming) segment shown in Figure 1-5(b) violates all these constraints: variable y in the conditional test is uninitialized during a read access, its subsequent assignment to x is type-incompatible, and variable z is undefined.

It is quite telling that despite the popularity and generality of grammatical evolution, we were able to uncover only a single case of evolution using a real-world, unrestricted phenotypic language—involving a semantically simple *hardware* description language (HDL). (Mizoguchi et al., 1994) implemented the complete grammar of SFL (Structured Function description Language) (Nakamura et al., 1991) as production rules of a rewriting system, using approximately 350(!) rules for a language far simpler than Java. The semantic constraints of SFL—an object-oriented, register-transfer-level language—are sufficiently weak for using its BNF directly:

> By designing the genetic operators based on the production rules and by performing them in the chromosome, a grammatically correct SFL program can be generated. This eliminates the burden of eliminating grammatically incorrect HDL programs through the evolution process and helps to concentrate selective pressure in the target direction. (Mizoguchi et al., 1994)

(Arcuri, 2009) recently attempted to repair Java source code using syntax-tree transformations. His JAFF system is not able to handle the entire language—only an explicitly defined subset (Arcuri, 2009, Table 6.1), and furthermore, exhibits a host of problems that evolution of correct Java bytecode avoids inherently: individuals are compiled at each fitness evaluation, compilation errors occur despite the *syntax*-tree modifications being legal (cf. discussion above), lack of support for a significant part of the Java syntax (inner and anonymous classes, labeled `break` and `continue` statements, Java 5.0 syntax extensions, etc.), incorrect support of method overloading, and other problems:

> The constraint system consists of 12 basic node types and 5 polymorphic types. For the functions and the leaves, there are 44 different types of constraints. For each program, we added as well the constraints regarding local variables and method calls. Although the constraint system is quite accurate, it does not completely represent yet all the possible constraints in the employed subset of the Java language (i.e., a program that satisfies these constraints would not be necessarily compilable in Java). (Arcuri, 2009)

FINCH, through its clever use of Java bytecode, attains a scalability leap in evolutionarily manageable programming language complexity.

6. The Halting Issue

An important issue that must be considered when dealing with the evolution of unrestricted programs is whether they halt—or not (Langdon and Poli, 2006). Whenever Turing-complete programs with arbitrary control flow are evolved, a possibility arises that computation will turn out to be unending. A program that has acquired the undesirable non-termination property during evolution is executed directly by the JVM, and FINCH has nearly no control over the process.

A straightforward approach for dealing with non-halting programs is to limit the execution time of each individual during evaluation, assigning a minimal fitness value to programs that exceed the time limit. This approach, however, suffers from two shortcomings: First, limiting execution time provides coarse-time granularity at best, is unreliable in the presence of varying CPU load, and as a result is wasteful of computer resources due to the relatively high time-limit value that must be used. Second, applying a time limit to an arbitrary program requires running it in a separate thread, and stopping the execution of the thread once it exceeds the time limit. However, externally stopping the execution is either unreliable (when interrupting the thread that must then eventually enter a blocked state), or unsafe for the whole application (when attempting to kill the thread).[3]

Therefore, in FINCH we exercise a different approach, taking advantage of the lucid structure offered by Java bytecode. Before evaluating a program, it is temporarily *instrumented* with calls to a function that throws an exception if called more than a given number of times (steps). A call to this function is inserted before each backward branch instruction and before each method invocation. Thus, an infinite loop in any evolved individual program will raise an exception after exceeding the predefined steps limit. Note that this is not a coarse-grained (run)time limit, but a precise limit on the number of steps.

7.   (No) Loss of Compiler Optimization

Another issue that surfaces when bytecode genetic operators are considered is the apparent loss of compiler optimization. Indeed, most native-code producing compilers provide the option of optimizing the resulting machine code to varying degrees of speed and size improvements. These optimizations would presumably be lost during the process of bytecode evolution.

Surprisingly, however, bytecode evolution does *not* induce loss of compiler optimization, since there is no optimization to begin with! The common assumption regarding Java compilers' similarity to native-code compilers is simply incorrect. As far as we were able to uncover, with the exception of the IBM Jikes Compiler (which has not been under development since 2004, and which does not support modern Java), no Java-to-bytecode compiler is optimizing. Sun's Java Compiler, for instance, has not had an optimization switch since version 1.3.[4] Moreover, even the GNU Compiler for Java, which is part of the highly optimizing GNU Compiler Collection (GCC), does not optimize at the

---

[3] For the intricacies of stopping Java threads see http://java.sun.com/javase/6/docs/technotes/guides/concurrency/threadPrimitiveDeprecation.html.
[4] See the old manual page at http://java.sun.com/j2se/1.3/docs/tooldocs/solaris/javac.html, which contains the following note in the definition of the -O (Optimize) option: *the -O option does nothing in the current implementation of* javac.

bytecode-producing phase—for which it uses the Eclipse Compiler for Java as a front-end—and instead performs (optional) optimization at the native code-producing phase. The reason for this is that optimizations are applied at a later stage, whenever the JVM decides to proceed from interpretation to just-in-time compilation (Kotzmann et al., 2008).

The fact that Java compilers do not optimize bytecode does not preclude the possibility of doing so, nor render it particularly hard in various cases. Indeed, in FINCH we apply an automatic post-crossover bytecode transformation that is typically performed by a Java compiler: dead-code elimination. After crossover is done, it is possible to get a method with unreachable bytecode sections (e.g., a forward goto with no instruction that jumps into the section between the goto and its target code offset). Such dead code is problematic in Java bytecode, and it is therefore automatically removed from the resulting individuals by our system. This technique does not impede the ability of individuals to evolve introns, since there is still a multitude of other intron types that can be evolved (Brameier and Banzhaf, 2007) (e.g., any arithmetic bytecode instruction not affecting the method's return value, which is not considered dead-code bytecode, though it is an intron nonetheless).

8. A Summary of Results

Due to space limitations we only provide a brief description of our results, with the full account available in (Orlov and Sipper, 2009; Orlov and Sipper, 2010). To date, we have successfully tackled several problems:

- *Simple and complex symbolic regression*: Evolve programs to approximate the simple polynomial $x^4 + x^3 + x^2 + x$ and the more complex polynomial $\sum_{i=1}^{9} x^i$.

- *Artificial ant problem*: Evolve programs to find all 89 food pellets on the Santa Fe trail.

- *Intertwined spirals problem*: Evolve programs to correctly classify 194 points on two spirals.

- *Array sum*: Evolve programs to compute the sum of values of an integer array, along the way demonstrating FINCH's ability to handle loops and recursion.

- *Tic-tac-toe*: Evolve a winning program for the game, starting from a *flawed* implementation of the negamax algorithm. This example shows that programs can be improved.

Figure 1-6 shows two examples of Java programs evolved by FINCH.

```
Number simpleRegression(Number num) {        int sumlistrec(List list) {
  double d = num.doubleValue();                int sum = 0;
  return Double.valueOf(d + (d * (d * (d +     if (list.isEmpty())
    ((d = num.doubleValue()) +                   sum = sum;
      (((num.doubleValue() * (d = d) + d)        else
        * d + d) * d + d) * d)                     sum += ((Integer)list.get(0))
    * d) + d) + d) * d);                             .intValue() + sumlistrec(
}                                                    list.subList(1, list.size())));
                                               return sum;
                                             }

(a)                                          (b)
```

Figure 1-6. Examples of evolved programs for the degree-9 polynomial regression problem (a), and the recursive array sum problem (b). The Java code shown was produced by decompiling the respective evolved bytecode solutions.

9.   Concluding Remarks

A recent study commissioned by the US Department of Defense on the subject of futuristic ultra-large-scale (ULS) systems that have billions of lines of code noted, among others, that, "Judiciously used, digital evolution can substantially augment the cognitive limits of human designers and can find novel (possibly counterintuitive) solutions to complex ULS system design problems" (Northrop et al., 2006, p. 33). This study does not detail any actual research performed but attempts to build a road map for future research. Moreover, it concentrates on huge, futuristic systems, whereas our aim is at current systems of any size. Differences aside, both our work and this study share the vision of true software evolution.

Turing famously (and wrongly...) predicted that, "in about fifty years' time it will be possible, to programme computers [...] to make them play the imitation game so well that an average interrogator will not have more than 70 per cent. chance of making the right identification after five minutes of questioning" (Turing, 1950). Recently, Harman wrote that, "...despite its current widespread use, there was, within living memory, equal skepticism about whether compiled code could be trusted. If a similar change of attitude to evolved code occurs over time..." (Harman, 2010).

We wish to offer our own prediction for fifty years hence, in the hope that we shall *not* be wrong: We believe that in about fifty years' time it will be possible, to program computers by means of evolution. Not merely *possible* but indeed *prevalent*.

References

Arcuri, Andrea (2009). *Automatic Software Generation and Improvement Through Search Based Techniques*. PhD thesis, University of Birmingham, Birmingham, UK.

Brameier, Markus and Banzhaf, Wolfgang (2007). *Linear Genetic Programming*. Number XVI in Genetic and Evolutionary Computation. Springer.

Bruneton, Eric, Lenglet, Romain, and Coupaye, Thierry (2002). ASM: A code manipulation tool to implement adaptable systems (Un outil de manipulation de code pour la réalisation de systèmes adaptables). In *Adaptable and Extensible Component Systems (Systèmes à Composants Adaptables et Extensibles), October 17–18, 2002, Grenoble, France*, pages 184–195.

Engel, Joshua (1999). *Programming for the Java^{TM} Virtual Machine*. Addison-Wesley, Reading, MA, USA.

Gosling, James, Joy, Bill, Steele, Guy, and Bracha, Gilad (2005). *The Java^{TM} Language Specification*. The Java^{TM} Series. Addison-Wesley, Boston, MA, USA, third edition.

Harman, Mark (2010). Automated patching techniques: The fix is in. *Communications of the ACM*, 53(5):108.

Kotzmann, Thomas, Wimmer, Christian, Mössenböck, Hanspeter, Rodriguez, Thomas, Russell, Kenneth, and Cox, David (2008). Design of the Java HotSpot^{TM} client compiler for Java 6. *ACM Transactions on Architecture and Code Optimization*, 5(1):7:1–32.

Koza, John R. (1992). *Genetic Programming: On the Programming of Computers by Means of Natural Selection*. MIT Press, Cambridge, MA, USA.

Langdon, W. B. and Poli, R. (2006). The halting probability in von Neumann architectures. In Collet, Pierre, Tomassini, Marco, Ebner, Marc, Gustafson, Steven, and Ekárt, Anikó, editors, *Proceedings of the 9th European Conference on Genetic Programming*, volume 3905 of *Lecture Notes in Computer Science*, pages 225–237, Budapest, Hungary. Springer.

Lindholm, Tim and Yellin, Frank (1999). *The Java^{TM} Virtual Machine Specification*. The Java^{TM} Series. Addison-Wesley, Boston, MA, USA, second edition.

Miecznikowski, Jerome and Hendren, Laurie (2002). Decompiling Java bytecode: Problems, traps and pitfalls. In Horspool, R. Nigel, editor, *Compiler Construction: 11th International Conference, CC 2002, Held as Part of the Joint European Conferences on Theory and Practice of Software, ETAPS 2002, Grenoble, France, April 8–12, 2002*, volume 2304 of *Lecture Notes in Computer Science*, pages 111–127, Berlin / Heidelberg. Springer-Verlag.

Mizoguchi, Jun'ichi, Hemmi, Hitoshi, and Shimohara, Katsunori (1994). Production genetic algorithms for automated hardware design through an evolutionary process. In *Proceedings of the First IEEE Conference on Evolutionary Computation, ICEC'94*, volume 2, pages 661–664.

Nakamura, Yukihiro, Oguri, Kiyoshi, and Nagoya, Akira (1991). Synthesis from pure behavioral descriptions. In Camposano, Raul and Wolf, Wayne Hendrix, editors, *High-Level VLSI Synthesis*, pages 205–229. Kluwer, Norwell, MA, USA.

Northrop, Linda et al. (2006). *Ultra-Large-Scale Systems: The Software Challenge of the Future*. Carnegie Mellon University, Pittsburgh, PA, USA.

O'Neill, Michael and Ryan, Conor (2003). *Grammatical Evolution: Evolutionary Automatic Programming in a Arbitrary Language*, volume 4 of *Genetic programming*. Kluwer Academic Publishers.

Orlov, Michael and Sipper, Moshe (2009). Genetic programming in the wild: Evolving unrestricted bytecode. In Raidl, Günther et al., editors, *Proceedings of the 11th Annual Conference on Genetic and Evolutionary Computation, July 8–12, 2009, Montréal Québec, Canada*, pages 1043–1050, New York, NY, USA. ACM Press.

Orlov, Michael and Sipper, Moshe (2010). Flight of the FINCH through the Java wilderness. *IEEE Transactions on Evolutionary Computation*. In press.

Poli, Riccardo, Langdon, William B., and McPhee, Nicholas Freitag (2008). *A field guide to genetic programming*. Published via http://lulu.com and freely available at http://www.gp-field-guide.org.uk. (With contributions by J. R. Koza).

Spector, Lee and Robinson, Alan (2002). Genetic programming and autoconstructive evolution with the Push programming language. *Genetic Programming and Evolvable Machines*, 3(1):7–40.

Turing, Alan Mathison (1950). Computing machinery and intelligence. *Mind*, 59(236):433–460.

Wong, Man Leung and Leung, Kwong Sak (2000). *Data Mining Using Grammar Based Genetic Programming and Applications*, volume 3 of *Genetic Programming*. Kluwer, Norwell, MA, USA.

Woodward, John R. (2003). Evolving Turing complete representations. In Sarker, Ruhul et al., editors, *The 2003 Congress on Evolutionary Computation, CEC 2003, Canberra, Australia, 8–12 December, 2003*, volume 2, pages 830–837. IEEE Press.

Chapter 2

TOWARDS PRACTICAL AUTOCONSTRUCTIVE EVOLUTION: SELF-EVOLUTION OF PROBLEM-SOLVING GENETIC PROGRAMMING SYSTEMS

Lee Spector

Cognitive Science, Hampshire College, Amherst, MA, 01002-3359 USA.

Abstract   Most genetic programming systems use hard-coded genetic operators that are applied according to user-specified parameters. Because it is unlikely that the provided operators or the default parameters will be ideal for all problems or all program representations, practitioners often devote considerable energy to experimentation with alternatives. Attempts to bring choices about operators and parameters under evolutionary control, through self-adaptive algorithms or meta-genetic programming, have been explored in the literature and have produced interesting results. However, no systems based on such principles have yet been demonstrated to have greater practical problem-solving power than the more-standard alternatives. This chapter explores the prospects for extending the practical power of genetic programming through the refinement of an approach called *autoconstructive evolution*, in which the algorithms used for the reproduction and variation of evolving programs are encoded in the programs themselves, and are thereby subject to variation and evolution in tandem with their problem-solving components. We present the motivation for the autoconstructive evolution approach, show how it can be instantiated using the Push programming language, summarize previous results with the *Pushpop* system, outline the more recent *AutoPush* system, and chart a course for future work focused on the production of practical systems that can solve hard problems.

Keywords: genetic programming, meta-genetic programming, autoconstructive evolution, Push, PushGP, Pushpop, AutoPush

1.   Introduction

The work described in this chapter is motivated both by features of biological evolution and by the requirements for the high-performance problem-solving systems of the future.

Under common conceptions of biological evolution the variation of genotypes from parents to children, and hence the diversification of phenotypes from progenitors to their descendants, is essentially random prior to selection. Offspring vary randomly, it is said, and selection acts on the resulting diversity by allowing the better-adapted random variants to survive and reproduce. Such conceptions are held not only by the lay public but also by theorists such as Jerry Fodor and Massimo Piattelli-Palmarini who, in their book *What Darwin Got Wrong,* criticize Darwinian theory in part on the grounds that the random "generate and test" algorithm at its core is insufficiently powerful to account for the facts of natural history (Fodor and Piattelli-Palmarini, 2010).

But diversification in nature, while certainly random in some respects, is also clearly non-random in several others. If one were to modify DNA molecules in truly random ways, considering all chemical bonds to be equally good candidates for breakage and re-connection, then one would not end up with DNA molecules at all but instead with some other sort of organic soup. Cellular machinery copies DNA, and repairs copying errors, in ways that allow for certain kinds of "errors" but only within tightly constrained bounds. At higher levels of organization variation is constrained by genetic regulatory processes, the mechanics of sexual recombination, cell division and development, and, at a much higher level of organization, by social structures that guide non-random mate selection. All of these constraints emerge from reproductive processes that have themselves evolved over the course of natural history. There is a large literature on such constraints, including a recent theory of "facilitated variation" (Gerhart and Kirschner, 2007), and summaries of the evolution of variation from pre-biotic Earth to the present (Maynard Smith and Szathmáry, 1999).

Whether or not the evolved-non-randomness of biological variation constitutes a significant critique of neo-Darwinism or of the historical Darwin, as claimed by Fodor and Piattelli-Palmarini, is beyond the scope of the present discussion. For our purposes, however, two related points should be made. First, while truly random variation, filtered by selection, may be too weak of a mechanism to have produced the sequence of phenotypes observed over time in the historical record, it is possible for random variation, *when acting on the reproductive mechanisms themselves,* to produce variation mechanisms that are *not* purely random. This is presumably what happened in natural history. Second, this bootstrapping process, of the evolution of adaptive, not-entirely-random variation by means of the initially random variation *of the variation mechanisms*, might also be applied to evolutionary problem-solving technologies.

Why would we want to do this? One reason is that the problem-solving power of current evolutionary computing technologies is limited by the nature of the variation mechanisms that we build into these systems by hand. Consider, for example, the standard mutation operators used in genetic programming. Subtree replacement, applied uniformly to the nodes in a program tree (or uniformly to interior vs. leaf nodes with a specified probability), involving the replacement of subtrees with newly-generated random subtrees, provides a form of variation that leads to solutions in some but not all problem environments. This has led to the development of a wide range of alternative mutation operators; see, for example, the "Mutation Cookbook" section of (Poli et al., 2008, pp. 42–44). But which of these will be most helpful in which circumstances, and which others, perhaps not yet invented, may be needed to solve challenging new problems?

The field currently has no satisfying answer to this question, which will become all the more pressing as genetic programming systems incorporate more expressive and heterogeneous program representations. In the context of such representations it may well make sense for different program elements or program locations to have different variation rates or procedures, and it will not be obvious, in advance, how to make these choices. The question will also become all the more pressing as genetic programming systems are applied to ever more complex problems, about which the system designers will have less knowledge and intuition. And the question will be raised with even greater urgency with respect to recombination operators such as crossover, for which there even more open questions (e.g. about how to choose crossover partners) that currently require the user to make choices that may not be optimal.

Two approaches to these general issues that have previously been explored in the literature are "self-adaptation" and "meta-genetic programming." Many forms of self-adaptation have been investigated, both within genetic programming and in other areas of evolutionary computation (with many examples including (Angeline, 1995; Spears, 1995; Angeline, 1996; Eiben et al., 1999; MacCallum, 2003; Fry et al., 2005; Beyer and Meyer-Nieberg, 2006; Vafaee et al., 2008; Silva and Dignum, 2009)). In all of these systems the parameters of the evolutionary algorithm are varied and subjected to some form of selection, whether the variation and selection is accomplished by means of the overarching evolutionary algorithm, by a secondary evolutionary algorithm, or by some other machine learning technique. In some cases the parameters are adapted on an individual basis, while in others the self-adaptive system modifies global parameters that apply to an entire population. In general, however, these systems vary only pre-selected parameters of the variation operators in pre-specified ways, and they do not allow for the evolution of arbitrary methods of variation.

By contrast, the "meta-genetic programming" approach leverages the program-space search capabilities of genetic programming to search for variation operators—which are, after all, themselves programs—during the search for problem-solving programs (Schmidhuber, 1987; Kantschik et al., 1999; Edmonds, 2001; Tavares et al., 2004; Diosan and Oltean, 2009). These systems would appear to have more potential to evolve adaptive variation algorithms, but they have generally been subject to one or both of the following two significant limitations:

- The evolving genetic operators are not associated with specific evolving problem-solving programs; they are expected to apply to all evolving problem-solving programs equally well.

- The evolving genetic operators are restricted to being compositions of a small number of pre-designed components; many conceivable genetic operators will not be representable using these components.

The first of these limitations contrasts with some of the self-adaptive evolutionary algorithms mentioned previously, in which the values of parameters for genetic operators are encoded in individuals. That this "global" conception of the applicability of genetic operators might be a limitation should be evident from a cursory examination of the diversity of reproductive strategies in nature. For example, the reproductive strategies of the dandelion are quite different from those of the tiger, the oyster mushroom, and *Escherichia coli*; nobody would expect the strategies of any of these organisms to work particularly well for any of the others. Of course the diversity present in the Earth's biosphere dwarfs that of any current genetic programming system, but it would nonetheless be quite surprising if the same genetic operators worked equally well across a genetic programming population with any significant diversity. One could well imagine, for example, that a subset of the population might share one particular subtree in which a high degree of mutation is adaptive and a second subtree in which mutation is always deleterious. Other individuals in the population might lack either or both of these subtrees, or they might contain additional code that changes the effects of mutations within these particular subtrees.

The second of these limitations is probably mostly a reflection of the fact that most genetic programming representations limit the expressiveness of the programs that they can evolve more generally. Although several Turing complete representations have been described (for example, (Teller, 1994; Nordin and Banzhaf, 1995; Spector and Robinson, 2002a; Woodward, 2003; Yabuki and Iba, 2004; Langdon and Poli, 2006)), such representations are relatively rare and representations that can easily perform arbitrary transformations on variable-sized programs are rarer still. Nature appears to be quite flexible and inventive in the variation mechanisms that it employs (e.g., mechanisms involving gene duplication), and we can easily imagine cases in which genetic programming systems would benefit from the use of genetic operators that are not simple compositions of hand-designed operator components.

Another line of research that bears on the approach presented here generally appears in the artificial life literature. Systems such as Tierra (Ray, 1991), Avida (Ofria and Wilke, 2004), and SeMar (Suzuki, 2004) all involve the evolution of programs that are partially responsible for their own reproduction, and in which the reproductive mechanisms (including genetic operators) are therefore subject to variation and selection. However, in these systems diversification is generally driven by hand-designed "ancestor" replicators and/or by the effects of hand-designed mutation algorithms that are applied automatically to the results of all code manipulation operations. Furthermore, while some of these systems have been used to solve computational problems their problem-solving power has been quite limited; they have been used to evolve simple logic gates and arithmetic functions, but they have not been applied to the kinds of difficult problems that genetic programming practitioners are interested in solving. This is not surprising, as these systems have generally been developed primarily to study biological evolution, not to solve difficult computational problems.

Additional related work has conducted in the context of evolved self-reproduction (Taylor, 1999; Sipper and Reggia, 2001) although most of this work has been focused on the evolution of exact replication rather than the evolution of adaptive variation. An exception, and the closest work to that described below, is Koza's work on the "Spontaneous Emergence of Self-Replicating and Evolutionarily Self-Improving Computer Programs" (Koza, 1994). In that work Koza evolved programs that simultaneously solved problems (albeit simple Boolean problems) and produced variant offspring using template-based code self-modification in a "sea" or "Turing gas" of programs (Fontana, 1992).

This chapter describes an approach to self-adaptive genetic programming, called *autoconstructive evolution*, that combines several features of the approaches described above, with the long-term goal of producing a new generation of powerful problem solving systems. The potential advantage of the autoconstructive evolution approach is that it will allow variation mechanisms to co-evolve with the programs to which they are applied, thereby allowing the evolutionary system itself to adapt to its problem environments in significant ways. The autoconstructive evolution approach was first described in 2001 and 2002 (Spector, 2001; Spector, 2002; Spector and Robinson, 2002a; Spector and Robinson, 2002b), using the Pushpop system that leveraged features of the Push programming language for evolved programs. In the next section this earlier work is briefly described. The subsequent section describes more recent work on the approach, using better technology and a more explicit focus on the goal of high performance problem solving, implemented in a newer system called *AutoPush*. The final section of the chapter offers some brief conclusions.

2.   Push and Pushpop

An *autoconstructive evolution* system was defined in (Spector and Robinson, 2002a) as "any evolutionary computation system that adaptively constructs its own mechanisms of reproduction and diversification as it runs." In the context of the present discussion, however, that definition is too general, and a more specific definition that captures both the past and present usage would be "any genetic programming system in which the methods for reproduction and diversification are encoded in the individual programs themselves, and are thereby subject to variation and evolution." The goal in the previous work, as in the work described here, is for the ways in which children are produced to be evolved along with the programs to which they will be applied. This is done by encoding the mechanisms for reproduction and diversification *within* the programs themselves, which must be capable of producing children and, in principle, of solving the problem to which the genetic programming system is being applied. The space of possible reproduction and diversification methods is vast and an ideal system would allow evolving programs to reach new and uncharted reaches of this space. Human-designed diversification mechanisms, including human-designed genetic operators, human-specified automatic mutation during code-manipulation, and human-written ancestor programs, should all be avoided.

Of course it will generally be necessary for *some* features of any evolutionary system to be pre-specified; for example, all of the systems described here borrow several pre-specified elements of traditional genetic programming systems, including a generation-based evolutionary loop, a fixed-size population, and tournament selection with a pre-specified tournament size. The focus here is on the evolution of the means by which children are produced from parents, and it is this task for which we currently seek autoconstructive methods.

A prerequisite for this approach is a program representation in which problem-solving functions and child-production functions can both be easily expressed. The *Push* programming language was originally designed specifically for this purpose (Spector, 2001). Push is a stack-based language roughly in the tradition of Forth, but for which each data type has its own stack. Instructions generally take their arguments from the appropriate stacks and push their results onto the appropriate stacks.[1] If an instruction requires arguments that are not present on the appropriate stacks when it is called then it does nothing (it acts as a "no-op").

---

[1] Exceptions are instructions that draw their inputs from external data structures, for example instructions that access inputs, and instructions that act on external data structures, for example "developmental" instructions that add components to externally-developing representations of circuits or other structured objects.

These specifications mean that even though multiple data types may be present in a program no instruction will ever be called on arguments of the wrong type, regardless of its syntactic position in the program. Among other benefits, this means that there are essentially no syntax constraints on Push programs aside from a requirement that parentheses be balanced. This is particularly useful for systems in which child programs will be produced by evolving programs.

One of Push's most important features for autoconstructive evolution, and for genetic programming more generally, is the fact that "code" is a first-class data type. When a Push program is being executed the code that is queued for execution is stored on a special stack called the "exec" stack, and exec instructions in the program can manipulate the queued instructions in order to implement a wide variety of evolved control structures (Spector et al., 2005). Additional code stacks (including one called simply "code," and in some implementations others with names such as "child") can be used to store and manipulate code for a variety of other purposes. This feature has significant benefits for genetic programming even in a non-autoconstructive context (that is, even when standard, hard-coded genetic operators are used, as in the PushGP system), but here we focus on the use of Push for autoconstructive evolution. Space limits prevent full exposition of the Push language here; see (Spector et al., 2005) and the references therein for further details.[2]

The first autoconstructive evolution system built using Push, called Pushpop, can best be understood as an extension of a more-standard genetic programming system such as PushGP. In PushGP, when a program is being tested for fitness on a particular fitness case it is run and then the problem-solving outputs are collected from the relevant data stacks (typically integer or float) and tested for errors; Pushpop does this as well, but it also simultaneously collects a potential child from the child stack. If the problem to which the system is being applied involves n fitness cases then the testing of each program in the population will produce n potential children. In the reproductive phase tournaments are conducted among parents and children are selected randomly from the set of potential children of the winning parents. If there are insufficient children to fill the child population then newly generated random individuals are used.

In Pushpop, as in any autoconstructive evolution system, care must be taken to prevent the takeover of the population by perfect replicators or other pathological replicants. Because there is no automatic mutation in Pushpop a perfect replicator can rapidly fill the population with copies of itself, after which no evolution (and indeed no change at all) will occur. The production of perfect replicators in Push is generally trivial, because programs are pushed onto the code stack prior to execution. For this reason Pushpop includes a "no cloning" rule that specifies that exact clones will not be allowed into the child popula-

---

[2] See also http://hampshire.edu/lspector/push.html.

tion. Settings are also available that prohibit children that are identical to any of their ancestors or any other individuals in the population. The "no cloning" rule forces programs to diversify in *some* way, but it does not dictate the mode or extent of diversification. The pathology of perfect replicators in nature was presumably overcome with the aid of vast stretches of time and over vast expanses of the Earth, within which perfect replicators may have arisen but later been eliminated when changes occurred to which they could not adapt. Our resources are much more constrained, however, and so we must proactively cull the individuals that we know cannot possibly evolve.

Programs in a Pushpop population can reproduce using evolved forms of multi-parent recombination, accessing other individuals in the population through the use of a variety of instructions provided for this purpose and using them in any computable way to produce their children (Spector and Robinson, 2002a). In fact, evolving Pushpop programs can access *and then execute* code from other individuals in the population, which means that evolved programs may not work correctly when executed outside of the populations within which they evolved. This is unfortunate from the perspective of a practitioner who is primarily interested in producing a program that will solve a particular problem, since the "solution" may require the entire population to work and it may be exceptionally difficult to understand. The mechanisms for population access in Pushpop are also somewhat complex, and the presence of these mechanisms makes it particularly difficult to analyze the performance of the system. For these reasons the new work described here does not allow executing programs to access the other programs in the population; see below for further discussion.

Pushpop is capable of solving simple symbolic regression problems, and it has served as the basis for studies of the evolution of diversification. For example, one study showed that evolving populations that produce adaptive Pushpop programs—that is, programs that actually solve the problems presented to the system—are reliably more diverse than is required by the "no cloning" rule alone (Spector, 2002). But Pushpop's utility as a problem-solving system is limited, and the focus of the Push project in subsequent years has been on more traditional genetic programming systems such as PushGP. PushGP uses traditional genetic operators but the code-manipulation features of Push nonetheless provide benefits, for example by simplifying the evolution of novel control structures and modular architectures.

More recently, however, the use of Push for autoconstructive evolution has been revisited in light of improvements to the Push language (Spector et al., 2005), the availability of substantially faster hardware, and a clarified focus on the long-term potential of autoconstructive evolution to solve problems that cannot be solved with hand-coded diversification mechanisms.

3.   Practical Autoconstructive Evolution

AutoPush is a new autoconstructive genetic programming system, a successor to Pushpop built on the more expressive version 3 of the Push programming language and designed with a more explicit focus on problem-solving power. To that end, several sources of inessential complexity in Pushpop have been removed to aid in the analysis of AutoPush runs and their results.

AutoPush, like Pushpop, uses the basic generational loop of a standard genetic programming system and tournament selection with a pre-specified tournament size. Also like Pushpop it uses no pre-specified genetic operators, no ancestor replicators, and no pre-specified, automatic mutation. And like Pushpop it represents its programs in a Turing complete language so that children may be produced from parents by means of any computable function, modulo limits on execution steps or time.

The current version of AutoPush is asexual—that is, parents must construct their children without having access to other programs in the population—because this eliminates the complexity that may not be necessary and it also simplifies analysis. Asexual programs may be run in isolation, both to solve the target problem and to study the range of children that they produce, and it is easy to store all of their ancestors (of which there will be only as many as there have been generations, while each individual in a sexually-reproducing population may have exponentially many ancestors). Future versions of AutoPush may reintroduce the possibility of recombination by reintroducing instructions that provide access to other individuals in the population; it is our intention to explore this option once the dynamics of the asexual version are better understood. It is also worth noting that the role of sex in biological diversification is a subject of considerable debate, and that asexual organisms diversify in complex and significant ways (Barraclough et al., 2003).

The processes by which programs are tested for problem-solving performance and used to produce children also differ between Pushpop and Auto-Push. In Pushpop a potential child is produced for each fitness case, during the calculation of the problem-solving answer for that fitness case. This means that the number of children may depend on the number of fitness cases, which complicates analysis and also changes the way that the algorithm will perform on problems with different numbers of fitness cases. By contrast, in AutoPush no children are produced during fitness testing; any code left on the code stack after a fitness-testing run is ignored.[3] Instead, when an individual is selected

---

[3] In Pushpop a special child stack is used for the production of children because the code stack is needed for the expression of evolved control structures in Push1, in which Pushpop was implemented. AutoPush is implemented in Push3, in which the new exec stack can be used for evolved control structures, freeing up the code stack for child production.

for autoconstructive reproduction in a tournament it is run again, with an input of 0, to produce a child program for the next generation.[4]

The most significant innovation in AutoPush is a new approach to constraints on birth and selection. Pushpop incorporates a "no cloning" rule but AutoPush goes further, adding more constraints on birth and selection to facilitate the evolution of adaptive diversification. Following the lead of meta-genetic programming developers who judged the fitness of evolving operators by "some measure of success in increasing the fitness of the population they operate on" (Edmonds, 2001), AutoPush incorporates factors based on the history of improvement within the ancestry of an individual.

There are many ways in which one might measure "history of improvement" and many ways in which such measurements might be used in an evolutionary algorithm. For example, Smits et al. define "activity" or "potential to improve" as "the sum of the number of moves [in the program search space] that either improved the fitness or neutral moves that resulted in either no change in fitness or a change that was less than a given (dynamic) tolerance limit" (Smits et al., 2010). They use this measure to select candidates for further testing, crossover, and replacement. Additional comments on varieties and measures of self-improvement can be found in (Schmidhuber, 2006).

In AutoPush the history of improvement is a scalar that summarizes the direction of problem-solving performance changes over the individual's ancestry, with greater weight given to more recent changes (see formula below). It would be tempting to use this measure of improvement only in selection, possibly as a second objective—in addition to problem-solving performance—in the context of a multi-objective selection scheme. But this, by itself, would not work well because selection cannot salvage a population that has become overrun by evolutionary "dead-enders" that can never produce improved descendants. Such dead-enders include not only cloners but also programs of several other categories. For example, consider a population full of programs that produce children that vary only in a subexpression that is never executed. This population is just as un-adaptive as a population of cloners, and it will do no good to select among its individuals on any basis whatsoever. Many other, more subtle categories of dead-enders exist, presenting challenges to any evolutionary system that relies only on selection to drive adaptation. The alternative approach taken in AutoPush is to prevent such dead-enders, when they can be detected, from reproducing at all, and to make room in the population for the children of improvers or at least for new random individuals.

---

[4]The input value of 0 is arbitrary, and an input value is provided only for the minor convenience of avoiding re-definition of the input-pushing instruction. None of this should be significant as long as we are consistent in the ways that we conduct the autoconstructive reproduction runs.

As a result, we place a variety of constraints on birth and selection which act collectively to promote the evolution of adaptive diversification without specifying the form(s) that the actual diversification algorithms will take. More specifically, we conduct selection using tournaments, with comparisons within the tournament set computed as follows:[5]

- Prefer reproductively competent parents: Individuals that were generated by other individuals beat randomly-generated individuals, and individuals that are "grandchildren" beat all others that are not. If both individuals being compared are grandchildren then the lengths of their lineages are not otherwise decisive.

- Prefer parents with non-stagnant lineages: A lineage is considered stagnant if it has persisted for at least some preset number of generations (6 in the experiments described here) and if problem-solving performance has not changed in the most recent half of the lineage.

- Prefer parents with good problem-solving performance: If neither reproductive competence nor lineage stagnation are decisive then select the parent that does a better job on the target problem.

The constraints on birth make use of two auxiliary definitions, for "improvement" and "code discrepancy." Improvement is a measure of how much the problem-solving performance of a lineage has improved, with greater weight being given to the most recent steps in the lineage. We first compute a normalized vector of changes in problem-solving performance, with improvements represented as 1, declines represented as -1, and repeats of the same value represented as 0. The overall improvement value is then calculated as the weighted average of the elements of this vector, with the weights produced by following function (with decay factor $\delta = 0.1$ for the runs described here):

$$w_{g=current-gen} = 1$$
$$w_{g-1} = w_g * (1 - \delta)$$

Code discrepancy is a measure of the difference between two programs, calculated as the sum, over all unique expressions and sub-expressions in either of the programs, of the difference between the numbers of occurrences of the expression in the two programs. In the context of these definitions we can state the constraints on birth as follows:

---

[5]These constraints, and those mentioned for birth below, are stated using the numerical parameter values that were chosen, more or less arbitrarily, for the runs described here. Other values may perform better, and further study may provide guidance on setting these values or eliminating the parameters altogether.

- Prevent birth from lineages with at least a preset threshold number of ancestors (4 here) and an improvement of less than some preset minimum (0.1 here).

- Prevent birth from lineages with at least a preset threshold number of ancestors (3 here) and constant discrepancy between parent and child in all generations.

- Prevent birth from parents that received disqualifying fitness penalties, e.g. for nontermination or non-production of result values.

- Prevent birth of children with sizes outside of the specified legal range (here 10–100 points).

- Prevent birth of children that are identical to any of their ancestors.

- Prevent birth of children that are identical to potential siblings; for this test the parent program is run a second time to produce an additional child that is used only for this comparison.

4.   Preliminary results

While the approach described here has not yet been shown to solve problems that are out of reach of more conventional genetic programming systems— indeed, it is currently weaker than the more-standard PushGP system—it has solved simple problems and produced illuminating data that may help to deepen our understanding.

For example, in one run on a symbolic regression problem with the target function $y = x^3 - 2x^2 - x$ AutoPush found a solution that descended from the following randomly generated program:[6]

```
((code_if (code_noop) boolean_fromfloat (2) integer_fromfloat)
(code_rand integer_rot) exec_swap code_append integer_mult)
```

While it is difficult to tell from inspection how this program works, even for those experienced in reading Push code, the specific code instructions that are included provide clues about how it constructs children. For example, the code_rand instruction generates new random code, and the code_append instruction combines two pieces of code on the code stack. It is even more revealing to look at the code outputs from several runs of this program. In this case they are all of the form:

```
(RANDOM-INSTRUCTION (code_if (code_noop) boolean_fromfloat
```

---

[6]Space limitations prevent full description of the run parameters or the instruction set; see (Spector et al., 2005) and the source code at http://hampshire.edu/lspector/gptp10 for more information.

```
(2) integer_fromfloat) (code_rand integer_rot) exec_swap code_append
integer_mult)
```

where "RANDOM-INSTRUCTION" is some particular randomly chosen instruction. So this program's reproductive strategy is merely to add a new, random instruction to the beginning of itself.

This strategy continues for several generations, with several improvements in problem-solving performance, until something new and interesting happens. In the sixth generation a child is produced with a new list added, rather than just a new instruction, and it also has a new reproductive strategy: it adds something new to the beginning of *both* of its top-level lists. In other words, the sixth-generation individual is of this form:

```
(SUB-EXPRESSION-1 SUB-EXPRESSION-2)
```

where each "SUB-EXPRESSION-n" is a different sub-expression, and the seventh-generation children of this program are all of the form:

```
((RANDOM-INSTRUCTION-1 (SUB-EXPRESSION-1))
 (RANDOM-INSTRUCTION-2 (SUB-EXPRESSION-2)))
```

where each "RANDOM-INSTRUCTION-n" is some particular randomly chosen instruction.

One generation later the problem was solved, by the following program:

```
((integer_stackdepth (boolean_and code_map)) (integer_sub
(integer_stackdepth (integer_sub (in (code_wrap (code_if (code_noop)
boolean_fromfloat (2) integer_fromfloat) (code_rand integer_rot)
exec_swap code_append integer_mult))))))
```

This program inherits the altered reproductive strategy of its parent, augmenting both of its primary sub-expressions with new initial instructions in its children.

In the run described above the only available code-manipulation instructions were those in the standard Push specification, which are modeled loosely on Lisp list-manipulation primitives. In some runs, however, we have added a "perturb" instruction that changes symbols and constants in a program to other random symbols or constants with a probability derived from an integer popped from the integer stack. Perturb, which was also used in some Pushpop runs, is itself a powerful mutation operator, but its availability does not dictate if or how or where it will be used; for example, it would be possible for an evolved reproductive strategy to use perturb on only one part of its code, or to use it with different probabilities on different parts of its code, or to use it conditionally or in conjunction with other code-manipulation instructions. With the perturb instruction included we have been able to solve somewhat more difficult problems such as the symbolic regression of $y = x^6 - 2x^4 + x^2 - 2$, and we are actively exploring application to more difficult problems and analysis of the resulting programs and lineages, with the hypothesis that more complex and adaptive reproductive strategies will emerge in the context of more challenging problem environments.

5.   Conclusions

The specific results reported here are preliminary, and the hypothesis that autoconstructive evolution will extend the problem-solving power of genetic programming is still speculative. However, the hypothesis has been refined, the means for testing it have been simplified, the principles that underlie it have been better articulated, and the prospects for analysis of incremental results have been improved. We have shown (again) that mechanisms of adaptive variation can evolve as components of evolving problem-solving systems, and we have described reasons to believe that the best problem-solving systems of the future will make use of some such techniques. Only further experimentation will determine whether and when autoconstructive evolution will become the most appropriate technique for solving difficult problems of practical significance.

Acknowledgments

Kyle Harrington, Paul Sawaya, Thomas Helmuth, Brian Martin, Scott Niekum and Rebecca Neimark contributed to conversations in which some of the ideas used in this work were refined. Thanks also to the GPTP reviewers, to William Josiah Erikson for superb technical support, and to Hampshire College for support for the Hampshire College Institute for Computational Intelligence.

References

Angeline, Peter J. (1995). Adaptive and self-adaptive evolutionary computations. In Palaniswami, Marimuthu and Attikiouzel, Yianni, editors, *Computational Intelligence: A Dynamic Systems Perspective*, pages 152–163. IEEE Press.

Angeline, Peter J. (1996). Two self-adaptive crossover operators for genetic programming. In Angeline, Peter J. and Kinnear, Jr., K. E., editors, *Advances in Genetic Programming 2*, chapter 5, pages 89–110. MIT Press, Cambridge, MA, USA.

Barraclough, Timothy G., Birky, C. William Jr., and Burt, Austin (2003). Diversification in sexual and asexual organisms. *Evolution*, 57:2166–2172.

Beyer, Hans-Georg and Meyer-Nieberg, Silja (2006). Self-adaptation of evolution strategies under noisy fitness evaluations. *Genetic Programming and Evolvable Machines*, 7(4):295–328.

Diosan, Laura and Oltean, Mihai (2009). Evolutionary design of evolutionary algorithms. *Genetic Programming and Evolvable Machines*, 10(3):263–306.

Edmonds, Bruce (2001). Meta-genetic programming: Co-evolving the operators of variation. *Elektrik*, 9(1):13–29. Turkish Journal Electrical Engineering and Computer Sciences.

Eiben, Agoston Endre, Hinterding, Robert, and Michalewicz, Zbigniew (1999). Parameter control in evolutionary algorithms. *IEEE Transations on Evolutionary Computation*, 3(2):124–141.

Fodor, Jerry and Piattelli-Palmarini, Massimo (2010). *What Darwin got wrong*. New York: Farrar, Straus and Giroux.

Fontana, Walter (1992). Algorithmic chemistry. In Langton, C. G., Taylor, C., Farmer, J. D., and Rasmussen, S., editors, *Artificial Life II*, pages 159–210. Addison-Wesley.

Fry, Rodney, Smith, Stephen L., and Tyrrell, Andy M. (2005). A self-adaptive mate selection model for genetic programming. In *Proceedings of the 2005 IEEE Congress on Evolutionary Computation*, volume 3, pages 2707–2714, Edinburgh, UK. IEEE Press.

Gerhart, John and Kirschner, Marc (2007). The theory of facilitated variation. *Proceedings of the National Academy of Sciences*, 104:8582–8589.

Kantschik, Wolfgang, Dittrich, Peter, Brameier, Markus, and Banzhaf, Wolfgang (1999). Meta-evolution in graph GP. In *Genetic Programming, Proceedings of EuroGP '99*, volume 1598 of *LNCS*, pages 15–28, Goteborg, Sweden. Springer-Verlag.

Koza, John R. (1994). Spontaneous emergence of self-replicating and evolutionarily self-improving computer programs. In Langton, Christopher G., editor, *Artificial Life III*, volume XVII of *SFI Studies in the Sciences of Complexity*, pages 225–262. Addison-Wesley, Santa Fe, New Mexico, USA.

Langdon, William B. and Poli, Riccardo (2006). On turing complete T7 and MISC F–4 program fitness landscapes. In Arnold, Dirk V., Jansen, Thomas, Vose, Michael D., and Rowe, Jonathan E., editors, *Theory of Evolutionary Algorithms*, Dagstuhl, Germany. Internationales Begegnungs- und Forschungszentrum fuer Informatik (IBFI), Schloss Dagstuhl, Germany.

MacCallum, Robert M. (2003). Introducing a perl genetic programming system: and can meta-evolution solve the bloat problem? In *Genetic Programming, Proceedings of EuroGP '2003*, volume 2610 of *LNCS*, pages 364–373, Essex. Springer-Verlag.

Maynard Smith, John and Szathmáry, Eörs (1999). *The origins of life*. Oxford: Oxford University Press.

Nordin, Peter and Banzhaf, Wolfgang (1995). Evolving turing-complete programs for a register machine with self-modifying code. In *Genetic Algorithms: Proceedings of the Sixth International Conference (ICGA95)*, pages 318–325, Pittsburgh, PA, USA. Morgan Kaufmann.

Ofria, Charles and Wilke, Claus O. (2004). Avida: A software platform for research in computational evolutionary biology. *Artificial Life*, 10(2):191–229.

Poli, Riccardo, Langdon, William B., and McPhee, Nicholas Freitag (2008). *A field guide to genetic programming.* http://lulu.com and freely available at http://www.gp-field-guide.org.uk. (With contributions by J. R. Koza).

Ray, Thomas S. (1991). Is it alive or is it GA. In *Proceedings of the Fourth International Conference on Genetic Algorithms*, pages 527–534, University of California - San Diego, La Jolla, CA, USA. Morgan Kaufmann.

Schmidhuber, Jurgen (1987). Evolutionary principles in self-referential learning. on learning now to learn: The meta-meta-meta...-hook. Diploma thesis, Technische Universitat Munchen, Germany.

Schmidhuber, Jurgen (2006). Gödel machines: Fully self-referential optimal universal self-improvers. In Goertzel, B. and Pennachin, C., editors, *Artificial General Intelligence*, pages 119–226. Springer.

Silva, Sara and Dignum, Stephen (2009). Extending operator equalisation: Fitness based self adaptive length distribution for bloat free GP. In *Proceedings of the 12th European Conference on Genetic Programming, EuroGP 2009*, volume 5481 of *LNCS*, pages 159–170, Tuebingen. Springer.

Sipper, Moshe and Reggia, James A. (2001). Go forth and replicate. *Scientific American*, 265(2):27–35.

Smits, Guido F., Vladislavleva, Ekaterina, and Kotanchek, Mark E. (2010). Scalable symbolic regression by continuous evolution with very small populations. In Riolo, Rick L., McConaghy, Trent, and Vladislavleva, Ekaterina, editors, *Genetic Programming Theory and Practice VIII*. Springer.

Spears, William M. (1995). Adapting crossover in evolutionary algorithms. In *Proceedings of the Fourth Annual Conference on Evolutionary Programming*, pages 367–384. MIT Press.

Spector, Lee (2001). Autoconstructive evolution: Push, pushGP, and pushpop. In *Proceedings of the Genetic and Evolutionary Computation Conference (GECCO-2001)*, pages 137–146, San Francisco, California, USA. Morgan Kaufmann.

Spector, Lee (2002). Adaptive populations of endogenously diversifying pushpop organisms are reliably diverse. In *Proceedings of Artificial Life VIII, the 8th International Conference on the Simulation and Synthesis of Living Systems*, pages 142–145, University of New South Wales, Sydney, NSW, Australia. The MIT Press.

Spector, Lee, Klein, Jon, and Keijzer, Maarten (2005). The push3 execution stack and the evolution of control. In *GECCO 2005: Proceedings of the 2005 conference on Genetic and evolutionary computation*, volume 2, pages 1689–1696, Washington DC, USA. ACM Press.

Spector, Lee and Robinson, Alan (2002a). Genetic programming and autoconstructive evolution with the push programming language. *Genetic Programming and Evolvable Machines*, 3(1):7–40.

Spector, Lee and Robinson, Alan (2002b). Multi-type, self-adaptive genetic programming as an agent creation tool. In *GECCO 2002: Proceedings of the Bird of a Feather Workshops, Genetic and Evolutionary Computation Conference*, pages 73–80, New York. AAAI.

Suzuki, Hideaki (2004). *Design Optimization of Artificial Evolutionary Systems*. Doctor of informatics, Graduate School of Informatics, Kyoto University, Japan.

Tavares, Jorge, Machado, Penousal, Cardoso, Amilcar, Pereira, Francisco B., and Costa, Ernesto (2004). On the evolution of evolutionary algorithms. In *Genetic Programming 7th European Conference, EuroGP 2004, Proceedings*, volume 3003 of *LNCS*, pages 389–398, Coimbra, Portugal. Springer-Verlag.

Taylor, Timothy John (1999). *From Artificial Evolution to Artificial Life*. PhD thesis, Division of Informatics, University of Edinburgh, UK.

Teller, Astro (1994). Turing completeness in the language of genetic programming with indexed memory. In *Proceedings of the 1994 IEEE World Congress on Computational Intelligence*, volume 1, pages 136–141, Orlando, Florida, USA. IEEE Press.

Vafaee, Fatemeh, Xiao, Weimin, Nelson, Peter C., and Zhou, Chi (2008). Adaptively evolving probabilities of genetic operators. In *Seventh International Conference on Machine Learning and Applications, ICMLA '08*, pages 292–299, La Jolla, San Diego, USA. IEEE.

Woodward, John (2003). Evolving turing complete representations. In *Proceedings of the 2003 Congress on Evolutionary Computation*, pages 830–837, Canberra. IEEE Press.

Yabuki, Taro and Iba, Hitoshi (2004). Genetic programming using a Turing complete representation: recurrent network consisting of trees. In de Castro, Leandro N. and Von Zuben, Fernando J., editors, *Recent Developments in Biologically Inspired Computing*, chapter 4, pages 61–81. Idea Group Publishing.

Chapter 3

THE RUBIK CUBE AND GP TEMPORAL SEQUENCE LEARNING: AN INITIAL STUDY

Peter Lichodzijewski and Malcolm Heywood

Faculty of Computer Science, Dalhousie University, 6050 University Av., Halifax, NS, B3H 1W5. Canada.

Abstract   The 3×3 Rubik cube represents a potential benchmark for temporal sequence learning under a discrete application domain with multiple actions. Challenging aspects of the problem domain include the large state space and a requirement to learn invariances relative to the specific colours present the latter element of the domain making it difficult to evolve individuals that learn 'macro-moves' relative to multiple cube configurations. An initial study is presented in this work to investigate the utility of Genetic Programming capable of layered learning and problem decomposition. The resulting solutions are tested on 5,000 test cubes, of which specific individuals are able to solve up to 350 (7 percent) cube configurations and population wide behaviours are capable of solving up to 1,200 (24 percent) of the test cube configurations. It is noted that the design options for generic fitness functions are such that users are likely to face either reward functions that are very expensive to evaluate or functions that are very deceptive. Addressing this might well imply that domain knowledge is explicitly used to decompose the task to avoid these challenges. This would augment the described generic approach currently employed for Layered learning/ problem decomposition.

Keywords: bid-based cooperative behaviours, problem decomposition, Rubik cube, symbiotic coevolution, temporal sequence learning.

1.   Introduction

Evolutionary Computation as applied to temporal sequence learning problems generally assumes a phylogenetic framework for learning (Barreto et al., 2009). That is to say, policies are evaluated in their entirety on the problem domain before search operators are applied to produce new policies. Conversely, the ontogenetic approach to temporal sequence learning performs incremental refinement over a single candidate solution with respect to each state–action pair

(Barreto et al., 2009). The latter is traditionally referred to as reinforcement learning. However, the distinction is often ignored, with reinforcement learning frequently used as a general label for any scenario in which the temporal credit assignment problem/ delayed reward exists; not least because algorithms are beginning to appear which combine both phylogenetic and ontogenetic mechanisms of learning (Whiteson and Stone, 2006).[1] Examples of the temporal sequence learning problem appear in many forms, from control style formulations in which the goal is to learn a policy for controlling a robot or vehicle to games in which the general objective is to learn a strategy. In this work we are interested in the latter domain, specifically the case of learning a strategy to solve multiple configurations of the 3×3 Rubik cube.

The problem of learning to solve Rubik cube configurations presents multiple challenges of wider interest to the temporal sequence learning community. Specific examples might include: 1) a large number of states ranging from trivial to demanding, 2) the problem is known to challenge human players, 3) a wide variation in start states exists, therefore resilient to self play dynamics that might simplify board games such as back-gammon (Pollack and Blair, 1998), 4) generalization to learn invariances/ symmetries implicit in the game.

Approaches for finding solutions to scrambled configurations of a Rubik cube fall into one of two general approaches: optimal solvers or macro-moves. In the case of solving a cube using a minimal (optimal) number of moves, extensive use is made of lookup tables to provide an exact evaluation function as deployed relative to a game tree summary of the cube state. Thus with respect to the eight corner cubies, the position and orientation of a single cubie is defined by the other 7; or $8! \times 3^7 = 88,179,840$ combinations. An iterative deepening breadth first search would naturally enumerate all such paths between goal and possible configurations for the corner cubies, forming a "pattern database" for later use. Most emphasis is therefore on the utilization of appropriate hash codings and graph symmetries to extend this enumeration over all possible legal states of a cube (in total there are 4.3252×10^{19} legal states in a 3×3 cube). Such an approach recently identified an upper bound on the number of moves necessary to solve a worst case cube configuration as 26 (Kunkle and Cooperman, 2007).

Conversely, non-optimal methods rely on 'macro-moves' which establish the correct location for specific cubies without disrupting the location of perviously positioned cubies. This is the approach most widely assumed by both human players and 'automated' solvers. Such strategies generally take 50 to 100 moves to solve a scrambled cube (Korf, 1997). The advantage this gives is that "general purpose" strategies might result that are appropriate to a wide range of

---

[1]In the following we will use the terms reinforcement and temporal sequence learning interchangeably, particularly where there is a previous established history of terminology e.g., as in hierarchical reinforcement learning.

scenarios, thus giving hope for identifying machine learning approaches that generalize. However, from the perspective of cube 'state' we can also see that once one face of a cube is completed the completion of the remaining faces will increasingly result in periods when the relative entropy of the cube will go up considerably.[2] Moreover, from a learning system perspective macro-moves need to be associated with any color combination to be effective, a problem that represents a requirement for learning invariances in a scalable manner.

Two previous published attempts to evolve solutions to the Rubik cube using evolutionary methods have taken rather different approaches to the problem. One attempts to evolve a generic strategy under little a priori information (Baum and Durdanovic, 2000); whereas the second concentrates on independently evolving optimal move sequences to each scrambled cube (El-Sourani et al., 2010), making use of domain knowledge to formulate appropriate constraints and objectives. In this work we assume the motivation of the former, thus the goal is to evolve a program able to provide solutions to as many scrambled cubes as possible.

The approach taken by (Baum and Durdanovic, 2000) employed a domain specific language under the Hayek framework for phylogenetic temporal sequence learning. A domain specific representation included the capability to 'address' specific faces of the cube and compare content with other faces as well as tests for the number of correct cubies. Two approaches to training were considered, either incrementally increasing the difficulty of cube configurations (e.g., one or two twist modifications relative to a solved cube) with binary (solved/ not solved) feedback or cubes with a 100 twist 'scrambling' and feedback proportional to the number of correctly placed cubies. Two different formulations for actions applied to a cube were also considered, with an action space of either three (90 degree turn of the front face, and row or column twists of the cube) or a fixed 3-dimensional co-ordinate frame on which a total of twelve 90 degree turns are applied (the scheme employed here). The most notable result from Hayek relative to this work was that up to 10 cubies could be correctly placed (one face and some of the middle). In effect Hayek was building macro-moves, but could not work through the construction of the remaining cube faces without destroying the work done on the first face.

In the following we develop the Symbiotic Bid-Based (SBB) GP framework and introduce a generic approach to layered learning that does not rely on the a priori definition of different goal functions for each 'layer' (as per the classical definition of Layered learning (Stone, 2007)). The use of layering is supported by the explicitly symbiotic approach adopted to evolution. A discussion of the domain specific requirements will then be made, with results establishing the

---

[2]Consider the case of completing the final face if all other cubies are correctly positioned.

relative success of the initial approach adopted here, and conclusions discussing future work in the Rubik cube domain.

2.   Layered learning in Symbiotic Bid-Based GP

Symbiosis is a process by which symbionts of different species – in this case computer programs – receive sufficient ecological pressure to cooperate in a common host compartment (Heywood and Lichodzijewski, 2010). Over a period of time the symbionts will either develop the fitness of the host or not, as per natural selection. Thus, fitness evaluation takes place at the level of hosts not at the level of individual symbionts, or a serial dependence between host and symbionts (Figure 3-1).

In the case of this work, hosts are represented by an independent population – a Genetic Algorithm in this case – each host individual defining a compartment by indexing a subset of individuals from an independent symbiont population (Figure 3-1). However, rather than symbionts from the same host having their respective outcomes combined in some form of a voting policy – as in ensemble methods – we explicitly require each symbiont to learn the specific context in which they operate. To do so, symbionts assume the bid-based GP framework (Lichodzijewski and Heywood, 2007). Thus, each symbiont consists of a program and a scalar. The program is used to evolve a *bidding strategy* and the scalar expresses a domain dependent *action*, say class label or 'turn right'. The program evolves whereas the action does not. Within the context of a host individual each symbiont executes their program on the current state of the world/ training instance. The symbiont with the largest bid winning the right to present its action as the outcome from that host under the current state. Under a reinforcement learning domain this action would update the state of the world and the process repeats, with a new round of bidding between symbionts from the same host w.r.t. the updated state of the world. Fitness evaluation is performed over the worlds/ training instances defined by the point population (Algorithm 1, Step 10). Competitive coevolution therefore facilitates the development of point and host populations, with co-operative coevolution developing the interaction between symbionts within a host. Competitive coevolution again appears between hosts in the host population (speciation) to maintain host diversity. This latter point is deemed particularly important in supporting 'intrinsic motivation' in the behaviours evolved,[3] where this represents a central tenet for hierarchical reinforcement learning in general (Oudeyer et al., 2007).

---

[3] Intrinsic motivations or goals are considered to be those central to supporting the existence of an organism. In addition to behaviour diversity, the desire to reproduce is considered an intrinsic motivation/ goal. Conversely, 'extrinsic motivations' are secondary factors that might act in support of the original intrinsic factors such as food seeking behaviours, where these are learnt during the lifetime of the organism and might be specific to that particular organism.

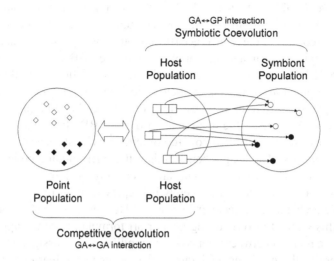

Figure 3-1. Generic architecture of Symbiotic Bid-Based GP (SBB). A *point population* represents the subset of training scenarios over which a training epoch is performed. The *host population* conducts a combinatorial search for the best symbiont partnerships; whereas the *symbiont population* contains the bid-based GP individuals who attempt to learn a good context for their corresponding actions.

Algorithm 1 The core SBB training algorithm. P^t, H^t, and S^t refer to the point, host, and symbiont populations at time t.

1: **procedure** TRAIN
2:    $t = 0$ ▷ Initialization
3:    initialize point population P^t
4:    initialize host population H^t (and symbiont population S^t)
5:    **while** $t \leq t_{max}$ **do**   ▷ Main loop
6:       create new points and add to P^t
7:       create new hosts and add to H^t (add new symbionts to S^t)
8:       **for all** $h_i \in H^t$ **do**
9:          **for all** $p_k \in P^t$ **do**
10:             evaluate h_i on p_k
11:          **end for**
12:       **end for**
13:       remove points from P^t
14:       remove hosts from H^t (remove symbionts from S^t)
15:       $t = t + 1$
16:    **end while**
17: **end procedure**

The above Symbiotic Bid-Based GP or 'SBB' framework – as summarized by Figure 3-1 and Algorithm 1 – provides a natural scheme for layered learning by letting the content of the (converged) host population represent the actions for a new set of symbionts in a second application of the SBB algorithm; hereafter 'Layered SBB'. The association between the next population of symbionts and the earlier population of hosts is explicitly hierarchical. However, there is no explicit requirement to re-craft fitness functions at each layering (although this is also possible). Instead, the reapplication of the SBB algorithm results in a second layer of hosts that learn how to combine previously learnt behaviours in specific contexts. The insight behind this is that SBB bidding policies under a temporal sequence learning domain are effectively evolving the conditions under which an action begins and ends its deployment. This is the general goal of hierarchical reinforcement learning. However, the SBB framework achieves this without also requiring an a priori formulation of the appropriate subtasks, the relation between subtasks, or a modified credit assignment policy; as is generally the case under hierarchical reinforcement learning (Oudeyer et al., 2007). In the following we summarize the core SBB algorithm, where this extends the original SBB framework presented in (Lichodzijewski and Heywood, 2008) and was applied elsewhere in a single layer supervised learning context (Lichodzijewski and Heywood, 2010a); the reader is referred to the latter for additional details of regarding host–symbiont variation operators.

Point Population

As indicated in the above generic algorithm description, a competitive co-evolutionary relationship is assumed between point and host population (Figure 3-1). Specifically, variation in the point population supports the necessary development in the host population. This implies that points have a fitness and are subject to variation operators. Thus, points are created in two phases on account of assuming a breeder style of replacement in which the worst P_{gap} points are removed (Step 13) – hereafter all references to specific 'Steps' are w.r.t. Algorithm 1 – and a corresponding number of new points are introduced (Step 6) at each generation. New points are created under one of two paths. Either a point is created as per the routine utilized at initialization (no concept of a parent point) or offspring are initialized relative to a parent point, with the parent selected under fitness proportional selection. The relative frequency of each point creation scheme is defined by a corresponding probability, p_{genp}. Discussion of the point population variation operators is necessarily application dependent, and is therefore presented later (Section 3).

The evaluation function of Step 10 assumes the application of a domain specific reward that is a function of the interaction between point (p_k) and host

(h_i) individuals, or $G(h_i, p_k)$. This is therefore defined later (Equation (3.6), Section 3) as a weighted distance relative to the ideal target state.

The global / base point fitness, f_k, may now be defined relative to the count of hosts, c_k, within a neighbourhood (Lichodzijewski and Heywood, 2010a), or

$$f_k = \begin{cases} 1 + \frac{1-c_k}{H_{size}} & \text{if } c_k > 0 \\ 0 & \text{otherwise} \end{cases} \tag{3.1}$$

where H_{size} is the host population size, and count c_k is relative to the arithmetic mean μ_k of outcomes on point p_k or,

$$\mu_k = \frac{\sum_{h_i} G(h_i, p_k)}{H_{size}} \tag{3.2}$$

where $\mu \to 0$ implies that hosts are failing on point p_k and c_k is set to zero. Otherwise, c_k is defined by the number of hosts satisfying $G(h_i, p_k) \geq \mu_k$; that is the number of hosts with an outcome reaching the mean performance on point p_k.

Equation (3.1) establishes the global fitness of a point. However, unlike classification problem domains, points frequently have context under reinforcement learning domains i.e., a geometric interpretation. This enables us to define a local factor by which the global reward is modulated in proportion to the relative 'local' uniqueness of the candidate point. Specifically, each point is rewarded in proportion to the distance from the point to a subset of its nearest neighbours using ideas from outlier detection (Harmeling et al., 2006). To do so, all the points are first normalized by the maximum pair-wise Euclidean distance – as estimated across the point population content, therefore limiting local reward to the unit interval – after which the following reward scheme is adopted:

1. The set of K points nearest to p_k is identified;

2. The local reward r_k is calculated as,

$$r_k = \left(\frac{\sum_{p_l} (D(p_k, p_l))^2}{K} \right)^2 \tag{3.3}$$

   where the summation is taken over the set of K points nearest to p_k and $D(\cdot, \cdot)$ is the application specific distance function (Equation (3.7), Section 3).

3. The corresponding final fitness for point p_k is defined in terms of both global and local rewards or

$$f'_k = f_k \cdot r_k \tag{3.4}$$

With the normalized fitness f'_k established we can now delete the worst performing P_{gap} points (Step 13).

Host and Symbiont Population

Hosts are also subject to the removal and addition of a fixed number of H_{gap} individuals per generation, Steps 14 and 7 respectively. However, in order to also promote diversity in the host population behaviours, we assume a fitness sharing formulation. Thus, shared fitness, s_i of host h_i has the form,

$$s_i = \sum_{p_k} \left(\frac{G(h_i, p_k)}{\sum_{h_j} G(h_j, p_k)} \right)^3 \tag{3.5}$$

Thus, for point p_k the shared fitness score s_i re-weights the reward that host h_i receives on p_k relative to the reward on the same point as received by all hosts. As per the earlier comments regarding the role of fitness sharing in supporting 'intrinsic motivation,' a strong bias for diversity is provided through the cubic power. Evaluation takes place at Step 10, thus all hosts, h_i, are evaluated on all points, p_k.

Once the shared score for each host is calculated, the H_{gap} lowest ranked hosts are removed. Any symbionts that are no longer indexed by hosts are considered ineffective and are therefore also deleted. Thus, the symbiont population size may dynamically vary, with variation operators having the capacity to add additional symbionts (Lichodzijewski and Heywood, 2010a), whereas the point and host populations are of a fixed size.

3. Domain specific design decisions

Cube representation and actions

The representation assumed directly indexes all 54 facelets comprising the 3×3 Rubik cube. Indexing is sequential, beginning at the centre face with cubie colours differentiated in terms of integers over the interval $[0, ..., 5]$. Such a scheme is simplistic with no explicit support for indicating which facelets are explicitly connected to make corner or edges. Actions in layer 0 define a 90 degree clock-wise or counter clock-wise twists to each face; there are 6 faces resulting in a total of 12 actions. When additional layers are added under SBB, the population of host behaviours from the previous population represent the set of candidate actions. As such additional layers attempt to evolve new contexts for previously evolved behaviours/ build larger macro-moves.

Reward and distance functions

The reward function applies a simple weighting scheme to the number of quarter turn twists (i.e., actions) necessary to move the final cube state to a solved cube. Naturally, such a test becomes increasingly expensive as the number of moves applied in the 'search' about the final cube state increases. Hence, the search is limited to testing for up to 2 moves away from the solution, resulting in the following reward function,

$$G(h_i, p_k) = \frac{1}{(1 + D(s_f, s^*))^2} \tag{3.6}$$

where s_f is the final state of the cube relative to cube configuration p_k and sequence of moves defined by host h_i; s^* is the ideal solved cube configuration, and; $D(s_2, s_1)$ defines the weighted distance function, or

$$D(s_2, s_1) = \begin{cases} 0, & \text{when 0 quarter twists match state } s_2 \text{ with } s_1 \\ 1, & \text{when 1 quarter twists match state } s_2 \text{ with } s_1 \\ 4, & \text{when 2 quarter twists match state } s_2 \text{ with } s_1 \\ 16, & \text{when} > 2 \text{ quarter twists match state } s_2 \text{ with } s_1 \end{cases} \tag{3.7}$$

Naturally, curtailing the 'look-ahead' to 2 quarter turn twists from the presented solution casts the fitness function into that of a highly deceptive 'needle in a haystack' style reward i.e., feedback is only available when you have all but provided a perfect solution. Adding additional twist tests however would result in tens of thousands of cube combinations potentially requiring evaluation before fitness could be defined. Other functions such as counting the number of correct facelets or cube entropy generally appeared to be less informative. The utility of combined metrics or a priori defined constraints might be of interest in future work.

Symbiont representation

Symbionts take the form of a linear GP representation, with instruction set for the Bid-Based GP individuals consisting of the following generic set of operators $\{+, -, \times, \div, ln(\cdot), cos(\cdot), exp(\cdot), if\}$. The conditional operator '*if*' applies an inequality operator to two registers and interchanges the sign of the first register if its value is smaller than the second. There are always 8 registers and a maximum of 24 instructions per symbiont.

Point initialization and offspring

Initialization of points – cube configurations used during evolution (Step 3) – takes the form of: (1) uniform sampling from the interval $[1, ..., 10]$ to define the number of twists applied to a solved cube; (2) stochastic selection of the sequence of quarter twist actions used to 'scramble' the cube, and; (3) test for a return to the solved cube configuration (in which case the quarter twist step is repeated). Thereafter, new points introduced during breeding (Step 6) follow one of two scenarios: adding twists to a parent point to create a child with probability p_{genp} or create a new point as per the aforementioned point initialization algorithm with probability $1 - p_{genp}$. The point offspring/ parent-wise creation is governed by the following process:

1. Select parent point, $p_i \in P^t$, under fitness proportional selection (point fitness defined by Equation (3.4), Section 2);

2. Define the number of additional twists, w_i, applied to create the child from the parent in terms of a normal p.d.f., or

$$w_i = abs(N(0, \sigma_{genTwist})) + 1 \qquad (3.8)$$

where $N(0, \sigma_{genTwist})$ is a normal p.d.f. with zero mean and variance $\sigma_{genTwist}$. Naturally, this is rounded to the nearest integer value;

3. Until the twist limit (w_i) is reached, select faces and clockwise/ counter clockwise twists with uniform probability relative to the parent cube configuration, p_i;

4. Should the resulting cube be a solved cube, the previous step is repeated.

4.   Results

Parameterization

Runs are performed over 60 initializations for both the case of Layered SBB (two layers) and single layer SBB base cases. The latter are parameterized to provide the same number of fitness evaluations/ upper bound on the number of instructions executed as per the total Layered SBB requirement. In the case of this work this implies a limit of 72000 evaluations or a $maxProgSize$ limit of 36 under the single layer baseline; hereafter '*big prog*'. Likewise reasoning brings about a team size limit (ω) of 36 under the single layer SBB baseline; hereafter '*big team*'. Relative to the sister work in which the current SBB formulation was applied to data sets from the supervised learning domain of classification (Lichodzijewski and Heywood, 2010a), three additional parameters are introduced for point generation (Section 2): (1) outlier parameter $K = 13$; (2) the probability of creating points $p_{genp} = 0.9$; and, (3) the variance for defining the number of additional twists necessary to create an offspring from a parent point $\sigma_{genTwist} = 3$. All other parameters are unchanged relative to those of the classification study (Table 3-1).

Table 3-1. Parameterization at Host (GA) and Symbiont (GP) populations. As per Linear GP, a fixed number of general purpose registers are assumed ($numRegisters$) and variable length programs subject to a max. instruction count ($maxProgSize$).

Host (solution) level			
Parameter	Value	Parameter	Value
t_{max}	1 000	ω	24
P_{size}, H_{size}	120	P_{gap}, H_{gap}	20, 60
p_{md}	0.7	p_{ma}	0.7
p_{mm}	0.2	p_{mn}	0.1
Symbiont (program) level			
numRegisters	8	*maxProgSize*	24
p_{delete}, p_{add}	0.5	p_{mutate}, p_{swap}	1.0

Sampled Test Set

Post training test performance is evaluated w.r.t. 5,000 unique 'random' test cubes, created as per the point initialization algorithm. Table 3-2 summarizes the distribution of cubes relative to the number of twists used to create them. A combined violin / quartile box plot is then used to express the total number of cube configurations solved. Figures 3-2 and 3-3 summarize this in terms of a single champion individual from each run[4] and corresponding cumulated population wide performance.

It is immediately apparent that the population wide behaviour (Figure 3-3) provides a significant source of useful diversity relative to that of the corresponding individual-wise performance (Figure 3-2). This is a generic property of fitness sharing implicit in the base SBB algorithm; Equation (3.5). However, it is also clear that under SBB 1 – in which second layer symbionts assume the hosts from layer 0 as their actions – the champion individuals are *unable* to directly build on the cumulative population wide behaviour from SBB 0. Conversely, under the case of real-valued reinforcement problem domains – such as the truck backer-upper (Lichodzijewski and Heywood, 2010b) – SBB 1 individuals were capable of producing champions that subsumed the SBB 0 population-wise performance. We attribute this to the more informative fitness function available under the truck backer-upper domain than that available under the Rubik cube.

Relative to the non-layered SBB base cases, no real trend appears under the individual-wise performance (Figure 3-2). Conversely, under the cumulative population wide behaviour (Figure 3-3), SBB 1 provides a significant

---

[4]Identified post training on an independent validation set generated as per the stochastic process used to identify the independent test set.

Table 3-2. Distribution of test cases. Samples selected over 1 to 10 random twists relative to solved cube resulting in 5,000 unique test configurations.

Number of twists	# of test cases	Number of twists	# of test cases
1	9	6	662
2	86	7	640
3	403	8	728
4	527	9	673
5	588	10	683

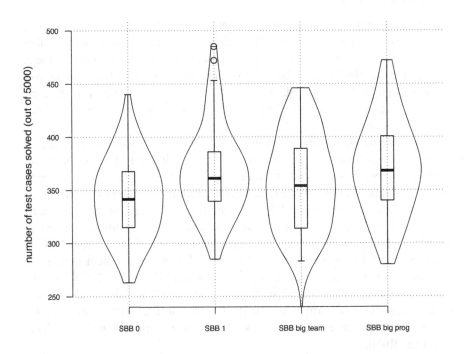

Figure 3-2. Total test cases solved by single best individual per run under SBB with and without layering under the stochastic sampling of 5,000 1 to 10 twist cubes. '*SBB 0*' and '*SBB 1*' denote first and second layer Layered SBB solutions. '*big team*' and '*big prog*' represent single layer SBB runs with either larger host or symbiont instruction limits.

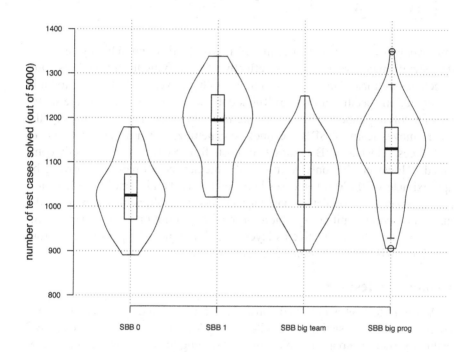

Figure 3-3. Total test cases solved by cumulated population wide performance per run under SBB with and without layering under the stochastic sampling of 5,000 1 to 10 twist cubes. '*SBB 0*' and '*SBB 1*' denote first and second layer Layered SBB solutions. '*big team*' and '*big prog*' represent single layer SBB runs with either larger host or symbiont instruction limits.

Table 3-3. Two-tailed Mann-Whitney test comparing total solutions under the Sampled Test Set provided by Layered SBB (second level) against single layer SBB parameterizations (big team (SBB-bt) and big program (SBB-bp)). The table reports *p*-values for the pair-wise comparison of distributions from Figures 3-2 and 3-3. Cases where the Layered SBB medians are higher (better) than non-layered SBB medians are noted with a ⋆.

Test Case	Champion individual	Population wide
Layered SBB vs SBB-0	0.002499⋆	3.11e-15⋆
Layered SBB vs SBB-bt	0.1519⋆	1.003e-10⋆
Layered SBB vs SBB-bp	0.5566	0.0002617⋆

improvement as measured in terms of a two-tailed Mann-Whitney test with 0.01 significance level (Table 3-3), effectively identifying the most consistently effective solutions. This appears to indicate that Layered SBB is able to build configuration specific sub-sets of Rubik cube solvers – that is to say, the strategies for solving cube configurations are not colour invariant. Specifically, the macro moves learnt at SBB 0 cannot be generalized over all permutations of cube faces. Thus, at SBB 1, subsets of hosts from SBB 0 can be usefully combined. However, this only results in the median performance improving by approximately 50 (200) test cases between layers 0 and 1 under single champion (respectively population-wise) test counts. Overall, neither increasing the instruction count limit per symbiont or maximum limit on the number of symbionts per host is as effective as layering at leveraging the performance from individual-wise to population wide performance.

Exhaustive test set

A second test set is designed consisting of all 1, 2 and 3 quarter twist cube configurations – consisting of 12, 114 and 1,068 unique test cubes respectively.[5] Naturally, there is no a priori bias towards solving these during training, cubes being configured stochastically relative to points selected under fitness proportional selection. Figure 3-4 summarizes this as a percentage of the number of 1, 2 and 3 twist configurations solved by the single best individual in each run.[6] The impact of layering is again evident, both from a consistency perspective and in terms of incremental improvements to the number of cases solved with each additional layer. Relative to the baseline single layer models, it is interesting to note that both 'SBB big team' and 'SBB big prog' had difficulty consistently solving the 1 twist configurations, whereas all SBB 1 first quartile performance

---

[5]These counts are somewhat lower than those reported in (Korf, 1997) because we do not include 180° twists in the set of permitted actions.
[6]The same 'champion' individual as identified under the aforementioned validation sample a priori to application of the sampled test set.

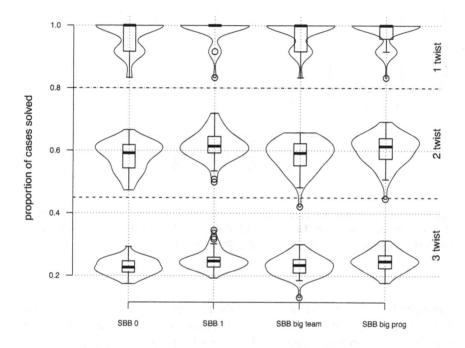

Figure 3-4. Percent of cases solved by single best SBB individuals as estimated under the exhaustive enumeration of 1, 2 and 3 quarter twist test cases. SBB 0 and SBB 1 denote the first and second layer solutions under Layered SBB; 'big team' and 'big prog' denote the base case SBB configurations without layering.

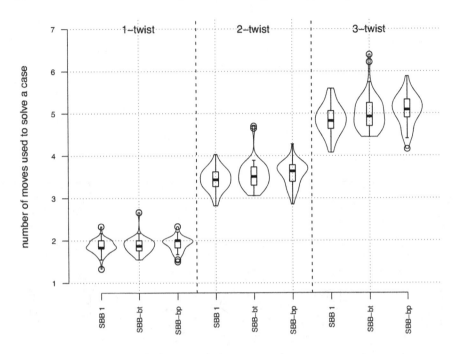

Figure 3-5. Number of moves used by champion individual to solve 1-, 2- and 3-twist points.
'*SBB 1*' is the second layer from Layered SBB, '*SBB-bt*' and '*SBB-bp*' denote the corresponding
single layer SBB big team and big program parameterizations.

corresponds to all test cases solved. Of the two baseline configurations, 'SBB
big prog' was again the more effective, implying that more complexity in the
symbionts was more advantageous than larger host–symbiont capacity.

Finally, we can also review the (mean) number of twists used to provide
solutions to each test configuration (Figure 3-5). The resulting distributions are
grouped by the original twist count. The move counts are averaged over all
cases solved by an individual, thus although some, say, 1 twist test cases might
be solved in one twist, cases that used three moves would naturally increase the
average move count above the ideal. Application of a two-tailed Man-Whitney
test indicates that the 'SBB 1' move counts are lower than the 'SBB-bp' ('big
program') move counts on 2- and 3-twist test cases at a 0.01 significance level
(Table 3-4). Thus, although Layered SBB and SBB big program solved a similar
total number of test cases (Figure 3-4), Layered SBB is able to solve them using
a statistically significant lower number of moves. Conversely, SBB big team
was not able to solve as many test cases, but when it did provide solutions, a
similar number of moves as Layered SBB where used.

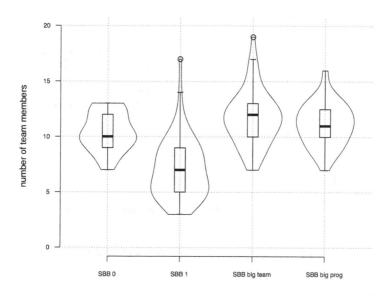

Figure 3-6. Number of symbionts per host over SBB runs.

Table 3-4. Two-tailed Mann-Whitney test results comparing solution move counts for champion individuals with Layered SBB (second level) against single layer SBB parameterizations (big team (SBB-bt) and big program (SBB-bp)). The table reports *p*-values for the pair-wise comparison of distributions from Figure 3-5. Cases where the single layer SBB medians are higher (worse) than Layered SBB medians are noted with a ⋆.

Test Case	1-twist	2-twist	3-twist
Layered SBB vs SBB-bt	0.4976⋆	0.1374⋆	0.0534⋆
Layered SBB vs SBB-bp	0.02737⋆	0.001951⋆	0.0007957⋆

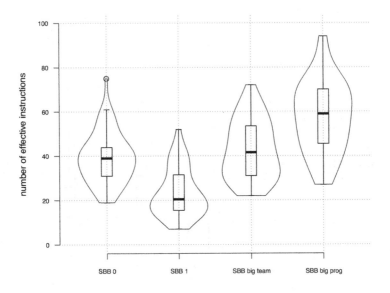

Figure 3-7. Number of instructions per host over SBB runs.

Model complexity

Finally, we can also consider model complexity, post intron removal. Relative to the typical number of symbionts utilized per host (Figure 3-6), layer 0 clearly utilizes more symbionts per host than layer 1. This implies that at layer 1 there are 5 to 8 hosts from layer 0 being utilized. As indicated in Section 2, this is possible because each of the hosts from layer 0 is now associated with a symbiont bidding behaviour as evolved at level 1. Further analysis will be necessary to identify what the specific patterns of behaviour associated with these combinations of hosts represent. Both base cases appear to use more symbionts per host, understandable given that they do not have the capacity to make use of additional layers. The same bias towards simplicity again appears relative to instruction count (Figure 3-7), thus SBB 1 uses a significantly lower instruction count than SBB 0 and the 'SBB big prog' naturally results in the most complex symbiont programs. Needless to say, SBB 1 solutions will use some combination of SBB 0 solutions, however, relative to any one move, only two hosts are ever involved in defining each action.

5.   Conclusions

Temporal sequence learning represents the most challenging scenario for establishing effective mechanisms for credit assignment. Indeed, specific challenges under the temporal credit assignment problem are generally a superset of those experienced under supervised learning domains. Layered learning represents one potential way of extending the utility of machine learning algorithms in general to temporal sequence learning (Stone, 2007). However, in order to do so effectively, solutions from any one 'layer' need to be both diverse and self-contained; properties that evolutionary computation may naturally support. Moreover, when building a new layer of candidate solutions the problem of automatic context association must be explicitly addressed. The SBB algorithm provides explicit support for these features and thus is able to construct layered solutions without recourse to hand designed objectives for each candidate component contributing to a solution (Lichodzijewski and Heywood, 2010b). This is in marked contrast to the original Layered learning methodology or the more recent developments in hierarchical reinforcement learning (Stone, 2007).

The Rubik cube as a whole is certainly not a 'solved' problem from a learning algorithm perspective. The current state-of-the-art evolves solutions for each cube configuration (El-Sourani et al., 2010), or as in the work reported here, provides a general strategy for solving a subset of scrambled cubes (Baum and Durdanovic, 2000). The discrete nature of the Rubik problem domain makes the design of suitable fitness and distance functions less intuitive/ more challenging than in the case of continuous valued domains. Indeed, specific examples of the effectiveness of SBB style layered learning under continuous valued reinforcement learning tasks are beginning to appear (Lichodzijewski and Heywood, 2010b). It is therefore anticipated that future developments will need to make use of more structural adaptation to the point population and/ or make use of a priori constraints in the formulation of different fitness functions per layer, as in the case of more classical approaches to building Rubik cube 'solvers'.

Acknowledgments

Peter Lichodzijewski has been a recipient of Precarn, NSERC-PGSD and a Killam Postgraduate Scholarships. Malcolm Heywood holds research grants from NSERC, MITACS, CFI, SwissCom Innovations SA. and TARA Inc.

References

Barreto, A. M. S., Augusto, D. A., and Barbosa, H. J. C. (2009). On the characteristics of sequential decision problems and their impact on Evolutionary Computation and Reinforcement learning. In *Proceedings of the International Conference on Artificial Evolution*, page in press.

Baum, E. B. and Durdanovic, I. (2000). Evolution of cooperative problem-solving in an artificial economy. *Neural Computation*, 12:2743–2775.

El-Sourani, N., Hauke, S., and Borschbach, M. (2010). An evolutionary approach for solving the Rubik's cube incorporating exact methods. In *EvoApplications Part – 1: EvoGames*, volume 6024 of *LNCS*, pages 80–89.

Harmeling, S., Dornhge, G., Tax, F., Meinecke, F., and Muller, K. R. (2006). From outliers to prototypes: Ordering data. *Neurocomputing*, 69(13-15):1608–1618.

Heywood, M. I. and Lichodzijewski, P. (2010). Symbiogenesis as a mechanism for building complex adaptive systems: A review. In *EvoApplications: Part 1 (EvoComplex)*, volume 6024 of *LNCS*, pages 51–60.

Korf, R. (1997). Finding optimal solutions to rubik's cube using pattern databases. In *Proceedings of the Workshop on Computer Games (IJCAI)*, pages 21–26.

Kunkle, D. and Cooperman, G. (2007). Twenty-six moves suffice for rubik's cube. In *Proceedings of ACM International Symposium on Symbolic and Algebraic Computation*, pages 235–242.

Lichodzijewski, P. and Heywood, M. I. (2007). Pareto-coevolutionary Genetic Programming for problem decomposition in multi-class classification. In *Proceedings of the Genetic and Evolutionary Computation Conference*, pages 464–471.

Lichodzijewski, P. and Heywood, M. I. (2008). Managing team-based problem solving with Symbiotic Bid-based Genetic Programming. In *Proceedings of the Genetic and Evolutionary Computation Conference*, pages 363–370.

Lichodzijewski, P. and Heywood, M. I. (2010a). Symbiosis, complexification and simplicity under gp. In *Proceedings of the Genetic and Evolutionary Computation Conference*. To appear.

Lichodzijewski, P. and Heywood, M.I. (2010b). A symbiotic coevolutionary framework for layered learning. In *AAAI Symposium on Complex Adaptive Systems*. Under review.

Oudeyer, P.Y., Kaplan, F., and V.V. Hafner, V. V. (2007). Intrinsic motivation systems for autonomous mental development. *IEEE Transactions on Evolutionary Computation*, 11:265–286.

Pollack, J. B. and Blair, A. D. (1998). Co-evolution in the successful learning of backgammon strategy. *Machine Learning*, 32:225–240.

Stone, P. (2007). Learning and multiagent reasoning for autonomous agents. In *Proceedings of the International Joint Conference on Artificial Intelligence*, pages 13–30.

Whiteson, S. and Stone, P. (2006). Evolutionary function approximation for reinforcement learning. *Journal of Machine Learning Research*, 7:887–917.

Chapter 4

ENSEMBLE CLASSIFIERS: ADABOOST AND ORTHOGONAL EVOLUTION OF TEAMS

Terence Soule[1], Robert B. Heckendorn[1], Brian Dyre[1], and Roger Lew[1]

[1] *University of Idaho, Moscow, ID 83844, USA.*

Abstract   AdaBoost is one of the most commonly used and most successful approaches for generating ensemble classifiers. However, AdaBoost is limited in that it requires independent training cases and can only use voting as a cooperation mechanism. This paper compares AdaBoost to Orthogonal Evolution of Teams (OET), an approach for generating ensembles that allows for a much wider range of problems and cooperation mechanisms. The set of test problems includes problems with significant amounts of noise in the form of erroneous training cases and problems with adjustable levels of epistasis. The results demonstrate that OET is a suitable alternative to AdaBoost for generating ensembles. Over the set of all tested problems OET with a hierarchical cooperation mechanism, rather than voting, is slightly more likely to produce better results. This is most apparent on the problems with very high levels of noise - suggesting that the hierarchical approach is less subject to over-fitting than voting techniques. The results also suggest that there are specific problems and features of problems that make them better suited for different training algorithms and different cooperation mechanisms.

Keywords: ensembles, teams, classifiers, OET, AdaBoost

1.   Introduction

Classification, the ability to classify a case based on attribute values, is a commonly studied problem with many practical applications. Approaches based on the evolution of classifiers have been widely used and proven to be quite successful (see for example (Muni et al., 2004; Kishore et al., 2000; Paul and Iba, 2009)). However, as the complexity of the classification problem increases, and particularly as the number of attributes increases, the performance of monolithic classifiers often degrades. Thus, researchers have introduced the idea of ensemble classifiers, in which multiple classifiers vote on each case (Polikar, 2006). The general idea is that the individual classifiers can partition the attribute space into simpler, overlapping sub-domains for which individual classifiers can be more readily trained. Perhaps the most successful and widely used of these ensemble technqies is AdaBoost (Freund et al., 1999; Schapire et al., 1998).

Recently, we introduced an alternative approach, called Orthogonal Evolution of Teams (Soule and Komireddy, 2006), for generating ensembles, or teams[1]. A significant advantage of Orthogonal Evolution of Teams (OET) over AdaBoost is that, unlike AdaBoost, it does not require independent training cases or voting as a cooperation mechanism. Thus, OET can be applied in cases when the agents must function simultaneously, such as search and exploration problems, swarms, and problems with non-voting cooperation mechanisms.

In previous research we have shown that the OET algorithm produces ensemble members whose errors are inversely correlated demonstrating that they cooperate effectively (Soule and Komireddy, 2006). In addition, repeated tests have shown that OET performs well on traditional multi-agent search problems that are not within the traditional domain of AdaBoost (Soule and Heckendorn, 2007a; Soule and Heckendorn, 2007b; Thomason et al., 2008). However, a systematic comparison of OET and AdaBoost on classification problems has not been performed. We present that comparison here using a range of data sets. The data sets include noisy cases with errors added to the training set and data sets with adjustable levels of epistasis. The goal is to determine whether and, if so, under what circumstances, either of the two algorithms performs better.

2.   Background

Here we present the two ensemble based learning techniques, AdaBoost and OET and briefly describe the strengths and weaknesses of each.

AdaBoost

AdaBoost, developed by Freud and Schapire, is an ensemble building technique based on the idea of combining *weak learners* (Freund et al., 1999). It uses a combination of repeated training and re-weighting of training cases to generate cooperative ensembles. The basic algorithm is as follows:

```
Assign each training example a weight
```

---

[1]The term 'ensemble' is most commonly applied to classifiers with multiple, voting members; whereas the term 'team' is commonly applied to multiple agents that work cooperatively on problems other than classification and/or that do not involve a vote. The term 'swarm' is commonly used for very large teams. Unlike AdaBoost, OET can be applied to all three types of problems.

```
For the ensemble size $N$ do
    Train a weak learner
    Calculate the error of the weak learner
    If the error $>$ 0.5 discard the learner and continue
    Calculate the normalized error of the learner
    Re-weight the training examples
Create the ensemble of the $N$ learners using a vote
weighted according to each learners' normalized error.
```

AdaBoost has several significant advantages for generating ensembles. First, it can be use in conjunction with most learning techniques. Second, theoretical results have shown that a) the ensemble error is bounded above, b) the ensemble error is less than the best ensemble member, and c) additional ensemble members lower the ensemble error - on the training set (and when members with error > 0.5 are discarded) (Polikar, 2006). These strengths make AdaBoost a very powerful and hence widely used technique for generating ensembles.

However, AdaBoost has several weaknesses. First, because of the re-weighting step it potentially has difficulty with noisy data sets in which some of the examples are mis-classified. In this case increasing emphasis may be placed on the erroneous cases: the early learners ignore them as not fitting the general pattern, their weight then increases to where later learners are effectively forced to consider them. However, in general, AdaBoost has proven surprisingly resistant to overfitting; a strength the some researchers feel has not been satisfactorily explained (Mease and Wyner, 2008). Part of the goal of this research is to compare AdaBoost and OET's ability to resist overfitting specifically when the training examples are noisy.

Second, because AdaBoost trains each ensemble member independently it's possible that problems with high levels of epistasis may confound it. The members of the ensemble may need to cooperate to overcome the high levels of epistasis in a way that is not possible when the members are trained sequentially. In contrast an algorithm that evolves all ensemble members in parallel may be able to leverage the capabilities of the members simultaneously to more successfully address high levels of epistasis. We use a synthetic problem with adjustable levels of epistasis to test this possibility.

Finally, AdaBoost is restricted to problems in which individuals can train independently and cooperate via a vote. This means that it cannot be applied to problems where more than one member is required to actually make progress. A typical example of such a problem is collective foraging where multiple members must work together to collect 'large' items or other problems in which members have heterogeneous, complementary capabilities and must be trained collectively to make progress. Similarly, AdaBoost depends on a (weighted) vote for cooperation. It is not directly applicable to ensembles using other forms of cooperation. An example of an alternative cooperative mechanism is the *leader* mechanism, in which the first ensemble member (the leader) 'examines' each input case and assigns it to one of the other ensemble members to classify. AdaBoost's sequential, vote based, ensemble generation algorithm can not be applied to ensembles using leaders for cooperation. This is a fundamental limitation of AdaBoost's incremental approach to building ensembles and cannot be readily overcome without fundamentally rewriting the algorithm.

Orthogonal Evolution of Teams

Other than AdaBoost common evolutionary ensemble training has fallen into two categories: team based and island based. In team based approaches the entire ensemble is treated as a single individual: the team receives a single fitness value and the selection process is applied entire teams (Luke and Spector, 1996; Soule, 1999; Brameier and Banzhaf, 2001; Platel et al., 2005). Crossover techniques vary, but approaches in which team members in the same 'position' within the team are crossed seem to have the most success (Haynes et al., 1995; Luke and Spector, 1996). In island based techniques the individuals are evolved in independent populations, i.e. islands, and best individuals from each island are combined into a single ensemble (see for example, (Imamura et al., 2004)).

Both of these techniques suffer from unique strengths and weaknesses. In team based approaches the ensemble members learn to cooperate well (similar to AdaBoost). It has been shown that they can evolve inversely correlated error - the errors of one member are explicitly covered by the other members (Soule and Komireddy, 2006). However, the individual members perform relatively poorly, i.e. their average fitness is often significantly poorer than the fitness of individuals evolved independently (Soule and Komireddy, 2006). In contrast, in island based approaches the individual members have relatively high fitness. However, they cooperate more poorly than in team based approaches; at best their errors are independent and in some cases their errors are correlated undermining the advantage of the ensemble (Imamura et al., 2004; Imamura, 2002; Soule and Komireddy, 2006).

The Orthogonal Evolution of Teams approach is an attempt to combine the strengths and avoid the weaknesses of the team and island approaches. A single population is created, but it is alternatively treated as independent islands (columns in the population, see Figure 4-1) or as teams (rows in the population, see Figure 4-1). A number of OET approaches are possible depending on whether the population is treated as rows or columns during selection and replacement (Thomason et al., 2008). In this paper we take one of the most straight-forward approaches: during the selection step the population is treated as islands i.e. selection is applied to each column creating a new team consisting of highly fit individuals. This is done twice to create two "all-star" teams. These teams undergo crossover, with crossover applied to individuals from the same column, and mutation, to create two offspring teams. These teams are evaluated and reinserted into the population, replacing two poorly fit teams.

Thus, during the selection stage the population is treated as islands and during the replacement stage the population is treated as teams. This places direct selection pressure on both individuals, so they can be selected for the all-star parent teams, and on teams, to avoid being replaced.

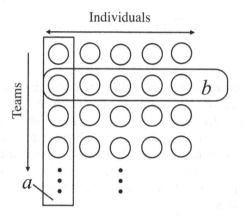

Figure 4-1. A population of individuals. Selection can be applied to members, keeping selection and replacement within the columns (a) in an island approach with each column serving as an island. Alternatively selection can be applied to whole rows (b) a team-based approach. Finally, selection can be varied between the two; these are the OET approaches.

3.   Problem Instances

To compare the ensemble classifiers we selected two data sets from the UCI Machine Learning Database (Asuncion and Newman, 2007). The sets are the Parkinson's Telemonitoring Data Set (Tsanas et al., 2009) and the Ionosphere data set (Sigillito et al., 1989). In addition, we used data collected as part of a research project conducted at the University of Idaho to assess cognitive workload (described in detail below) and from a synthetic problem with adjustable levels of epistasis. Each of these data sets represents a binary classification problem with numerical attributes (both integer and real). Table 4-1 summarizes the problems.

Assessing Cognitive Workload

This data set was generated as part of a research project conducted at the University of Idaho to measure cognitive workload. Subjects' skin conductance

Table 4-1. Number of attributes and number of cases for each of the test problems. Attributes are numerical (integer and real). The cognitive workload case consists of two separate data sets from two different test subjects. For each of the problems 50% of the cases are used for training and 50% for testing.

Problem	Number of Attributes	Number of Cases
Ionosphere	34	351
Parkinson's	22	195
Cognitive Workload (2 subjects)	20	2048
Synthetic Problem	20	1000

(SC, also known as galvanic skin response, GSR) and pupil diameter were measured while they performed a task with two distinct levels of difficulty. Changes in SC are generally believed to reflect autonomic responses to anxiety or stress, while changes in pupil diameter have been linked to differences in difficulty of tasks including sentence processing, mental calculations and user interface evaluation (Just and Carpenter, 1993; Nakayama and Katsukura, 2007). Thus, it was hypothesized that these physiological indicators could be used to determine which phase of the task the subject was in.

Stimuli and Apparatus.   Participants used a black cursor to chase a intensity balanced dot moving in a pseudo random fashion against a gray background. A balanced dot was used as precaution against having pupil dilations due to luminance changes. Participants controlled the cursor using a joystick. For the first minute of the experiment the control mappings were normal: moving the joystick forward moved the cursor up, moving the joystick right moved the cursor right, etc. After 60 seconds the joystick control mappings were abruptly rotated 90 clockwise, such that moving the joystick forward-backward moved the cursor right-left, and moving the joystick left-right moved the cursor upward-downward. The control dynamics were switched between normal and rotated by 90 degrees every 60 seconds for the eight minute duration of the experiment.

The abrupt changes in control mappings were hypothesized to elicit transient physiological responses, and the rotated mappings were hypothesized to cause physiological indicators reflecting increased workload. The goal was to train classifiers to use these physiological indicators to determine the control phase, normal or rotated. For this analysis data was used from the last 2 minutes of the experiment (covering one normal and one rotated period), by which time the subjects had obtained some practice with both sets of controls. Data was collected 18 times per second for a total of 2048 separate cases for each subject.

For a more detailed explanation of the experimental conditions please see (Lew et al., 2010).

Participants.   The data used is from two university students who participated in this experiment. Both had normal or corrected to normal Snellen visual acuity (20/30 or better). The participants were naive to the hypotheses of the experiment.

Synthetic Problem

The synthetic function was designed to allow control of the amount of epistasis in the problem. Each problem is defined in terms of a z-function, which are random Embedded Landscapes (Heckendorn, 2002). These are generalizations of NK-Landscapes in that the sub function masks are not guaranteed to cover the domain of the function and the number of sub-functions is not constrained to be equal to the number of bits in the domain as they are in NK-Landscapes. The range of values of the sub-functions are between -1 and 1.

The functions denoted by names of the form: **z-N-K-P**. They are randomly generated, but are of the form:

$$f(x) = positive\left(\sum_{i=1}^{P} g_i(pack(x, m_i))\right)$$

where:

- N is the number of bits (or binary valued features).

- P is the number of sub-functions to sum.

- K is the number of bits (or features) in the domain of g_i.

- m_i is an N bit mask that selects K bits out of N bits by using the pack function to extract the bits selected by the 1's in m_i. In a given f: $m_i \neq m_j \; \forall i, j$ such that $i \neq j$.

- g_i is a function that maps its K bit domain into the reals. This function is fully epistatic in that all Walsh coefficients are nonzero. The values of g_i are random in the range between -1 and $+1$. This where the randomness in the function is created.

- *positive* takes a real argument and returns 1 if its argument is positive and 0 otherwise.

This creates a function f that has the property that it has at most K bits of epistasis in P groups of interrelated bits that may overlap. Therefore, as K goes up, the amount of epistasis goes up and as P goes up the complexity of the constraint satisfaction problem created by the overlapping fully epistatic g's goes up when treated as a function to optimize.

Noisy Training Data

For many real-world data sets noisy cases - cases with the incorrect classification - are common. These cases can easily mislead training algorithms or lead to overfitting, as the training algorithm is forced to 'memorize' cases that don't fit the general solution because the class is incorrect. Thus, in addition to the basic data sets we ran experiments with noisy versions of each of the problems except the synthetic problem. For the noisy cases 0 (no noise), 10, 20, 30, or 40 percent of the training case answers were changed to the opposite (incorrect) case. The erroneous cases in the training set are kept the same through the evolutionary process to maximize the chance of mis-leading the learners. All of the test cases were unchanged, i.e. all are correct.

4.   Cooperation Mechanisms

With AdaBoost the ensemble members cooperate - collectively determine the classification for each input set - via a weighted vote. With OET two different cooperation mechanisms are tested. The first is a simple majority vote. The second is the leader approach in which the first ensemble member (the leader) 'examines' each input case and assigns it to one of the other ensemble members to classify. It is important to note that AdaBoost's sequential, vote based, ensemble generation algorithm can not be applied to ensembles using leaders for cooperation (or to most other cooperation mechanisms that do not use a vote).

5.   Genetic Program

For these experiments the ensemble size is always 3. One of the potential advantages of GP techniques is its ability to generate (somewhat) human-readable solutions. This advantage is lost if the ensemble size is large, hence the small value used here. The results are the average of 20 trials (synthetic problem) or 10 trials (other problems).

The basic GP used in both the AdaBoost and OET experiments is steady-state with a population size of 500, run for either 50000 iterations (synthetic problems) or 12500 iterations (all others). For OET this is the total number of iterations. For AdaBoost this is the number of iterations used to generate each of the three ensemble members. With OET each iteration requires evaluating six trees, three trees for each of the two offspring teams. Because AdaBoost only generates one tree at a time, it only evaluates two trees per iteration. Thus, to equalize the number of tree evaluations AdaBoost uses the full number of

Table 4-2. Summary of the GP parameters.

Algorithm	Steady-state
Iterations	50000 (synthetic problem) or 12500 (all others)
Population Size	500
Non-terminals	iflte, +, -, *, /
Terminals	Attributes, Random constants
Crossover Rate	100%
Mutation Rate	1/size
Trials	20 (synthetic problem) or 10 (all others)
Ensemble Size	3

evaluations to generate *each* of the ensemble members effectively tripling the total number of iterations used with AdaBoost.

The non-terminal set consists of if-less-than-else, addition, subtraction, multiplication, and protected division (if the absolute value of the divisor is less than 0.00001 it returns 1). The terminal set consists of the N attributes of the problem and real-valued random constants generated in the range -2.0 to 2.0. Table 4-2 summarizes the GP's parameters.

6.   Results

Figure 4-2 presents the results on the ionosphere problem. For this problem the OET-leader approach performs significantly worse for low levels of noise (all significant tests use a two-tailed, Student's t-test, with significance defined as $P < 0.05$). OET-leader's relative performance improves as noise increases, but does not reach statistically better performance.

Figure 4-3 presents the results on the Parkinson's problem. OET-vote is significantly worse that both other techniques with 30% noise and OET-leader is significantly better with 40% noise.

Figure 4-4 presents the results for the cognitive workload problem with subject 1. At 0% noise AdaBoost is significantly worse than the other two approaches and OET-vote is significantly better. At 40% noise OET-leader is significantly better than other two approaches.

Figure 4-5 presents the results for the cognitive workload problem with subject 2. At 0% noise AdaBoost is significantly worse than OET-vote. At 20% and 30% noise AdaBoost is significantly better than other two approaches.

Figure 4-6 presents the results on the synthetic functions. OET-leader is significantly better than the other two algorithms on 4 of the 7 functions (2-30, 5-10, 5-30, 10-30). OET-vote is significantly better than the other two algorithms on 1 of the functions (2-3).

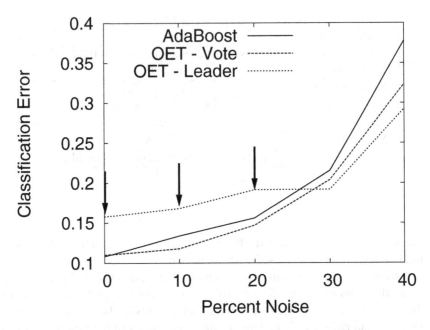

Figure 4-2. Results on the ionosphere problem for varying levels of noise in the training data. Arrows show significant differences. For this problem the OET-leader approach is significantly worse (Student's two-tailed, t-test P < 0.05) than the other two approaches for low levels of noise. It's relative performance improves for higher levels of noise, but the differences do not reach significance.

Overall the results are mixed. For the majority of cases the performance of the two algorithms are statistically indistinguishable. Generally, OET-leader performs better on the noisiest cases, suggesting that it is less prone to overfitting, but often performs more poorly on the low noise cases. OET-vote performs better on some of the simplest cases (0% noise and the 2-3 function) and AdaBoost's performance tends to fall in the middle.

7.   Conclusions

In general the results confounded the expectations. The goal of this research was to compare AdaBoost, a well established and widely used ensemble training technique, to OET, a newer approach that has proven successful on a number of problems. Given the nature of AdaBoost it was hypothesized that OET was most likely to perform better under one of two conditions. First, on cases with significant noise, because AdaBoost's re-weighting approach would force it to focus on erroneous cases causing it to overfit. Second, on cases with high levels of epistasis, because AdaBoost's incremental approach to building an ensemble

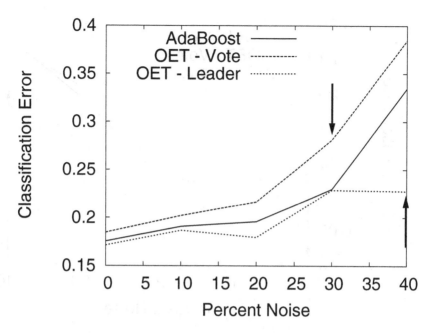

Figure 4-3. Results on the Parkinson's problem for varying levels of noise in the training data. Arrows show significant differences. For this problem the OET-vote approach is significantly worse (Student's two-tailed, t-test $P < 0.05$) than the other two approaches for 30% noise and the OET-leader approach is significantly better with 40% noise.

could interfere with its ability to leverage multiple members simultaneously to 'untangle' high epistasis problems.

The results do strongly suggest that performance depends both on the training algorithm and the cooperation method, but confounded the specific hypotheses regarding noise and epistasis. OET with voting ensemble members only performed better with zero error and the least epistasis, whereas OET with hierarchical cooperation (the leader approach described previously) had the best performance with high levels of noise and epistasis. AdaBoost's performance generally fell between OET-vote and OET-leader and showed the best results for the mid-range of noise.

However, for the majority of cases the algorithms' performance was statistically indistinguishable. This suggests that the performance of the algorithms is generally comparable, if not identical. Based on the results it seems plausible that further testing would show that there are specific types of problems or features of problems that make them better suited for one or another of the algorithms and/or cooperation mechanisms.

Most importantly, these results strongly suggest that OET is generally on par with AdaBoost, but, as noted previously, OET can be applied to problems and

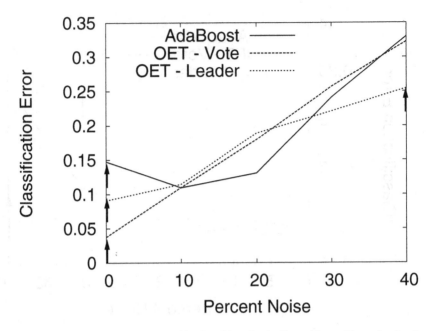

Figure 4-4. Results on the cognitive workload problem for the first subject with varying levels of noise in the training data. Arrows show significant differences. For this problem the results between all three approaches are significantly different with no noise in the training set (Student's two-tailed t-test $P < 0.05$). The OET-leader approach is significantly better than the other two approaches with 40% noise.

cooperation mechanisms that are not suitable for AdaBoost. Thus, researchers can confidently apply OET in cases where AdaBoost is inappropriate.

References

Asuncion, A. and Newman, D.J. (2007). UCI machine learning repository.

Brameier, Markus and Banzhaf, Wolfgang (2001). Evolving teams of predictors with linear genetic programming. *Genetic Programming and Evolvable Machines*, 2(4):381–408.

Freund, Y., Schapire, R., and Abe, N. (1999). A short introduction to boosting. *JOURNAL-JAPANESE SOCIETY FOR ARTIFICIAL INTELLIGENCE*, 14:771–780.

Haynes, Thomas, Sen, Sandip, Schoenefeld, Dale, and Wainwright, Roger (1995). Evolving a team. In Siegel, Eric V. and Koza, John, editors, *Working Notes of the AAAI-95 Fall Symposium on GP*, pages 23–30. AAAI Press.

Heckendorn, Robert B. (2002). Embedded landscapes. *Evolutionary Computation*, 10(4):345–376.

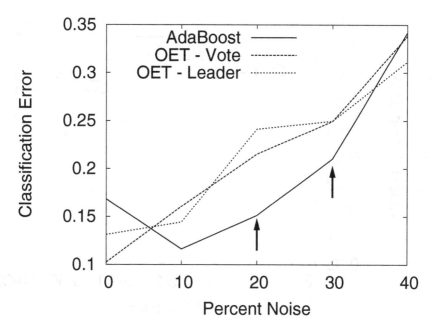

Figure 4-5. Results on the cognitive workload problem for the second subject with varying levels of noise in the training data. Arrows show significant differences. For this problem AdaBoost is significantly better with noise levels of 20% and 30%. Additionally, OET-vote is significantly better than AdaBoost (but not OET-leader) with 0% noise.

Imamura, Kosuke (2002). *N-version Genetic Programming: A probabilistic Optimal Ensemble.* PhD thesis, University of Idaho.

Imamura, Kosuke, Heckendorn, Robert B., Soule, Terence, and Foster, James A. (2004). Behavioral diversity and a probabilistically optimal gp ensemble. *Genetic Programming and Evolvable Machines*, 4:235–253.

Just, M.A. and Carpenter, P.A. (1993). The intensity dimension of thought: Pupillometric indices of sentence processing. *Canadian Journal of Experimental Psychology*, 47(2):310–339.

Kishore, JK, Patnaik, LM, Mani, V., and Agrawal, VK (2000). Application of genetic programming for multicategory pattern classification. *IEEE Transactions on Evolutionary Computation*, 4(3):242–258.

Lew, R., P., Dyre B., Soule, T., Werner, S., and Ragsdale, S. A. (2010). Assessing mental workload from skin conductance and pupillometry using wavelets and genetic programming. In *Proceedings of the 54th Annual Meeting of the Human Factors and Ergonomics Society.*

Luke, Sean and Spector, Lee (1996). Evolving teamwork and coordination with genetic programming. In Koza, John R., Goldberg, David E., Fogel, David B.,

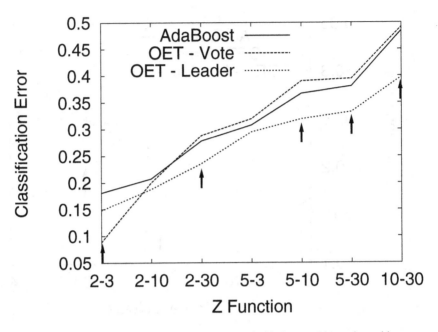

Figure 4-6. Results on the z functions. No noise was used with these problems, the problems are arranged along the x-axis in approximate order of difficulty. Arrows show significant differences in performance (Student's two-tailed, t-test $P < 0.05$). For the 2-3 function the OET-vote approach is significantly better than both other approaches. For the 2-30, 5-10, 5-30, and 10-30 problems the OET-leader approach is significantly better than the other two approaches Additionally, the OET-leader approach is significantly better than AdaBoost (but not OET-vote) for the 2-10 problem and significantly better than OET-vote (but not AdaBoost) for the 5-3 problem.

and Riolo, Rick R., editors, *Genetic Programming 1996: Proceedings of the First Annual Conference on Genetic Programming*, pages 150–156. Cambridge, MA: MIT Press.

Mease, D. and Wyner, A. (2008). Evidence contrary to the statistical view of boosting. *The Journal of Machine Learning Research*, 9:131–156.

Muni, DP, Pal, NR, and Das, J. (2004). A novel approach to design classifiers using genetic programming. *IEEE transactions on evolutionary computation*, 8(2):183–196.

Nakayama, M. and Katsukura, M. (2007). Feasibility of assessing usability with pupillary responses. *Proc. of AUIC 2007, 15*, 22.

Paul, T.K. and Iba, H. (2009). Prediction of cancer class with majority voting genetic programming classifier using gene expression data. *IEEE/ACM Transactions on Computational Biology and Bioinformatics (TCBB)*, 6(2):353–367.

Platel, Michael Defoin, Chami, Malik, Clergue, Manuel, and Collard, Philippe (2005). Teams of genetic predictors for inverse problem solving. In *Proceeding of the 8th European Conference on Genetic Programming – EuroGP 2005*.

Polikar, R. (2006). Ensemble based systems in decision making. *IEEE Circuits and systems magazine*, 6(3):21–45.

Schapire, R.E., Freund, Y., Bartlett, P., and Lee, W.S. (1998). Boosting the margin: A new explanation for the effectiveness of voting methods. *Annals of statistics*, 26(5):1651–1686.

Sigillito, V G, Wing, S P, Hutton, L V, and Baker, K B (1989). Classification of radar returns from the ionosphere using neural networks. *Johns Hopkins APL Tech. Dig*, vol. 10:262–266. in.

Soule, T. and Heckendorn, R.B. (2007a). Improving Performance and Cooperation in Multi-Agent Systems. In *Proceedings of the Genetic Programming Theory and Practice Workshop*. Springer.

Soule, Terence (1999). Voting teams: A cooperative approach to non-typical problems. In Banzhaf, Wolfgang, Daida, Jason, Eiben, Agoston E., Garzon, Max H., Honavar, Vasant, Jakiela, Mark, and Smith, Robert E., editors, *Proceedings of the Genetic and Evolutionary Computation Conference*, pages 916–922, Orlando, Florida, USA. Morgan Kaufmann.

Soule, Terence and Heckendorn, Robert B. (2007b). Evolutionary optimization of cooperative heterogeneous teams. In *SPIE Defense and Security Symposium*, volume 6563.

Soule, Terence and Komireddy, Pavankumarreddy (2006). Orthogonal evolution of teams: A class of algorithms for evolving teams with inversely correlated errors. In Riolo, Rick L., Soule, Terence, and Worzel, Bill, editors, *Genetic Programming Theory and Practice IV*, volume 5 of *Genetic and Evolutionary Computation*, chapter 8, pages –. Springer, Ann Arbor.

Thomason, Russell, Heckendorn, Robert B., and Soule, Terence (2008). Training time and team composition robustness in evolved multi-agent systems. In O'Neill, Michael, Vanneschi, Leonardo, Gustafson, Steven, Esparcia Alcazar, Anna Isabel, De Falco, Ivanoe, Della Cioppa, Antonio, and Tarantino, Ernesto, editors, *Proceedings of the 11th European Conference on Genetic Programming, EuroGP 2008*, volume 4971 of *Lecture Notes in Computer Science*, pages 1–12, Naples. Springer.

Tsanas, A., Little, M.A., McSharry, P.E., and Ramig, L.O. (2009). Accurate telemonitoring of Parkinson's disease progression by non-invasive speech tests. *Scientific Commons*.

Chapter 5

COVARIANT TARPEIAN METHOD FOR BLOAT CONTROL IN GENETIC PROGRAMMING

Riccardo Poli[1]

[1]*School of Computer Science and Electronic Engineering, University of Essex, Wivenhoe Park, CO4 3SQ, UK.*

Abstract   In this paper a simple modification of the Tarpeian bloat-control method is presented which allows one to dynamically set the parameters of the method in such a way to guarantee that the mean program size will either keep a particular value (e.g., its initial value) or will follow a schedule chosen by the user. The mathematical derivation of the technique as well as its numerical and empirical corroboration are presented.

Keywords: Bloat control, Tarpeian Method, Price's theorem, Size-evolution equation

1. Background

Many techniques to control bloat have been proposed in the last two decades (for recent reviews see (Poli et al., 2008; Luke and Panait, 2006; Alfaro-Cid et al., 2010; Silva, 2008)). One with a theoretically-sound basis is the Tarpeian method introduced in (Poli, 2003). This is the focus of this paper.

The Tarpeian method is extremely simple in its implementation. All that is needed is a wrapper for the fitness function like the following algorithm:

Tarpeian Wrapper:
if size(program) > average_program_size **and** random() < p_t **then**
    return(f_{bad});
else
    return(fitness(program));

were p_t is a real number between 0 and 1, random() is a function which returns uniformly distributed random numbers in the range $[0, 1)$ and f_{bad} is a constant which represents an extremely low (or high, if minimising) fitness value such that individuals with such fitness are almost guaranteed not to be selected. The method got its name after the Tarpeian Rock in Rome, which in Roman times was the infamous execution place for traitors and criminals (above average size individuals), who would be led to its top and then hurled down to their death.

A feature of this algorithm is that it does not require *a priori* knowledge of the size of the potential solutions to a problem. If programs need to grow in order to improve fitness, the original Tarpeian method will not prevent this. It will occasionally hit some individuals that, *if evaluated*, would result in being fitter than average and this may slow down a little the progress of a run. However, because the wrapper *does not* evaluate the individuals being given a low fitness, very little computation is wasted. Even at a high anti-bloat intensity, p_t, a better-than-average longer-than-average individual has still a chance of making it into the population. If enough individuals of this kind are produced (w.r.t. the individuals which are better-than-average but also shorter-than-average), eventually the average size of the programs in the population may grow. However, when this happens the Tarpeian method will immediately adjust so as to discourage further growth.

After its proposal, the Tarpeian method has started being used in a variety of studies and applications. For example, in (Mahler et al., 2005) its performance and generalisation capabilities were studied, while it was compared with other bloat-control techniques in (Luke and Panait, 2006; Wyns and Boullart, 2009; Alfaro-Cid et al., 2010). The method has been used with success in the evolution of bin packing heuristics (Burke et al., 2007; Allen et al., 2009), in the evolution of image analysis operators (Roberts and Claridge, 2004), in artificial financial markets based on GP (Martinez-Jaramillo and Tsang, 2009), in predicting protein networks (Garcia et al., 2008a), in the design of passive analog filters using GP (Chouza et al., 2009), in the prediction of protein-protein functional associations (Garcia et al., 2008b) and in the simplification of decision trees via GP (Garcia-Almanza and Tsang, 2006).

In all cases the Tarpeian method has been a solid and efficient choice. All studies and applications, however, have had to determine by trial and error the value of the parameter p_t best suited to their problem(s).[1] This is not really a drawback of this method: virtually all anti-bloat techniques require setting one or more parameters. For example, also the parsimony pressure method (Koza, 1992; Zhang and Mühlenbein, 1995; Zhang and Mühlenbein, 1993; Zhang et al., 1997) requires setting one parameter (the parsimony coefficient).

In recent research (Poli and McPhee, 2008), we developed a method, called *covariant parsimony pressure*, that allows one to dynamically and optimally set the parsimony coefficient for the parsimony pressure method in such a way to completely control the evolution of the mean program size. The aim of this

---

[1] In principle also f_{bad} needs to be set. However, this is normally easily done (more on this later) and requires virtually no tuning.

paper is to achieve the same level of control for the Tarpeian method. We will do this partly by following the tracks of (Poli and McPhee, 2008). We therefore start our journey by briefly summarising the main ideas that led to the covariant parsimony pressure method.

2. Covariant Parsimony Pressure

Let us start by considering the size evolution equation developed in (Poli, 2003; Poli and McPhee, 2003), which, as shown in (Poli and McPhee, 2008), with trivial manipulations can be rewritten as follows

$$E[\mu'] = \sum_{\ell} \ell p(\ell) \tag{5.1}$$

where the index ℓ ranges over all program sizes, μ' is a stochastic variable which represents the average size of the programs at the next generation and $p(\ell)$ is the probability of selecting a program of size ℓ from the current generation. The equation applies to GP systems with independent selection and symmetric sub-tree crossover.[2]

If $\phi(\ell)$ represents the proportion of programs of size ℓ in the current generation, then, clearly, the average size of the programs in the current generation is given by $\mu = \sum_{\ell} \ell \phi(\ell)$. Thus one can simply express the expected change in average size of programs between two generations as

$$E[\Delta\mu] = E[\mu'] - \mu = \sum_{\ell} \ell \left(p(\ell) - \phi(\ell) \right). \tag{5.2}$$

In (Poli and McPhee, 2008), we showed that if we restrict our attention to fitness proportionate selection, we can express $p(\ell) = \phi(\ell)\frac{f(\ell)}{\bar{f}}$, where $f(\ell)$ is the average fitness of the programs of size ℓ and $\bar{f}$ is the average fitness of the programs in the population. Then, with some algebraic manipulations, one finds that Equation (5.2) is actually equivalent to Price's theorem (Price, 1970). That is

$$E[\Delta\mu] = \frac{\mathrm{Cov}(\ell, f)}{\bar{f}}. \tag{5.3}$$

Let us imagine that a fitness function incorporating parsimony, $f_p = f - c\ell$, is used, where c is the parsimony coefficient, ℓ is the size of a program and f is its raw fitness (problems-solving performance). Feeding this into Equation (5.3), then setting its l.h.s. ($E[\Delta\mu]$) to zero and solving for c, one finds

$$c = \frac{\mathrm{Cov}(\ell, f)}{\mathrm{Var}(\ell)}. \tag{5.4}$$

---

[2]In a symmetric operator the probability of selecting particular crossover points in the parents does not depend on the order in which the parents are drawn from the population.

This value of c guarantees that, in expectation, the size of the programs in the next generation will be the same as in the current generation (as long as the coefficient c is recomputed at each generation).

In (Poli and McPhee, 2008) we also showed that with simple further manipulations of Equation (5.3) one can even set c dynamically in such a way as to force the mean program size to vary according to any desired function of time, thereby providing complete control over the evolution of size.

3.   Covariant Tarpeian Method

Let us now model the effects on program size of the Tarpeian method in GP systems with independent selection and symmetric sub-tree crossover. In the Tarpeian method the fitness of individuals of size not exceeding the mean size μ is left unaffected. If p_t is the Tarpeian rate, on average individuals of size bigger than the mean will see their fitness set to a very low value, f_{bad}, in a proportion p_t of cases, while fitness will be unaffected with probability $1 - p_t$. In order to see what effects the Tarpeian method has on the expected change in program size $E[\Delta\mu]$, we need to verify how the changes in fitness it produces affect the terms in the size evolution equation (Equation (5.2)). In other words, we need to compute

$$E[\Delta\mu_t]   =   \sum_\ell \ell\, (p_t(\ell) - \phi(\ell)) \qquad (5.5)$$

or

$$E[\Delta\mu_t]   =   \frac{\mathrm{Cov}(\ell, f_t)}{\bar{f}_t}. \qquad (5.6)$$

where $\Delta\mu_t = \mu'_t - \mu$, μ'_t is the average program size in the next generation when the Tarpeian method is used, $p_t(\ell)$ is the probability of selecting individuals of size ℓ when the Tarpeian method is used, f_t is the fitness of individuals after the application of the Tarpeian method, and $\bar{f}_t$ is the mean program fitness after the application of the Tarpeian method.

Unfortunately, when attempting to study Equations (5.5) and (5.6) for the Tarpeian method things are significantly harder than for the parsimony pressure method. Under fitness proportionate selection, we have that $p_t(\ell) = \phi(\ell)\frac{f_t(\ell)}{\bar{f}_t}$ where $f_t(\ell)$ is the mean fitness of the programs of size ℓ after the application of the Tarpeian method. In the absence of Tarpeian bloat control (i.e., for $p_t = 0$), these quantities are *constants* (given that we have full information about the current generation). However, as soon as $p_t > 0$, they become *stochastic variables*. This is because the Tarpeian method is stochastic and, so, we cannot be certain as to precisely how many individuals will have their fitness reduced by it, how many individual in each length class will be affected and how many individuals in each fitness class will be affected. If $f_t(\ell)$ and $\bar{f}_t$ are stochastic variables then so are the selection probabilities $p_t(\ell)$ and, consequently, also the quantity $E[\Delta\mu_t]$ on the l.h.s. of Equations (5.5) and (5.6)

In other words Equations (5.5) and (5.6) give us the expectation of the change in mean program size from one generation to the next *conditionally* to the Tarpeian method modifying the fitness of a particular set of individuals. In formulae,

$$E[\Delta\mu_t|F_t = f_t] \quad = \quad \sum_\ell \ell\,(p_t(\ell) - \phi(\ell)) = \frac{\mathrm{Cov}(\ell, f_t)}{\bar{f}_t}. \qquad (5.7)$$

where F_t is a (vector) stochastic variable which represents the fitness associated to the individuals in the population after the application of the Tarpeian method.

The distribution $\Pr\{F_t = f_t\}$ of F_t depends on the fitness and size of the individuals in the population and the parameter p_t. In principle, we could determine the explicit expression for such a distribution and then compute

$$E[\Delta\mu_t] \quad = \quad \sum_{f_t} E[\Delta\mu_t|F_t = f_t]\Pr\{F_t = f_t\}. \qquad (5.8)$$

However, working out a closed form for this equation is difficult. The reason is that the fitness values f_t appear at the denominator of the selection probabilities $p_t(\ell)$ via the average fitness $\bar{f}_t$ in addition to appearing at the numerators.

To overcome the difficulty and obtain results which allow the application of the theory to the problem of optimally choosing the parameters of the Tarpeian method, we will use the following *approximation*:

$$\begin{aligned}
E[\Delta\mu_t] \quad &= \quad E\big[E[\Delta\mu_t|F_t = f_t]\big] \\
&= \quad E\left[\frac{\mathrm{Cov}(\ell, f_t)}{\bar{f}_t}\right] \cong \frac{E[\mathrm{Cov}(\ell, f_t)]}{E[\bar{f}_t]}. \qquad (5.9)
\end{aligned}$$

Later in the paper we will get an idea as to the degree of error introduced by the approximation. For now, however, let us see if we can find a closed form for this approximation.

Let us start from computing $E[\bar{f}_t]$:

$$
\begin{aligned}
E[\bar{f}_t] \\
&= E\Big[\sum_\ell \phi(\ell) f_t(\ell)\Big] \\
&= \sum_{\ell \le \mu} \phi(\ell) E[f_t(\ell)] + \sum_{\ell > \mu} \phi(\ell) E[f_t(\ell)] \\
&= \sum_{\ell \le \mu} \phi(\ell) f(\ell) + \sum_{\ell > \mu} \phi(\ell) [p_t \times f_{bad} + (1 - p_t) \times f(\ell)] \\
&= \sum_\ell \phi(\ell) f(\ell) - \sum_{\ell > \mu} \phi(\ell) f(\ell) + \sum_{\ell > \mu} \phi(\ell) [p_t \times f_{bad} + (1 - p_t) \times f(\ell)] \\
&= \bar{f} + \sum_{\ell > \mu} \phi(\ell) [p_t \times f_{bad} + (1 - p_t) \times f(\ell) - f(\ell)] \\
&= \bar{f} + \sum_{\ell > \mu} \phi(\ell) [p_t \times f_{bad} - p_t \times f(\ell)] \\
&= \bar{f} - p_t \sum_{\ell > \mu} \phi(\ell) (f(\ell) - f_{bad}) \\
&= \bar{f} - p_t \phi_> \sum_{\ell > \mu} \frac{\phi(\ell)}{\phi_>} (f(\ell) - f_{bad}) \\
&= \bar{f} - p_t \phi_> (\bar{f}_> - f_{bad}) \qquad\qquad\qquad (5.10)
\end{aligned}
$$

where $\phi_> = \sum_{\ell > \mu} \phi(\ell)$ is the proportion of above-average-size programs and $\bar{f}_>$ is the average fitness of such programs.

Let us now compute the expected covariance between ℓ and f_t:

$$E[\text{Cov}(\ell, f_t)]$$

$$= E\left[\sum_\ell \phi(\ell)(\ell - \mu)(f_t(\ell) - \bar{f_t})\right]$$

$$= \sum_\ell \phi(\ell)(\ell - \mu)E[(f_t(\ell) - \bar{f_t})]$$

$$= \sum_\ell \phi(\ell)(\ell - \mu)(E[f_t(\ell)] - E[\bar{f_t}])$$

$$= \sum_\ell \phi(\ell)(\ell - \mu)(E[f_t(\ell)] - \bar{f} + p_t\phi_>(\bar{f}_> - f_{bad}))$$

$$= \sum_\ell \phi(\ell)(\ell - \mu)(E[f_t(\ell)] - \bar{f})$$

$$+ \; p_t\phi_>(\bar{f}_> - f_{bad})\underbrace{\sum_\ell \phi(\ell)(\ell - \mu)}_{=0}$$

$$= \sum_\ell \phi(\ell)(\ell - \mu)(E[f_t(\ell)] - \bar{f})$$

$$= \sum_{\ell \leq \mu} \phi(\ell)(\ell - \mu)(E[f_t(\ell)] - \bar{f})$$

$$+ \; \sum_{\ell > \mu} \phi(\ell)(\ell - \mu)(E[f_t(\ell)] - \bar{f})$$

$$= \sum_{\ell \leq \mu} \phi(\ell)(\ell - \mu)(f(\ell) - \bar{f})$$

$$+ \; \sum_{\ell > \mu} \phi(\ell)(\ell - \mu)[p_t f_{bad} + (1 - p_t)f(\ell) - \bar{f}]$$

$$= \sum_\ell \phi(\ell)(\ell - \mu)(f(\ell) - \bar{f}) - \sum_{\ell > \mu} \phi(\ell)(\ell - \mu)(f(\ell) - \bar{f})$$

$$+ \; \sum_{\ell > \mu} \phi(\ell)(\ell - \mu)[p_t f_{bad} + (1 - p_t)f(\ell) - \bar{f}]$$

$$= \text{Cov}(\ell, f)$$

$$+ \; \sum_{\ell > \mu} \phi(\ell)(\ell - \mu)[p_t f_{bad} + (1 - p_t)f(\ell) - \bar{f} - f(\ell) + \bar{f}]$$

Thus

$$E[\text{Cov}(\ell, f_t)] = \text{Cov}(\ell, f) - p_t \sum_{\ell > \mu} \phi(\ell)(\ell - \mu)(f(\ell) - f_{bad}). \qquad (5.11)$$

If $\mu_>$ is the average size of the programs that are longer than μ, we can write

$$\sum_{\ell>\mu} \phi(\ell)(\ell - \mu)(f(\ell) - f_{bad})$$

$$= \sum_{\ell>\mu} \phi(\ell)(\ell - \mu_> - \mu + \mu_>)(f(\ell) - f_{bad})$$

$$= \sum_{\ell>\mu} \phi(\ell)(\ell - \mu_>)(f(\ell) - f_{bad}) - (\mu - \mu_>) \sum_{\ell>\mu} \phi(\ell)(f(\ell) - f_{bad})$$

$$= \sum_{\ell>\mu} \phi(\ell)(\ell - \mu_>)(f(\ell) - \bar{f}_> - f_{bad} + \bar{f}_>) - (\mu - \mu_>)\phi_>(\bar{f}_> - f_{bad})$$

$$= \sum_{\ell>\mu} \phi(\ell)(\ell - \mu_>)(f(\ell) - \bar{f}_>)$$

$$+ \sum_{\ell>\mu} \phi(\ell)(\ell - \mu_>)(\bar{f}_> - f_{bad}) - (\mu - \mu_>)\phi_>(\bar{f}_> - f_{bad})$$

$$= \phi_> \mathrm{Cov}_>(\ell, f)$$

$$+ (\bar{f}_> - f_{bad}) \underbrace{\sum_{\ell>\mu} \phi(\ell)(\ell - \mu_>)}_{=0} - (\mu - \mu_>)\phi_>(\bar{f}_> - f_{bad}),$$

$$= \phi_> \left[\mathrm{Cov}_>(\ell, f) + (\mu_> - \mu)(\bar{f}_> - f_{bad}) \right].$$

where $\mathrm{Cov}_>(\ell, f)$ is the covariance between program size and fitness *within* the programs which are of above-average size. Thus, we finally obtain

$$E[\mathrm{Cov}(\ell, f_t)] = \mathrm{Cov}(\ell, f) - p_t\phi_> \left[\mathrm{Cov}_>(\ell, f) + (\mu_> - \mu)(\bar{f}_> - f_{bad}) \right].$$
$$(5.12)$$

Substituting Equations (5.12) and (5.9) into Equation (5.8) we obtain

$$E[\Delta\mu_t] \cong \frac{\mathrm{Cov}(\ell, f) - p_t\phi_> \left[\mathrm{Cov}_>(\ell, f) + (\mu_> - \mu)(\bar{f}_> - f_{bad}) \right]}{\bar{f} - p_t\phi_>(\bar{f}_> - f_{bad})}. \quad (5.13)$$

With this explicit formulation of the expected size changes, following the same strategy as in the covariant parsimony pressure method (see Section 2), we can find out for what value of p_t we get $E[\Delta\mu_t] = 0$. By setting the l.h.s. of Equation (5.13) to 0 and solving for p_t, we obtain:

$$p_t \cong \frac{\mathrm{Cov}(\ell, f)}{\phi_> \left[\mathrm{Cov}_>(\ell, f) + (\mu_> - \mu)(\bar{f}_> - f_{bad}) \right]}. \quad (5.14)$$

This equation allows one to determine how often the Tarpeian method should be applied to modify the fitness of above-average-size programs as a function of a small set of descriptors of the current state of the population and of the parameter f_{bad}.

We should note that for some values of f_{bad} the method is unable to control bloat. For such values, one would need to set $p_t > 1$ which is clearly impossible (since p_t is a probability). Naturally, we can find out what such values of f_{bad} are by setting $p_t = 1$ in Equation (5.14) and solving for f_{bad} obtaining

$$f_{bad} \cong \bar{f}_> - \frac{\text{Cov}(\ell, f) - \text{Cov}_>(\ell, f)\phi_>}{\phi_>(\mu_> - \mu)}. \tag{5.15}$$

However, since we normally don't particularly care about the specific value of f_{bad}, as long as the method gets the job done, the obvious and safe choice $f_{bad} = 0$ is perhaps the most practical one.

What if we wanted $\mu(t)$ to follow, in expectation, a particular function $\gamma(t)$, e.g., the ramp $\gamma(t) = \mu(0) + b \times t$ or a sinusoidal function? The theory helps us in this case as well.

What we want is that $E[\mu_t'] = \gamma(g)$, where g is the generation number. Note that $E[\mu_t'] = E[\Delta \mu_t] + \mu$. So, adding μ to both sides of Equation (5.13) we obtain:

$$\gamma(g) \cong \frac{\text{Cov}(\ell, f) - p_t\phi_> \left[\text{Cov}_>(\ell, f) + (\mu_> - \mu)(\bar{f}_> - f_{bad})\right]}{\bar{f} - p_t\phi_>(\bar{f}_> - f_{bad})} + \mu.$$

Solving again for p_t yields:

$$p_t \cong \frac{\text{Cov}(\ell, f) - [\gamma(g) - \mu][\bar{f} - p_t\phi_>(\bar{f}_> - f_{bad})]}{\phi_> \left[\text{Cov}_>(\ell, f) + (\mu_> - \mu)(\bar{f}_> - f_{bad})\right]} \tag{5.16}$$

Note that, in the absence of sampling noise (i.e., for an infinite population), requiring that $E[\Delta\mu] = 0$ at each generation implies $\mu(g) = \mu(0)$ for all $g > 0$. However, in any finite population the parsimony pressure method can only achieve $\Delta\mu = 0$ *in expectation*, so there can be some random drift in $\mu(g)$ w.r.t. its starting value of $\mu(0)$. If tighter control over the mean program size is desired, one can use Equation (5.15) with the choice $\gamma(g) = \mu(0)$, which leads to the following formula

$$p_t \cong \frac{\text{Cov}(\ell, f) - [\mu(0) - \mu][\bar{f} - p_t\phi_>(\bar{f}_> - f_{bad})]}{\phi_> \left[\text{Cov}_>(\ell, f) + (\mu_> - \mu)(\bar{f}_> - f_{bad})\right]} \tag{5.17}$$

Note the similarities and differences between this and Equation (5.14). In the presence of any drift moving μ away from $\mu(0)$, this equation will actively strengthen the size control pressure to push the mean program size back to its initial value.

4. Example and Numerical Corroboration

As an example, let us consider the small population in the first two columns of Table 5-1 and let us apply Equation (5.3) to it. We have that $\text{Cov}(\ell, f) = 6.75$

Table 5-1. The effects of the covariant Tarpeian method on a small sample population of 4 individuals. The size and raw fitness of the individuals in the population are shown in the first two columns. The remaining columns report the fitness associated to each such individuals after the application of the Tarpeian method with optimal p_t.

		Trials									
Size	f	f_t	f_t	f_t	f_t	f_t	f_t	f_t	f_t	f_t	f_t
5	9	0	0	0	0	0	9	0	9	0	0
2	1	1	1	1	1	1	1	1	1	1	1
2	2	2	2	2	2	2	2	2	2	2	2
7	8	0	0	8	0	8	0	0	0	8	0
$E[\Delta\mu]$	1.35	-2.00	-2.00	1.64	-2.00	1.64	0.25	-2.00	0.25	1.64	-2.00
		Average $E[\Delta\mu] = -0.46$									

and $\bar{f} = 5$. So, in the absence of bloat control we will have an expected increase in program size of $E[\Delta\mu] = 1.35$ at the next generation. This is to be expected given the strong correlation between fitness and size in our sample population.

Let us now compute p_t using Equation (5.14). Since in our population $\mu = 4$, we have that $\phi_> = 0.5$, the programs of size 5 and 7 being of above-average size. Their average size is $\mu_> = 6$ and their average fitness is $\bar{f}_> = 8.5$. Finally, the covariance between their size and their fitness is $\text{Cov}_>(\ell, f) = -0.5$. Using these values and the covariance between size and fitness which we computed previously, and taking the safe value $f_{bad} = 0$, we obtain $p_t \cong 0.818182$.

Let us now imagine that we adopt this particular value of p_t and let us recompute the Tarpeian fitness of the members of our population based on the application of the Tarpeian method (with $f_{bad} = 0$). Since the method is stochastic we will do it multiple times, so as to get an idea of its expected behaviour. The results of these trials are shown in columns 3–12 of Table 5-1. Computing the expected change in program size after the application of the Tarpeian method shows that in 5 out of 10 cases it is negative, in 2 cases it is marginally positive and only in the remaining cases it is comparable (in fact slightly bigger) than expected when the Tarpeian method is not used. Indeed, on average we expect a slight contraction in the mean program size of -0.46. In other words, the estimate for p_t has exceeded the value required to achieve a zero expected change in program size. Errors such as this have to be expected given the tiny population we have used.

To corroborate the theory presented in the previous section and evaluate how population size affects the accuracy of our estimate of p_t, we need to perform many more trials (so as to avoid small sample errors) with a variety of population sizes. For these tests we will create populations with an extremely high correlation between fitness and size.

Table 5-2. Errors in $E[\Delta\mu_t]$ resulting from the approximations in the calculation of p_t for different population sizes and for a fitness function where $f(\ell) = \ell$. Statistics were computed over 1,000 independent repetitions of the application of the Tarpeian method to a population including programs from size 1 to M, M being the population size.

Population size M	$E[\Delta\mu]$ without Tarpeian	Estimated optimal p_t	Average $E[\Delta\mu_t]$ with Tarpeian	Standard deviation of $E[\Delta\mu_t]$
10	15.00	0.750	-3.050	10.74
100	16.51	0.795	-0.275	3.64
1000	16.80	0.804	0.026	1.16
10000	16.83	0.805	-0.004	0.36
100000	16.83	0.805	-0.003	0.12

Our populations include $M = 10$, 100, 1000, 10000, and 100,000 individuals. In each population individual i has size $\ell_i = \lfloor \frac{i}{M} \times 100 \rfloor$ and fitness $f_i = \ell_i$. These choices would be expected to produce very strong bloat. Indeed, as shown in the second column of Table 5-2 we expect to see the mean size of programs to increase by between 15 and 16.83 at the next generation.

We now apply the Tarpeian method with the optimal p_t computed via Equation (5.14) on our test populations 1000 times. The optimal p_t obtained for each population size is shown in the third column of Table 5-2. Each time different individuals are hit by the reduction of fitness associated with the method. So, different expected changes in program size $E[\Delta\mu_t]$ will be produced. The fourth and fifth columns of Table 5-2 show the mean and standard deviations of $E[\Delta\mu_t]$ over the 1000 repetitions of the test. As we can see from these values, in all cases bloat is entirely under control, although, for this problem, Equation (5.14) consistently overestimates p_t thereby leading to slightly shrinking individuals on average. Note how rapidly the mean error becomes very small as the population size grows towards the typical values used in realistic GP runs. The standard deviations also rapidly drop, indicating that the method becomes almost deterministic for very large population sizes. This is confirmed by the distributions of $E[\Delta\mu_t]$ for different population sizes shown in Figure 5-1.

5. Empirical Tests

To further corroborate the theory, we conducted experiments using a linear register-based GP system. The system we used is a generational GP system. It initialises the population by repeatedly creating random individuals with lengths uniformly distributed between 1 and 200 primitives. The primitives are drawn randomly and uniformly from a problem's primitive set. The system uses fitness proportionate selection and crossover applied with a rate of 90%. The remaining 10% of the population is created via selection followed by point

Table 5-3. Primitive set used in our experiments.

Instructions
R1 = RIN
R2 = RIN
R1 = R1 + R2
R2 = R1 + R2
R1 = R1 * R2
R2 = R1 * R2
Swap R1 R2

mutation (with a rate of 1 mutation per program). Crossover creates offspring by selecting two random crossover points, one in each parent, and taking the first part of the first parent and the second part of the second w.r.t. their crossover points. This is a form of sub-tree crossover for linear structures/trees. We used populations of size 1,000 and 10,000. In each condition we performed 100 independent runs, each lasting either 50 or 100 generations.

With this system we solved a classical symbolic regression problem: the quintic polynomial. In other words, the objective was to evolve a function which fits a polynomial of the form $x + x^2 + \cdots + x^d$, where $d = 5$ is the degree of the polynomial, for x in the range $[-1, 1]$. In particular we sampled the polynomials at the 21 equally spaced points $x \in \{-1, -0.9, \ldots, 0.9, 1.0\}$. Polynomials of this type have been widely used as benchmark problems in the GP literature.

Fitness (to be maximised) was $1/(1 + \text{error})$ where error is the sum of the absolute differences between the target polynomial and the output produced by the program under evaluation over these 21 fitness cases. The primitive set used to solve these problems is shown in Table 5-3. The instructions refer to three registers: the input register RIN which is loaded with the value of x before a fitness case is evaluated and the two registers R1 and R2 which can be used for numerical calculations. R1 and R2 are initialised to x and 0, respectively. The output of the program is read from R1 at the end of its execution.

Figure 5-2 shows the results of our runs for populations of size 1000 and 10,000 in the absence of bloat control and when using the version of the Co-variant Tarpeian method in Equation (5.17). Figure 5-3 shows the results for a population of size 1000 when using the version of the Covariant Tarpeian method in Equation (5.15) where $\gamma(g)$ is the following triangle wave of period 50 generations:

$$\gamma(g) = 100 \times \left(0.75 + 0.5 \times \left| \frac{g + 12.5}{50} - \left\lfloor \frac{g + 12.5}{50} + 0.5 \right\rfloor \right| \right). \quad (5.18)$$

Table 5-4. Comparison of success rates in the quintic polynomial regression for different population sizes with and without Tarpeian bloat control. Runs were declared successful if the sum of absolute errors in the best individual fell below 1. Tarpeian bloat control was exerted using Equation (5.15) with $\gamma(g) = \mu(0)$ ("Covariant Tarpeian constant") or with the $\gamma(g)$ function in Equation (5.18) ("Covariant Tarpeian triangle").

Bloat control	pop size	success rate
None	1,000	94%
Covariant Tarpeian constant	1,000	92%
Covariant Tarpeian triangle	1,000	95%
None	10,000	100%
Covariant Tarpeian constant	10,000	100%

It is apparent that in the absence of bloat control there is very substantial bloat, while the Covariant Tarpeian method provides almost total control over the size dynamics.

It has sometimes been suggested that bloat control techniques can harm performance. One may wonder, then, if performance was affected by the use of the covariant Tarpeian method. In the quintic polynomial regression there was very little variation in the success rate (for a given population size) across techniques, as illustrated in Table 5-4. This is very encouraging, but it would be surprising if in other problems and for other parameter settings there weren't some performance differences. Future research will need to explore this.

6. Conclusions

There are almost as many anti-bloat recipes as there are researchers in genetic programming. Very few, however, have a theoretical pedigree. The Tarpeian method (Poli, 2003) is one of them. In recent years, the method has started becoming more and more widespread, probably because of its simplicity. The method, however, like most others, requires setting one main parameter (and one secondary one) for it to perform appropriately. Until now this parameter had to be set by trial and error.

In this paper we integrate the theory that led to the development of the original Tarpeian method with ideas that recently led to the covariant parsimony pressure method (Poli and McPhee, 2008) (another theoretically derived method), to obtain equations which allow one to optimally set the parameter(s) of the method so as to achieve almost full control over the evolution of the mean program size in runs of genetic programming. Although the complexity of the task has forced us to rely on approximations to make progress, numerical and empirical corroboration confirm that the quality of the approximation is good. Experiments have also confirmed the effectiveness of the Covariant Tarpeian method.

References

Alfaro-Cid, Eva, Merelo, J. J., Fernandez de Vega, Francisco, Esparcia-Alcazar, Anna I., , and Sharman, Ken (2010). Bloat control operators and diversity in genetic programming: A comparative study. _Evolutionary Computation_, 18(2):305–332.

Allen, Sam, Burke, Edmund K., Hyde, Matthew R., and Kendall, Graham (2009). Evolving reusable 3D packing heuristics with genetic programming. In Raidl, Guenther, Rothlauf, Franz, Squillero, Giovanni, Drechsler, Rolf, Stuetzle, Thomas, Birattari, Mauro, Congdon, Clare Bates, Middendorf, Martin, Blum, Christian, Cotta, Carlos, Bosman, Peter, Grahl, Joern, Knowles, Joshua, Corne, David, Beyer, Hans-Georg, Stanley, Ken, Miller, Julian F., van Hemert, Jano, Lenaerts, Tom, Ebner, Marc, Bacardit, Jaume, O'Neill, Michael, Di Penta, Massimiliano, Doerr, Benjamin, Jansen, Thomas, Poli, Riccardo, and Alba, Enrique, editors, _GECCO '09: Proceedings of the 11th Annual conference on Genetic and evolutionary computation_, pages 931–938, Montreal. ACM.

Burke, Edmund K., Hyde, Matthew R., Kendall, Graham, and Woodward, John (2007). Automatic heuristic generation with genetic programming: evolving a jack-of-all-trades or a master of one. In Thierens, Dirk, Beyer, Hans-Georg, Bongard, Josh, Branke, Jurgen, Clark, John Andrew, Cliff, Dave, Congdon, Clare Bates, Deb, Kalyanmoy, Doerr, Benjamin, Kovacs, Tim, Kumar, Sanjeev, Miller, Julian F., Moore, Jason, Neumann, Frank, Pelikan, Martin, Poli, Riccardo, Sastry, Kumara, Stanley, Kenneth Owen, Stutzle, Thomas, Watson, Richard A, and Wegener, Ingo, editors, _GECCO '07: Proceedings of the 9th annual conference on Genetic and evolutionary computation_, volume 2, pages 1559–1565, London. ACM Press.

Chouza, Mariano, Rancan, Claudio, Clua, Osvaldo, , and Garcia-Martinez, Ramon (2009). Passive analog filter design using GP population control strategies. In Chien, Been-Chian and Hong, Tzung-Pei, editors, _Opportunities and Challenges for Next-Generation Applied Intelligence: Proceedings of the International Conference on Industrial, Engineering & Other Applications of Applied Intelligent Systems (IEA-AIE) 2009_, volume 214 of _Studies in Computational Intelligence_, pages 153–158. Springer-Verlag.

Garcia, Beatriz, Aler, Ricardo, Ledezma, Agapito, and Sanchis, Araceli (2008a). Genetic programming for predicting protein networks. In Geffner, Hector, Prada, Rui, Alexandre, Isabel Machado, and David, Nuno, editors, _Proceedings of the 11th Ibero-American Conference on AI, IBERAMIA 2008_, volume 5290 of _Lecture Notes in Computer Science_, pages 432–441, Lisbon, Portugal. Springer. Advances in Artificial Intelligence.

Garcia, Beatriz, Aler, Ricardo, Ledezma, Agapito, and Sanchis, Araceli (2008b). Protein-protein functional association prediction using genetic programming. In Keijzer, Maarten, Antoniol, Giuliano, Congdon, Clare Bates, Deb, Kalyanmoy, Doerr, Benjamin, Hansen, Nikolaus, Holmes, John H., Hornby, Gregory S., Howard, Daniel, Kennedy, James, Kumar, Sanjeev, Lobo, Fernando G., Miller, Julian Francis, Moore, Jason, Neumann, Frank, Pelikan, Martin, Pollack, Jordan, Sastry, Kumara, Stanley, Kenneth, Stoica, Adrian, Talbi, El-Ghazali, and Wegener, Ingo, editors, *GECCO '08: Proceedings of the 10th annual conference on Genetic and evolutionary computation*, pages 347–348, Atlanta, GA, USA. ACM.

Garcia-Almanza, Alma Lilia and Tsang, Edward P. K. (2006). Simplifying decision trees learned by genetic programming. In *Proceedings of the 2006 IEEE Congress on Evolutionary Computation*, pages 7906–7912, Vancouver. IEEE Press.

Koza, John R. (1992). *Genetic Programming: On the Programming of Computers by Means of Natural Selection*. MIT Press, Cambridge, MA, USA.

Luke, Sean and Panait, Liviu (2006). A comparison of bloat control methods for genetic programming. *Evolutionary Computation*, 14(3):309–344.

Mahler, Sébastien, Robilliard, Denis, and Fonlupt, Cyril (2005). Tarpeian bloat control and generalization accuracy. In Keijzer, Maarten, Tettamanzi, Andrea, Collet, Pierre, van Hemert, Jano I., and Tomassini, Marco, editors, *Proceedings of the 8th European Conference on Genetic Programming*, volume 3447 of *Lecture Notes in Computer Science*, pages 203–214, Lausanne, Switzerland. Springer.

Martinez-Jaramillo, Serafin and Tsang, Edward P. K. (2009). An heterogeneous, endogenous and coevolutionary GP-based financial market. *IEEE Transactions on Evolutionary Computation*, 13(1):33–55.

Poli, Riccardo (2003). A simple but theoretically-motivated method to control bloat in genetic programming. In Ryan, Conor, Soule, Terence, Keijzer, Maarten, Tsang, Edward, Poli, Riccardo, and Costa, Ernesto, editors, *Genetic Programming, Proceedings of EuroGP'2003*, volume 2610 of *LNCS*, pages 204–217, Essex. Springer-Verlag.

Poli, Riccardo, Langdon, William B., and McPhee, Nicholas Freitag (2008). *A field guide to genetic programming*. Published via http://lulu.com and freely available at http://www.gp-field-guide.org.uk. (With contributions by J. R. Koza).

Poli, Riccardo and McPhee, Nicholas (2008). Parsimony pressure made easy. In Keijzer, Maarten, Antoniol, Giuliano, Congdon, Clare Bates, Deb, Kalyanmoy, Doerr, Benjamin, Hansen, Nikolaus, Holmes, John H., Hornby, Gregory S., Howard, Daniel, Kennedy, James, Kumar, Sanjeev, Lobo, Fernando G., Miller, Julian Francis, Moore, Jason, Neumann, Frank, Pelikan, Martin, Pollack, Jordan, Sastry, Kumara, Stanley, Kenneth, Stoica, Adrian, Talbi, El-Ghazali, and Wegener, Ingo, editors, *GECCO '08: Proceedings of the 10th annual conference on Genetic and evolutionary computation*, pages 1267–1274, Atlanta, GA, USA. ACM.

Poli, Riccardo and McPhee, Nicholas Freitag (2003). General schema theory for genetic programming with subtree-swapping crossover: Part II. *Evolutionary Computation*, 11(2):169–206.

Price, George R. (1970). Selection and covariance. *Nature*, 227, August 1:520–521.

Roberts, Mark E. and Claridge, Ela (2004). Cooperative coevolution of image feature construction and object detection. In Yao, Xin, Burke, Edmund, Lozano, Jose A., Smith, Jim, Merelo-Guervós, Juan J., Bullinaria, John A., Rowe, Jonathan, Kabán, Peter Tiňo Ata, and Schwefel, Hans-Paul, editors, *Parallel Problem Solving from Nature - PPSN VIII*, volume 3242 of *LNCS*, pages 902–911, Birmingham, UK. Springer-Verlag.

Silva, Sara (2008). *Controlling Bloat: Individual and Population Based Approaches in Genetic Programming*. PhD thesis, Coimbra University, Portugal. Full author name is Sara Guilherme Oliveira da Silva.

Wyns, Bart and Boullart, Luc (2009). Efficient tree traversal to reduce code growth in tree-based genetic programming. *Journal of Heuristics*, 15(1):77–104.

Zhang, Byoung-Tak and Mühlenbein, Heinz (1993). Evolving optimal neural networks using genetic algorithms with Occam's razor. *Complex Systems*, 7:199–220.

Zhang, Byoung-Tak and Mühlenbein, Heinz (1995). Balancing accuracy and parsimony in genetic programming. *Evolutionary Computation*, 3(1):17–38.

Zhang, Byoung-Tak, Ohm, Peter, and Mühlenbein, Heinz (1997). Evolutionary induction of sparse neural trees. *Evolutionary Computation*, 5(2):213–236.

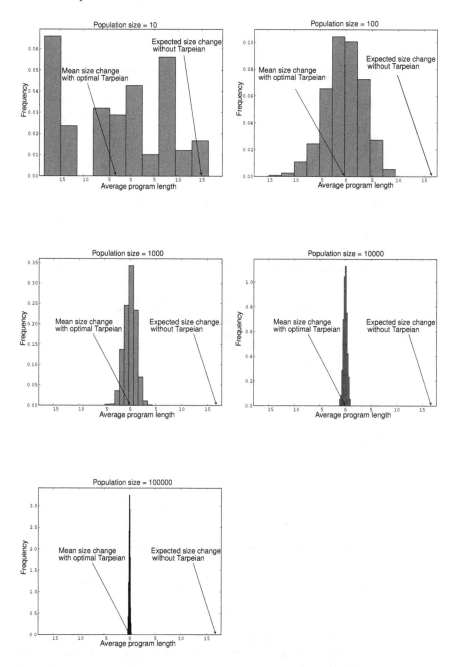

Figure 5-1. Distributions of $E[\Delta \mu_t]$ resulting from the application of the Covariant Tarpeian method for populations of size 10 (top left), 100 (top right), 1,000 (middle left), 10,000 (middle right) and 100,000 (bottom) with our sample fitness function.

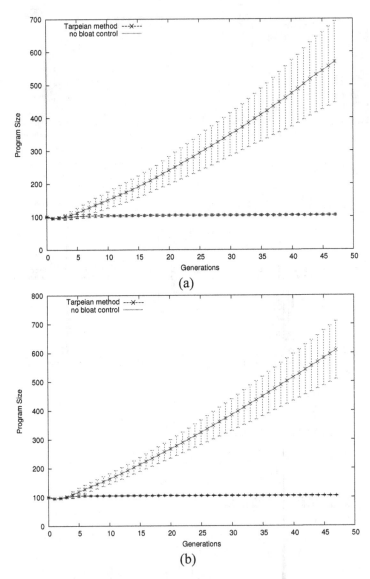

Figure 5-2. Mean program size for populations of size 1000 (a) and 10,000 (b) as a function of the generation number on the quintic polynomial symbolic regression in the absence of bloat control and when using the version of the Covariant Tarpeian method in Equation (5.17).

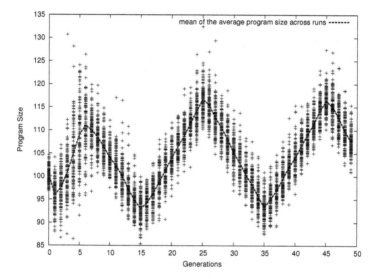

Figure 5-3. Average program size for populations of size 1000 and runs lasting 100 generations with the quintic polynomial symbolic regression when using the version of the Covariant Tarpeian method in Equation (5.15) where $\gamma(g)$ is a triangle wave. The dashed line represents the mean of the average program size across runs.

Chapter 6

A SURVEY OF SELF MODIFYING CARTESIAN GENETIC PROGRAMMING

Simon Harding[1], Wolfgang Banzhaf[1] and Julian F. Miller[2]

[1]*Department Of Computer Science, Memorial University, Canada;* [2]*Department Of Electronics, University of York, UK.*

Abstract

Self-Modifying Cartesian Genetic Programming (SMCGP) is a general purpose, graph-based, developmental form of Cartesian Genetic Programming. In addition to the usual computational functions found in CGP, SMCGP includes functions that can modify the evolved program at run time. This means that programs can be iterated to produce an infinite sequence of phenotypes from a single evolved genotype. Here, we discuss the results of using SMCGP on a variety of different problems, and see that SMCGP is able to solve tasks that require scalability and plasticity. We demonstrate how SMCGP is able to produce results that would be impossible for conventional, static Genetic Programming techniques.

Keywords: Cartesian genetic programming, developmental systems

1. Introduction

In evolutionary computation (EC) scalability has always been an important issue. An evolutionary technique is scalable if the generational time it takes to evolve a satisfactory solution to a problem increases relatively weakly with increasing problem size. As in EC, scalability is an important issue in Genetic Programming (GP). In GP important methods for improving scalability are modularity and re-use. Modularity is introduced through sub-functions or sub-procedures. These are often called Automatically Defined Functions (ADFs) (Koza, 1994a). The use of ADFs improves the scalability of GP by allowing solutions of larger or more difficult instances of particular classes of problems to be evolved. However, GP methods in general have largely employed genotype representations whose length (number of genes) is proportional to the size of the anticipated problem solutions. This has meant that *evolutionary operators* (e.g. crossover or mutation) have been used as the mechanism for building large genotypes. The same idea underlies approaches to evolve artificial neural networks. For instance, a well known method called NEAT uses evolutionary operators to introduce new neurons and connections, thus expanding the size of the genotype (Stanley and Miikkulainen, 2002).

It is interesting to contrast these approaches to mechanisms employed in evolution of biological organisms. Multicellular organisms, having possibly enormous phenotypes, are developed from *relatively* simple genotypes. Development implies an unfolding in space and time. It is clearly promising to consider employing an analogue of biological development in genetic programming (Banzhaf and Miller, 2004). There are, of course, many possible aspects of developmental biology that could be adopted to construct a developmental GP method. In this chapter we discuss one such approach. It is called Self Modifying Cartesian Genetic Programming (SMCGP). It is based on a simple underlying idea. Namely, that a phenotype can unfold over time from a genotype by allowing the genotype to include primitive functions which act on the genotype itself. We refer to this as self-modification. As far as the authors are aware, self-modification is included in only one existing GP system: Lee Spector's Push GP language (Spector and Robinson, 2002). One of the attractive aspects of introducing primitive self-modification functions is that it is relatively easy to include them in any GP system.

Since 2007, SMCGP has been applied to a variety of computational problems. In the ensuing time the actual details of the SMCGP implementation have changed, however the key concepts and philosophy have remained the same. Here we present the latest version. We explain the essentials of how SMCGP works in section 2. Section 3 discusses briefly examples of previous work with SMCGP. In section 4 we compare and contrast the way other GP systems include iteration with the iterative unrolling that occurs in SMCGP. We end the chapter with conclusions and suggestions for future work.

2.   Self Modifying Cartesian Genetic Programming

As the name suggests, SMCGP is based on the Cartesian Genetic Programming technique. In CGP, programs are encoded in a partly connected, feed forward graph. A full description can be found in (Miller and Thomson, 2000). The genotype encodes this graph. Associated with each node in the graph are genes that represent the node function and genes representing connections to either other nodes or terminals. The representation has a number of interesting features. Firstly, not all of the nodes in the genotype need to be connected to the output, so there is a degree of neutrality which has been shown to be very useful (Miller and Thomson, 2000; Vassilev and Miller, 2000; Yu and Miller,

2001; Miller and Smith, 2006). Secondly, as the genotype encodes a graph there is reuse of nodes, which makes the representation very compact and also distinct from tree based GP.

Although CGP has been used in various ways in developmental systems (Miller, 2004; Miller and Thomson, 2003; Khan et al., 2007), the programs that it produces are not themselves developmental. Instead, these approaches used a fixed length genotype to represent the programs defining the behaviour of cells.

SMCGP's representation is similar to CGP in some ways, but has extensions that allow it to have the self modifying features. SMCGP genotypes are a linear string of nodes. That is to say, only one row of nodes is used (in contrast to CGP which can have a rectangular grid of nodes). In contrast to CGP in which connection genes are absolute addresses, indicating where the data supplied to a node is to be obtained, SMCGP uses *relative* addressing. Each node obtains its data inputs from its connection genes by counting back from its position in the graph. To prevent cycles, nodes can only connect to previous nodes (on their left). The relative addressing allows section of the graph to be moved, duplicated, deleted etc without breaking constraints of the structure whilst allowing some sort of modularity. In addition to CGP, SMCGP has some extra genes that are used by self-modification functions to identify parts or characteristics of the graph that will be changed.

Another change from CGP is the way SMCGP handles inputs and outputs. Terminals are acquired through special functions (called INP, INPP, SKIPINP) and program outputs are taken from a special function called OUTPUT. This is an important change as it enables SMCGP programs to obtain and deliver as many inputs or outputs as required by the problem domain, during program execution. This allows the possibility of evolving general solutions to problems. For example, to find a program that can compute even-n parity, where n is arbitrary, one needs to be able to acquire an arbitrary number of inputs or terminals.

In summary: Each node in the SMCGP graph contains a number of evolvable elements:

- The function. Represented in the genotype as an integer.

- A list of (relative) connections addresses, again represented as integers.

- A set of 3 floating point number arguments used by self-modification functions.

There are also primitive *functions* that acquire or deliver inputs and outputs.

As with CGP, the number of nodes in the genotype is typically kept constant through an experiment. However, this means care has to be taken to ensure that the genotype is large enough to store the target program.

Executing a SMCGP Individual

SMCGP individuals are evaluated in a multi-step process, with the evolved program (the phenotype) executed several times. The evolved program in SM-CGP initially has the same structure as the genotype, hence the first step is to make a copy of the genotype and call it the phenotype. This graph is to be the 'working copy' of the program.

Each time the program is executed, the graph is first run and then any self modification operations required are invoked. The graph is executed in the following manner.

First, the node (or nodes) to be used as outputs are identified. This is done by reading through the graph looking at which nodes are of type OUTPUT. Once a sufficient number of these nodes has been found, the various nodes that they connect to are identified. If not enough output nodes are found, then the last n nodes in the graph are used, where n is the number of outputs required. If there are not enough nodes to satisfy this requirement, then the execution is aborted, and the individual is discarded.

At this point in the decoding, all the nodes that are actually used by the program have been identified and so their values can be calculated (the other nodes can simply be ignored). For the mathematical and binary operators, these functions are performed in the usual manner. However, as mentioned before SMCGP has a number of special functions. Table 6-1 shows an example of some of the functions used in previous work (see section 3).

The first special functions are the INP and INPP functions. Each time the INP function is called it returns the next available input (starting with the first, and returning to the first after reading the last input). The INPP function is similar, but moves backwards through the inputs. SKIPINP allows a number of inputs to be ignored, and then returns the next input. These functions help SMCGP to scale to handle increasing numbers of inputs through development. This also applies to the use of the OUTPUT function, which allows the number of outputs to change over time.

If a function is a self modification function, then it may be activated depending on the following rules. For binary functions they are always activated. For numeric function nodes, if the 1st input is larger than the 2nd input the node is activated. The self modification operation from an activated node is added to a list of pending operations - the 'ToDo' list. The maximum length of the list is a parameter of the system. After execution, the self modification functions on the ToDo list are applied to the current graph. The ToDo list is operated as a FIFO list in which the leftmost activated SM function is the first to be executed (and so on).

The self modification functions require arguments defining which parts of the phenotype the function operates on. These are taken from the arguments of the calling node. Many of the arguments are integers, so they may need to be cast. The arguments may be treated as an address (depending on the function) and like all SMCGP operations, these are relative addresses. The program can now be iterated again, if necessary.

3.   Summary of Previous Work in SMCGP

Early experiments

There are very few benchmark problems in the developmental system literature. In the first paper on SMCGP (Harding et al., 2007), we identified two possible challenges that had been described previously.

The first was to find a program that generates a sequence of squares (i.e. 0,1,2,4,9,16,25...) using a restricted set of mathematical operators such as + and −, but not multiplication or power. Without some form of self modification this challenge would be impossible to solve (Spector and Stoffel, 1996). SMCGP was easily able to solve this problem (89% success rate), and a large number of different solutions were found.

Typical solutions were similar to the program in table 6-2, where the program grew in length by adding new terms.

During evolution, solutions were only tested up to the first 10 iterations. However, after evolution the solutions were tested for generality by increasing the number of iterations to 50. 66% of the solutions are correct to 50 iterations. Thus SMCGP was able to find general solutions.

The next benchmark problem was the French Flag (FF) problem. Several developmental systems have been tested on generating the FF pattern (Miller, 2003; Miller and Banzhaf, 2003; Miller, 2004), and it is one of the few common problems tackled. In this problem, the task is to evolve a program that can assign the states of cells (represented as colours) into three distinct regions so that the complete set of cells looks like a French Flag. However, the design goals of SMCGP are very different to those the FF task demands. Many developmental systems are built around the idea of multi-cellularity and although they are capable of producing cellular patterns or even concentrations of simulated proteins, they are not explicitly computational in the sense of Genetic Programming. Often researchers have to devise somewhat arbitrary mappings from developmental outputs (i.e. cell states and protein levels) to those required for some computational application. SMCGP is designed to be an explicitly computational developmental system from the outset.

Typically, the FF is produced via a type of cellular automaton (CA), where each cell 'alive' contains a copy of an evolved program or set of update rules. We could have taken this approach with SMCGP, but we decided on a more abstract interpretation of the problem. In the CA version, each cell in the CA is analogous to a biological cell. In SMCGP, the biological abstractions

Basic	
Delete (DEL)	Delete the nodes between (P_0+x) and (P_0+x+P_1).
Add (ADD)	Add P_1 new random nodes after (P_0+x).
Move (MOV)	Move the nodes between (P_0+x) and (P_0+x+P_1) and insert after (P_0+x+P_2).
Duplication	
Overwrite (OVR)	Copy the nodes between (P_0+x) and (P_0+x+P_1) to position (P_0+x+P_2), replacing existing nodes in the target position.
Duplication (DUP)	Copy the nodes between (P_0+x) and (P_0+x+P_1) and insert after (P_0+x+P_2).
Duplicate Preserving Connections (DU3)	Copy the nodes between (P_0+x) and (P_0+x+P_1) and insert after (P_0+x+P_2). When copying, this function modifies the c_{ij} of the copied nodes so that they continue to point to the original nodes.
Duplicate and scale addresses (DU4)	Starting from position (P_0+x) copy (P_1) nodes and insert after the node at position (P_0+x+P_1). During the copy, c_{ij} of copied nodes are multiplied by P_2.
Copy To Stop (COPYTOSTOP)	Copy from x to the next "COPYTOSTOP" or 'STOP" function node, or the end of the graph. Nodes are inserted at the position the operator stops at.
Stop Marker (STOP)	Marks the end of a COPYTOSTOP section.
Connection modification	
Shift Connections (SHIFTCONNECTION)	Starting at node index (P_0+x), add P_2 to the values of the c_{ij} of next P_1.
Shift Connections 2 (MULTCONNECTION)	Starting at node index (P_0+x), multiply the c_{ij} of the next P_1 nodes by P_2.
Change Connection (CHC)	Change the $(P_1 mod 3)$th connection of node P_0 to P_2.
Function modification	
Change Function (CHF)	Change the function of node P_0 to the function associated with P_1.
Change Parameter (CHP)	Change the $(P_1 mod 3)$th parameter of node P_0 to P_2.
Miscellaneous	
Flush (FLR)	Clears the contents of the ToDo list

Table 6-1. Self modification functions. x represents the absolute position of the node in the graph, where the leftmost node has position 0. P_N are evolved parameters stored in each node.

Iteration (i)	Function	Result
0	$0 + i$	0
1	$0 + i$	1
2	$0 + i + i$	4
3	$0 + i + i + i$	9
4	$0 + i + i + i + i$	16
etc.		

Table 6-2. Program that generates sequence of squares. The program was found by reverse engineering a SMCGP phenotype. i, the current iteration, is the only input to the program.

are blurred, and the SMCGP phenotype itself could be viewed as a collection of cells. One way of viewing cells in SMCGP is to break the phenotype into 'modules' and then define these as the cells. In this way, SMCGP cells duplicate and differentiate using the various modifying functions. In a static program, this concept of cellularity does not exist.

To tackle the FF problem with SMCGP, we defined the target pattern to be a string of integers that could be visually interpreted as a French Flag pattern. In the CA model, the pattern would be taken as the output of the program at each cell. Here, since we can view SMCGP phenotypes as a collection of cells, we took the output pattern as the set of outputs from all the active (connected) nodes in the phenotype graph. The fitness of an individual is the count of how many of the sequence it got right after a certain number of iterations.

As the phenotype can change length when it is iterated, the number of active nodes can change and the length of the output pattern can also change. The value of the output of active nodes is dependent on the calculation it (and the nodes before it) does. So the French Flag pattern is effectively the side effect of some mathematical expression.

It was found that this approach was largely successful, but only in generating approximations to the flag. No exact solutions were found, which is similar to the findings of the CA solutions where exact results are uncommon.

The final task we explored in this paper was generating parity circuits, a challenge we return to in the next section.

Digital Circuits

Digital circuits have often been studied in genetic programming (Koza, 1994b; Koza, 1992b), and some systems have been used to produce 'general' solutions (Huelsbergen, 1998; Wong and Leung, 1996; Wong, 2005). A general solution in this sense is a program that can output a digital circuit for an arbitrary number of inputs, for example it may generate a parity circuit of any size [1]. Conveniently, many digital circuits are modular and hierarchical - and this fits the model of development that SMCGP implements.

In our first paper, we successfully produced parity circuits up to 8 inputs (Harding et al., 2007). We stopped at this size because, at the time, this was the maximum size we could find conventional CGP solutions for. In a subsequent paper (Harding et al., 2009a), we revisited the problem (using the latest version of SMCGP), and found that not only could we evolve larger parity circuits, but we could rapidly and consistently evolve provably general parity circuits.

We used an incremental fitness function to find programs that on the first iteration would solve 2 input parity, then 3 input parity on the next iteration and continue up to a maximum number of inputs. The fitness of an individual is the number of correct output bits over all iterations. To keep the computational costs down, we limited the evolution to 2 to 20 inputs, and then tested the final programs for generality by running up to 24 bits of input. We also stopped iterating programs if they failed to correctly produce all the output bits for the current table.

Note how if an individual fails to be successful on a particular iteration the evaluation is canceled. Not only did this reduce the computation time, but we hoped it would also help with producing generalized solutions. Our function set consisted of all the two-input Boolean functions and the self modifying functions. In 251 evolutionary runs we found that the average number of evaluations required to successfully solve the parity problems was (number of inputs in parentheses) are as follows: 1,429(2), 4,013 (3), 43,817 (6), 82, 936 (8), 107,586 (10), 110,216 (17). Here we have given an incomplete list that just illustrates the trend in problem difficulty.

We found that the number of evaluations stabilizes when the number of inputs is about 10. This is because after evolution has solved to a given number of inputs the solutions typically become generalized. We found that by the time that evolution had solved 5 inputs, more than half the solutions were generalizable up to 20 inputs, and by 10 inputs this was up to 90%. The percentage of runs that correctly computed even-parity 22 to 24 was approximately 96%. However, without analysis of the programs it was difficult to know whether they were truly general solutions.

The evolved programs can be relatively compact, especially when we place constraints on the initial size, the number of self modification operations allowed on the ToDo list and the overall length of the program. Figure 6-1 shows an example of an evolved parity circuit generating a program which we were able to prove is a general solution to even-parity.

---

[1] An even parity circuit takes a set of binary inputs and outputs true if an even number of the inputs are true, and false otherwise.

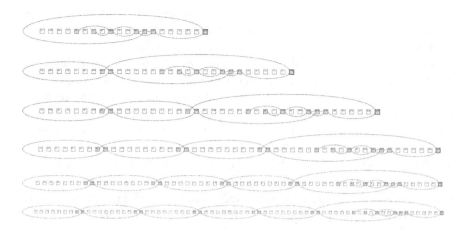

Figure 6-1. An example of the development of a parity circuit. Each line shows the phenotype graph at a given time step. The first graph solves the 2-input parity, the second solves 3-input and continues to 7-bits. The graph has been tested to generalise through to 24 inputs. This pattern of growth is typical of the programs investigated.

In recent work (to be published in (Harding et al., 2010a)) we have also shown general solutions for the digital adder circuit. A digital adder circuit of size n adds two binary n bit numbers together. This problem is much more complicated than parity, as the number of inputs scales twice as fast (i.e. it has to produce 1 bit+1 bit, 2+2, 3+3) and the number of outputs also grows with the number of inputs.

Mathematical problems

SMCGP has been applied to a variety of mathematical problems (Harding et al., 2009c; Harding et al., 2010b).

For the Fibonacci sequence, the fitness function is the number of correctly calculated Fibonacci numbers in a sequence of 50. The first two Fibonacci numbers are given as fixed inputs (these were 0 and 1). Thus the phenotypes are iterated 48 times. Evolved solutions were tested for generality by iterating up to 72 times (after which the numbers exceeds the long int). A success rate of 87.4% was acheived on 287 runs and 94.5% of these correctly calculated the suceeeding 24 Fibonacci numbers. We found that the average number of evaluations of 774,808 compared favourably with previously published methods and that the generalization rate was higher.

In the "list summation problem" we evolved programs that could sum an arbitrarily long list of numbers. At the n-th iteration, the evolved program should be able to take n inputs and compute the sum of all the inputs. We devised this problem because we thought it would be difficult for genetic programming without the addition of an explicit summation command. Koza used a summation operator called SIGMA that repeatedly evaluates its sole input until a predefined termination condition is realised (Koza, 1992a).

Input vectors consisted of random sequences of integers. The fitness is defined as the absolute cumulative error between the output of the program and the expected sum of the values. We evolved programs which were evaluated on input sequences of 2 to 10 numbers. The function set consisted of the self modifying functions and just the ADD operator. All 500 experiments were found to be successful, in that they evolved programs that could sum between 2 and 10 numbers (depending on the number of iterations the program is iterated). On average it took 6,922 evaluations to solve this problem. After evolution, the best individual for each run was tested to see how well it generalized. This test involved summing a sequence of 100 numbers. It was found that 99.03% solutions generalized. When conventional CGP was used it could only sum up to 7 numbers.

We also studied how SMCGP performed on a "Powers Regression" problem. The task is to evolve a program that, depending on the iteration, approximates the expression x^n where n is the iteration number. The fitness function applies x as integers from 0 to 20. The fitness is defined as the number of wrong outputs (i.e. lower is better). Programs were evolved to $n = 10$ and then tested for generality up to $n = 20$. As with many of the other experiments, the program is evolved with an incremental fitness function. We obtained 100% correct solutions (in 337 runs). The average number of evalutions was 869,699.

More recently we have looked at whether SMCGP could produce algorithms that can compute mathematical constants, like π and e, to arbitrary precision (Harding et al., 2010b). We were able to prove that two of the evolved formulae (one for π and one for e) rapidly converged to the constants in the limit of large iterations. We consider this work to be significant as evolving provable mathematical results is a rarity in evolutionary computation.

The fitness function was designed to produce a program where subsequent iterations of the program produced more accurate approximation to π or e. Programs were allowed to iterate for a maximum of 10 iterations. If the output after an iteration did not better approximate π, evaluation was stopped and a large fitness penalty applied. Note that it is possible that after the 10 iterations the output value diverges from the constant and the quality of the result would therefore worsen.

We analyzed one of the solutions that accurately converges to π. It had the generating function:

$$f(i) = \begin{cases} cos(sin(cos(sin(0)))) & i = 0 \\ f(i-1) + sin(f(i-1)) & i > 0 \end{cases} \qquad (6.1)$$

Equation 6.1 is a nonlinear recurrence relation and it can be proven formally that it is an exact solution in that it rapidly approaches π in the limit of large i.

Using the same fitness function as with π, evolving solutions for e was found to be significantly harder. In our experiments we chose the initial genotype to have 20 nodes and the ToDo list length to be 2. This meant that only two SM functions were used in each phenotype. We allowed the iteration number it as the sole program input. Defining $x = 4^{it}$ and $y = 4x = 4^{it+1}$ we evolved the solution for the output, z as

$$z = (1 + \frac{1}{y})^y \sqrt{1 + \frac{1}{y}} \tag{6.2}$$

Eqn 6.2 tends to the form of a well-known Bernoulli formula.

$$\lim_{y \to \infty} (1 + \frac{1}{y})^y \tag{6.3}$$

Evolving to Learn

In nature, we are used to the idea that plasticity (e.g., in the brain) can be used to learn during the lifetime of an organism. In the brain, the 'self-modification rules' are ultimately encoded in the genome. In (Harding et al., 2009b), we set out to use SMCGP to evolve a learning algorithm that could act on itself. The basic question being whether SMCGP can evolve a program that can learn - during the development phase - how to perform a given task. We chose the task of getting the same phenotype to learn all possible 2-input boolean truth tables. We took 16 copies of the same phenotype, and then tried to train each copy on a different truth table, with the fitness being how well the programs (after the learning phase) did at calculating the correct value based on a pair of inputs.

In SMCGP, the activation of a self modifying node is dependent on the values that it reads as inputs. Combined with the various mathematical operators, this allows the phenotype to develop differently in the presence of different sets of inputs. To support the mathematical operators, the Boolean tables were represented (and interpreted) as numbers, with -1.0 being false, +1.0 being true.

Figure 6-2 illustrates the process. The evolved genotype (a) is copied into phenotype space (b) where it can be executed. The phenotype is allowed to develop for a number of iterations (c). The number of iterations is defined by a special gene in the genotype. Copies of the developed phenotype are made (d) and each copy is assigned a different truth table to learn. The test set data is applied (e) as described in the following section. After learning (f) the phenotype can now be tested, and its fitness found. During (f), the individual is treated as a static individual - and is no longer allowed to modify itself. This fixed program is then tested for accuracy, and its fitness used as a component in the final fitness score of that individual.

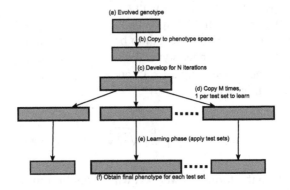

Figure 6-2. Fitness function flow chart, as described in section 3.

During the fitness evaluation stage, each row of the truth table is presented to a copy of the evolved phenotype (Figure 6-2.e). During this presentation, the error between the expected and actual output is fed back into the SMCGP program, in order to provide some sort of feedback. Full details of how this was implemented can be found in (Harding et al., 2009b).

During fitness calculation, we tested all 16 tables. However, we split the tables into two sets, one for deriving the fitness score (12 tables) and the other for a validation score (4 tables). It was found that 16% of experimental runs were successfully able to produce programs that correctly learned the 12 tables. None of the evolved programs was able to generalize to learn all the unseen truth tables. However, the system did come close with the best result having only 2 errors (out of a possible 16).

Figure 6-3 shows the form of the final phenotypes for the programs for each of the fitness truth tables. We can see both modularity and a high degree of variation - with the graphs for each table looking quite different from one another. This is in contrast to previous examples, such as the parity circuits, where we generally only see regular forms.

4.   Iteration in SMCGP and GP

One of the unique properties of SMCGP is how it handles iteration. Iteration is not new in genetic programming and there are several different forms. The most obvious form of GP with iteration is Linear Genetic Programming (LGP), where evolved programs can execute inside a kind of virtual machine in which the program counter can be modified using jump operations. LGP operates on registers (as in a CPU), and uses this memory to store state between iterations of the same section of program. It is also worth noting that in LGP sub-sections

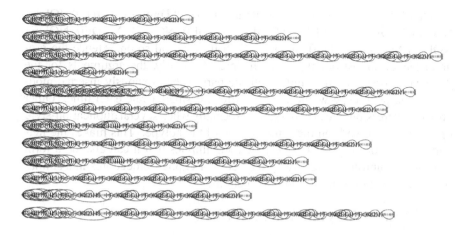

Figure 6-3. Phenotypes for each of the tables learned during evolution.

of code are executed repeatedly. This is different from most implementations of tree-based GP (and we restrict our discussion to the simple, common varieties found in the literature), as the tree represents an expression, and so any iteration has to be applied externally. Tree-based GP also typically does not have a concept of working registers to store state between iterations, so these must be added to the function set, or previous state information passed back via the tree's inputs. Tree-based GP normally only has one output, and no intermediate state information. So additional mechanisms would be required to select what information to store and pass to subsequent iterations. In LGP termination can be controlled by the evolved program itself, whereby with external iteration another mechanism needs to be defined - perhaps by enforcing a limit to the number of iterations or some form of conditional.

SMCGP handles its iteration in a very different manner. It can be viewed as something analogous to loop-unrolling in a compiler, whereby the contents of the loop are explicitly rewritten a number of times. In SMCGP, the duplication operator unrolls the phenotype. State information is passed between iterations by the connections made in the duplicated blocks. In compilers, it is done for program efficiency and is typically only done for small loops. In SMCGP, if the unrolling is excessive it will exceed the maximum permitted phenotype length. We speculate that this may help to evolve more efficient modularization. Because the activation of self modifying functions is determined by both the size of the ToDo list and the inputs to self modifying nodes, it is possible for SMCGP to self-limit when sections of code should be unrolled.

SMCGP's unrolling also has the possibility to grow exponentially, which forms a different kind of loop. For example, imagine a duplication operator that copied every node to its left and inserted it before itself : e.g NODE0

NODE1 DUPLICATE. On the next iteration it would produce NODE0 NODE1 NODE0 NODE1 DUPLICATE, then NODE0 NODE1 NODE0 NODE1 NODE0 NODE1 NODE0 NODE1 DUPLICATE and so on. Hence the program length almost doubles at each time. Similarly, the arguments for the duplication operation may only replicate part of the previously inserted module, so the phenotype would grow a different, smaller rate each time. Other growth progressions are also possible, especially when several duplication-style operators are at work on the same section of phenotype. This makes the iteration capabilities of SMCGP very rich and implies that it can also do a form of recursion unrolling - removing the need for explicit procedures in a similar way to the lack of need for loop instructions.

5.   Conclusions and Further Work

Self modification in Genetic Programming seems to be a useful property. With SMCGP we have shown that the implementation of such a system can be relatively straightforward, and that very good results can be achieved. In upcoming work, we will be demonstrating SMCGP on several other problems including generalized digital adders and a structural design problem.

Here we have discussed problems that require some sort of developmental process, as the problems require a scaling ability. One benefit of SMCGP is that if the problem does not need self modification, evolution can stop using it. When this happens, the representation reverts to something similar to classical CGP. In (Harding et al., 2009c), we showed that on a bio-informatics classification problem where there should be no benefit in using self modification, SMCGP behaved similarly to CGP. This result lets us be confident that in future work we can by default use SMCGP and automatically gain any advantages that development might bring.

The SMCGP representation has changed over time, whilst maintaining the same design philosophy. In future work we consider other variants as well. Currently we are investigating ways to simplify the genotype to make it easier for humans to understand. This should allow us to be able to prove general cases more easily, and perhaps explain how processes like the evolved learning algorithm function.

A whole world of self modifying systems seems to have become available now that the principle has been shown work successfully. We plan to investigate this world further and also encourage others to consider self modification in their systems.

6.   Acknowledgments

Funding from NSERC under discovery grant RGPIN 283304-07 to W.B. is gratefully acknowledged. S.H. was supported by an ACENET fellowship.

References

Banzhaf, W. and Miller, J. F. (2004). *The Challenge of Complexity*. Kluwer Academic.

Harding, S., Miller, J. F., and Banzhaf, W. (2009a). Self modifying cartesian genetic programming: Parity. In Tyrrell, Andy, editor, *2009 IEEE Congress on Evolutionary Computation*, pages 285–292, Trondheim, Norway. IEEE Computational Intelligence Society, IEEE Press.

Harding, Simon, Miller, Julian F., and Banzhaf, Wolfgang (2009b). Evolution, development and learning with self modifying cartesian genetic programming. In *GECCO '09: Proceedings of the 11th Annual conference on Genetic and evolutionary computation*, pages 699–706, New York, NY, USA. ACM.

Harding, Simon, Miller, Julian F., and Banzhaf, Wolfgang (2010a). Developments in cartesian genetic programming: Self-modifying cgp. *To be published in Genetic Programming and Evolvable Machines*.

Harding, Simon, Miller, Julian F., and Banzhaf, Wolfgang (2010b). Self modifying cartesian genetic programming: Finding algorithms that calculate pi and e to arbitrary precision. In *Genetic and Evolutionary Computation Conference, GECCO 2010. Accepted for publication.*

Harding, Simon, Miller, Julian Francis, and Banzhaf, Wolfgang (2009c). Self modifying cartesian genetic programming: Fibonacci, squares, regression and summing. In Vanneschi, Leonardo, Gustafson, Steven, et al., editors, *Genetic Programming, 12th European Conference, EuroGP 2009, Tübingen, Germany, April 15-17, 2009, Proceedings*, volume 5481 of *Lecture Notes in Computer Science*, pages 133–144. Springer.

Harding, Simon L., Miller, Julian F., and Banzhaf, Wolfgang (2007). Self-modifying cartesian genetic programming. In Thierens, Dirk, Beyer, Hans-Georg, Bongard, Josh, Branke, Jurgen, Clark, John Andrew, Cliff, Dave, Congdon, Clare Bates, Deb, Kalyanmoy, Doerr, Benjamin, Kovacs, Tim, Kumar, Sanjeev, Miller, Julian F., Moore, Jason, Neumann, Frank, Pelikan, Martin, Poli, Riccardo, Sastry, Kumara, Stanley, Kenneth Owen, Stutzle, Thomas, Watson, Richard A, and Wegener, Ingo, editors, *GECCO '07: Proceedings of the 9th annual conference on Genetic and evolutionary computation*, volume 1, pages 1021–1028, London. ACM Press.

Huelsbergen, Lorenz (1998). Finding general solutions to the parity problem by evolving machine-language representations. In Koza, John R., Banzhaf, Wolfgang, Chellapilla, Kumar, Deb, Kalyanmoy, Dorigo, Marco, Fogel, David B., Garzon, Max H., Goldberg, David E., Iba, Hitoshi, and Riolo, Rick, editors, *Genetic Programming 1998: Proceedings of the Third Annual Conference*, pages 158–166, University of Wisconsin, Madison, Wisconsin, USA. Morgan Kaufmann.

Khan, G.M., Miller, J.F, and Halliday, D.M. (2007). Coevolution of intelligent agents using cartesian genetic programming. In *Proceedings of the 9th annual conference on Genetic and evolutionary computation*, pages 269 – 276.

Koza, J. R. (1994a). *Genetic Programming II: Automatic Discovery of Reusable Programs*. MIT Press.

Koza, John R. (1992a). A genetic approach to the truck backer upper problem and the inter-twined spiral problem. In *Proceedings of IJCNN International Joint Conference on Neural Networks*, volume IV, pages 310–318. IEEE Press.

Koza, John R. (1994b). *Genetic Programming II: Automatic Discovery of Reusable Programs*. MIT Press, Cambridge Massachusetts.

Koza, J.R. (1992b). *Genetic Programming: On the Programming of Computers by Natural Selection*. MIT Press, Cambridge, Massachusetts, USA.

Miller, J. F. and Smith, S. L. (2006). Redundancy and computational efficiency in cartesian genetic programming. In *IEEE Transactions on Evoluationary Computation*, volume 10, pages 167–174.

Miller, Julian F. (2003). Evolving developmental programs for adaptation, morphogenesis, and self-repair. In Banzhaf, Wolfgang, Christaller, Thomas, Dittrich, Peter, Kim, Jan T., and Ziegler, Jens, editors, *Advances in Artificial Life. 7th European Conference on Artificial Life*, volume 2801 of *Lecture Notes in Artificial Intelligence*, pages 256–265, Dortmund, Germany. Springer.

Miller, Julian F. and Banzhaf, Wolfgang (2003). Evolving the program for a cell: from french flags to boolean circuits. In Kumar, Sanjeev and Bentley, Peter J., editors, *On Growth, Form and Computers*. Academic Press.

Miller, Julian F. and Thomson, Peter (2000). Cartesian genetic programming. In Poli, Riccardo, Banzhaf, Wolfgang, Langdon, William B., Miller, Julian F., Nordin, Peter, and Fogarty, Terence C., editors, *Genetic Programming, Proceedings of EuroGP'2000*, volume 1802 of *LNCS*, pages 121–132, Edinburgh. Springer-Verlag.

Miller, Julian F. and Thomson, Peter (2003). A developmental method for growing graphs and circuits. In *Proceedings of the 5th International Conference on Evolvable Systems: From Biology to Hardware*, volume 2606 of *Lecture Notes in Computer Science*, pages 93–104. Springer.

Miller, Julian Francis (2004). Evolving a self-repairing, self-regulating, french flag organism. In Deb, Kalyanmoy, Poli, Riccardo, Banzhaf, Wolfgang, Beyer, Hans-Georg, Burke, Edmund K., Darwen, Paul J., Dasgupta, Dipankar, Floreano, Dario, Foster, James A., Harman, Mark, Holland, Owen, Lanzi, Pier Luca, Spector, Lee, Tettamanzi, Andrea, Thierens, Dirk, and Tyrrell, Andrew M., editors, *GECCO (1)*, volume 3102 of *Lecture Notes in Computer Science*, pages 129–139. Springer.

Spector, L. and Robinson, A. (2002). Genetic programming and autoconstructive evolution with the push programming language. *Genetic Programming and Evolvable Machines*, 3:7–40.

Spector, Lee and Stoffel, Kilian (1996). Ontogenetic programming. In Koza, John R., Goldberg, David E., Fogel, David B., and Riolo, Rick L., editors, *Genetic Programming 1996: Proceedings of the First Annual Conference*, pages 394–399, Stanford University, CA, USA. MIT Press.

Stanley, K. O. and Miikkulainen, R. (2002). Evolving neural networks through augmenting topologies. *Evolutionary Computation*, 10(2):99–127.

Vassilev, Vesselin K. and Miller, Julian F. (2000). The advantages of landscape neutrality in digital circuit evolution. In *Proceedings of the Third International Conference on Evolvable Systems*, pages 252–263. Springer-Verlag.

Wong, Man Leung (2005). Evolving recursive programs by using adaptive grammar based genetic programming. *Genetic Programming and Evolvable Machines*, 6(4):421–455.

Wong, Man Leung and Leung, Kwong Sak (1996). Evolving recursive functions for the even-parity problem using genetic programming. In Angeline, Peter J. and Kinnear, Jr., K. E., editors, *Advances in Genetic Programming 2*, chapter 11, pages 221–240. MIT Press, Cambridge, MA, USA.

Yu, Tina and Miller, Julian (2001). Neutrality and the evolvability of boolean function landscape. In Miller, Julian F., Tomassini, Marco, Lanzi, Pier Luca, Ryan, Conor, Tettamanzi, Andrea G. B., and Langdon, William B., editors, *Genetic Programming, Proceedings of EuroGP '2001*, volume 2038 of *LNCS*, pages 204–217, Lake Como, Italy. Springer-Verlag.

Chapter 7

ABSTRACT EXPRESSION GRAMMAR SYMBOLIC REGRESSION

Michael F. Korns[1]

[1]*Korns Associates, 1 Plum Hollow, Henderson, Nevada 89052 USA.*

Abstract   This chapter examines the use of Abstract Expression Grammars to perform the entire Symbolic Regression process without the use of Genetic Programming per se. The techniques explored produce a symbolic regression engine which has absolutely no bloat, which allows total user control of the search space and output formulas, which is faster, and more accurate than the engines produced in our previous papers using Genetic Programming. The genome is an all vector structure with four chromosomes plus additional epigenetic and constraint vectors, allowing total user control of the search space and the final output formulas. A combination of specialized compiler techniques, genetic algorithms, particle swarm, aged layered populations, plus discrete and continuous differential evolution are used to produce an improved symbolic regression sytem. Nine base test cases, from the literature, are used to test the improvement in speed and accuracy. The improved results indicate that these techniques move us a big step closer toward future industrial strength symbolic regression systems.

Keywords: abstract expression grammars, differential evolution, grammar template genetic programming, genetic algorithms, particle swarm, symbolic regression.

1.   Introduction

This chapter examines techniques for improving symbolic regression systems with the aim of achieving entry-level industrial strength. In previous papers (Korns, 2006; Korns, 2007; Korns and Nunez, 2008; Korns, 2009), our pursuit of industrial scale performance with large-scale, symbolic regression problems, required us to reexamine many commonly held beliefs and to borrow a number of techniques from disparate schools of genetic programming and recombine them in ways not normally seen in the published literature. The techniques of abstract expression grammars were developed, but expored only tangentially.

While the techniques, described in detail in (Korns, 2009), produce a symbolic regression system of breadth and strength, lack of user control of the search space, bloated unreadable output formulas, accuracy, and slow convergence speed are all issues keeping an industrial strength symbolic regression system tantalizingly out of reach. In this chapter abstract expression grammars become the main focus and are promoted as the sole means of performing symbolic regression. Using the nine base test cases from (Korns, 2007) as a training set, to test for improvements in accuracy, we constructed our symbolic regression system using these important techniques:

- Abstract expression grammars
- Universal abstract goal expression
- Standard single point vector-based mutation
- Standard two point vector-based cross over
- Continuous vector differential evolution
- Discrete vector differential evolution
- Continuous particle swarm evolution
- Pessimal vertical slicing and out-of-sample scoring during training
- Age-layered populations
- User defined epigenetic factors
- User defined constraints

For purposes of comparison, all results in this paper were achieved on two workstation computers, specifically an Intel® Core™ 2 Duo Processor T7200 (2.00GHz/667MHz/4MB) and a Dual-Core AMD Opteron™ Processor 8214 (2.21GHz), running our Analytic Information Server software generating Lisp agents that compile to use the on-board Intel registers and on-chip vector processing capabilities so as to maximize execution speed, whose details can be found at *www.korns.com/Document_Lisp Language_Guide.html*. Furthermore, our Analytic Information Server is available in an open source software project at *aiserver.sourceforge.net*.

Testing Regimen and Fitness Measure

Our testing regimen uses only statistical best practices out-of-sample testing techniques. We test each of the nine test cases on matrices of 10000 rows samples by 5 columns inputs with no noise, and on matrices of 10000 rows by 20 columns with 40% noise, before drawing any conclusions. Taking all these combinations together, this creates a total of 18 separate test cases. For each test a training matrix is filled with random numbers between -50 and +50. The target expression for the test case is applied to the training matrix to compute the dependent variable and the required noise is added. The symbolic regression system is trained on the training matrix to produce the regression champion. Following training, a testing matrix is filled with random numbers between -50

Test	Minutes	Train-NLSE	Train-TCE	Test-NLSE	Test-TCE
linear	1	0.00	0.00	0.00	0.00
cubic	1	0.00	0.00	0.00	0.00
cross	145	0.00	0.00	0.00	0.00
elipse	1	0.00	0.00	0.00	0.00
hidden	3	0.00	0.00	0.00	0.00
cyclic	1	0.02	0.00	0.00	0.00
hyper	65	0.17	0.00	0.17	0.00
mixed	233	0.94	0.32	0.95	0.32
ratio	229	0.94	0.33	0.94	0.32

Table 7-1. Result For 10K rows by 5 columns no Random Noise.

and +50. The target expression for the test case is applied to the testing matrix to compute the dependent variable and the required noise is added. The regression champion is evaluated on the testing matrix for all scoring (i.e. out of sample testing).

Our two fitness measures are described in detail in (Korns, 2009) and consist of a standard least squared error which is normalized by dividing LSE by the standard deviation of Y (dependent variable). This normalization allows us to meaningfully compare the normalized least squared error (NLSE) between different problems. In addition we construct a fitness measure known as tail classification error, TCE, which measures how well the regression champion classifies the top 10% and bottom 10% of the data set. A TCE score of less than 0.20 is excellent. A TCE score of less than 0.30 is good; while, a TCE of 0.30 or greater is poor.

2. Previous Results on Nine Base Problems

The previously published results (Korns, 2009) of training on the nine base training models on 10,000 rows and five columns with no random noise and only 20 generations allowed, are shown in Table 7-1[1].

In general, training time is very reasonable given the difficulty of some of the problems and the limited number of training generations allowed. Average percent error performance varies from excellent to poor with the *linear* and *cubic* problems showing the best performance. Minimal differences between training error and testing error in the *mixed* and *ratio* problems suggest no over-fitting.

---

[1]The nine base test cases are described in detail in (Korns, 2007).

Table 7-2. Result for 10K rows by 20 columns with 40% Random Noise.

Test	Minutes	Train-NLSE	Train-TCE	Test-NLSE	Test-TCE
linear	82	0.11	0.00	0.11	0.00
cubic	59	0.11	0.00	0.11	0.00
cross	127	0.87	0.25	0.93	0.32
elipse	162	0.42	0.04	0.43	0.04
hidden	210	0.11	0.02	0.11	0.02
cyclic	233	0.39	0.11	0.35	0.12
hyper	163	0.48	0.06	0.50	0.07
mixed	206	0.90	0.27	0.94	0.32
ratio	224	0.90	0.26	0.95	0.33

Surprisingly, long and short classification is fairly robust in most cases including the very difficult *ratio*, and *mixed* test cases. The salient observation is the relative ease of classification compared to regression even in problems with this much noise. In some of the test cases, testing NLSE is either close to or exceeds the standard deviation of Y (not very good); however, in many of the test cases classification is below 0.20. (very good).

The previously published results (Korns, 2009) of training on the nine base training models on 10,000 rows and twenty columns with 40% random noise and only 20 generations allowed, are shown in Table 7-2.

Clearly the previous symbolic regression system performs most poorly on the test cases *mixed* and *ratio* with conditional target expressions. There is no evidence of over-fitting shown by the minimal differences between training error and testing error. Plus, the testing TCE is relatively good in both *mixed* and *ratio* test cases. Taken together, these scores portray a symbolic regression system which is ready to handle some industrial strength problems except for a few serious issues.

The output formulas are often so bloated, with intron expressions, that they are practically unreadable by humans. This seriously limits the acceptance of the symbolic regression system for many industrial applications. There is no user control of the search space, thus making the system impractical for most specialty applications. And of course we would love to see additional speed and accuracy improvements because industry is insatiable on those features.

A new architecture which will completely eliminate bloat, allow total user control over the search space and the final output formulas, improve our regression scores on the two conditional base test cases, and deliver an increase in learning speed, is the subject of the remainder of this chapter.

3.   New System Architecture

Our new symbolic regression system architecture is based entirely upon an Abstract Expression Grammar foundation. A single abstract expression, called the **goal expression**, defines the search space during each symbolic regression run. The objective of a symbolic regression run is to optimize the goal expression.

An example of a goal expression is: y = **f0(c0*x5)+(f1(c1)/(v0+3.14))**. As described in detail in (Korns 2009), the expression elements **f0, f1**, *, +, and / are abstract and concrete functions(*operators*). The elements **v0**, and x5 are abstract and concrete features. The elements **c0, c1**, and 3.14 are abstract and concrete real constants. Since the goal expression is abstract, there are many possible concrete solutions.

- y = **f0(c0*x5)+(f1(c1)/(v0+3.14))** (...to be solved...)
- y = **sin(-1.45*x5)+(log(22.56)/(x4+3.14))** (...possible solution...)
- y = **exp(38.16*x5)+(tan(-8.41)/(x0+3.14))** (...possible solution...)
- y = **square(-0.16*x5)+(cos(317.1)/(x9+3.14))** (...possible solution...)

The objective of symbolic regression is to find an *optimal* concrete solution to the abstract goal expression. In our architecture, each individual solution to the goal expression is implemented as a set of vectors containing the solution values for each abstract function, feature, and constant present in the goal expression. This allows the system to be based upon an all vector genome which is convenient for genetic algorithm, particle swarm, and differential evolution styled population operators. In addition to the regular vector chromosomes providing solutions to the goal expression, epigenetic wrappers and constraint vectors provide an important degree of control over the search process and will be discussed in detail later in this chapter. Taken all together our new symbolic regression system is based upon the following genome.

- Genome with four chromosome vectors
- Each chromosome has an epigenetic wrapper
- There are two user contraint vectors

The new system is constructed using these important techniques.

- Universal abstract goal expression
- Standard single point vector-based mutation
- Standard two point vector-based cross over
- Continuous vector differential evolution
- Discrete vector differential evolution
- Continuous particle swarm evolution
- Pessimal vertical slicing and out-of-sample scoring during training
- Age-layered populations

- User defined epigenetic factors
- User defined constraints

The *universal* abstract goal expression allows the system to be used for general symbolic regression and will be discussed in detail later in this chapter. Both single point vector-based mutation and two point vector-based cross over are discussed in (Man et al., 1999). Continuous and discrete vector differential evolution are discussed in (Price et al., 2005). Continuous particle swarm evolution is discussed in (Eberhart et al., 2001). Pessimal vertical slicing is discussed in (Korns, 2009). Age-layered populations are discussed in (Hornby, 2006) and (Korns, 2009). User defined epigenetic factors and user defined constraints will be discussed in detail later in this chapter.

However, before proceeding to discuss the details of the system impleme-nation, we will review abstract expression grammars as discussed in detail in (Korns, 2009).

Review of Abstract Expression Grammars

The simple concrete expression grammar we use in our symbolic regression system is a C-like functional grammar with the following basic elements.

- **Real Numbers**: 3.45, -.0982, 100.389, and *all other real constants.*
- **Row Features**: x1, x2, x9, and *all other features.*
- **Binary Operators**: +, *, /, %, max(), min(), mod()
- **Unary Operators**: sqrt(), square(), cube(), abs(), sign(), sigmoid()
- **Unary Operators**: cos(), sin(), tan(), tanh(), log(), exp()
- **Relational Operators**: $<, <=, ==, ! =, >=, >$
- **Conditional Operator**: *(expr < expr)* **?** *expr : expr)*
- **Colon Operator**: *expr : expr*
- **noop Operator**: noop()

Our numeric expressions are C-like containing the elements shown above and surrounded by regression commands such as, **regress()**, **svm()**, etc. Currently we support univariate regression, multivariate regression, and support vector regression. Our conditional expression operator (...) **?** (...) **:** (...) is the C-like conditional operator where the ? and : operators always come in tandem. Our **noop** operator is an idempotent which simply returns its first argument regardless of the number of arguments: noop(x7,x6/2.1) = x7. Our basic expression grammar is functional in nature, therefore all operators are viewed grammatically as function calls. Our symbolic regression system creates its regression champion using evolution; but, the final regression champion will be a compilation of a basic concrete expression such as:

- *(E1)*: f = (log(x3)/sin(x2*45.3))>x4 ? tan(x6) : cos(x3)

Computing an NLSE score for f requires only a single pass over every row of X and results in an attribute being added to f by executing the "score" method compiled into f as follows.

- f.NLSE = f.score(X,Y).

Suppose that we are satisfied with the form of the expression in (E1); but, we are not sure that the real constant 45.3 is optimal. We can enhance our symbolic regression system with the ability to optimize individual real constants by adding abstract constant rules to our built-in algebraic expression grammar.

- **Abstract Constants**: c1, c2, and c10

Abstract constants represent placeholders for real numbers which are to be optimized by the symbolic regression system. To further optimize f we would alter the expression in (E1) as follows.

- (*E2*): f = (log(x3)/sin(x2*c1))>x4 ? tan(x6) : cos(x3)

The compiler adds a new real number vector, C, attribute to f such that f.C has as many elements as there are abstract constants in (E2). Optimizing this version of f requires that the built-in "score" method compiled into f be changed from a single pass to a multiple pass algorithm in which the real number values in the abstract constant vector, f.C, are iterated until the expression in (E2) produces an optimized NLSE. This new score method has the side effect that executing f.score(X,Y) also alters the abstract constant vector, f.C, to optimal real number choices. Clearly the particle swarm (Eberhardt 2001) and differential evolution algorithms provide excellent candidate algorithms for optimizing f.C and they can easily be compiled into f.score by common compilation techniques currently in the main stream. Summarizing, we have a new grammar term, c1, which is a reference to the 1st element of the real number vector, f.C (in C language syntax c1 == f.C[1]). The f.C vector is optimized by scoring f, then altering the values in f.C, then repeating the process iteratively until an optimum NLSE is achieved. For instance, if the regression champion agent in (E2) is optimized with:

- f.C == < 45.396 >

Then the optimized regression champion agent in (E2) has a concrete conversion counterpart as follows:

- f = (log(x3)/sin(x2***45.396**))>x4 ? tan(x6) : cos(x3)

Suppose that we are satisfied with the form of the expression in (E1); but, we are not sure that the features, x2, x3, and x6, are optimal choices. We can enhance our symbolic regression system with the ability to optimize individual features by adding abstract feature rules to our built-in algebraic expression grammar.

- **Abstract Features**: v1, v2, and v10

Abstract features represent placeholders for features which are to be optimized by the nonlinear regression system. To further optimize f we would alter the expression in (E1) as follows.

- *(E3)*: f = (log(**v1**)/sin(**v2***45.3))>**v3** ? tan(**v4**) : cos(**v1**)

The compiler adds a new integer vector, V, attribute to f such that f.V has as many elements as there are abstract features in (E3). Each integer element in the f.V vector is constrained between 1 and M, and represents a choice of feature (in x). Optimizing this version of f requires that the built-in "score" method compiled into f be changed from a single pass to a multiple pass algorithm in which the integer values in the abstract feature vector, f.V, are iterated until the expression in (E3) produces an optimized NLSE. This new score method has the side effect that executing f.score(X,Y) also alters the abstract feature vector, f.V, to integer choices selecting optimal features (in x). Clearly the genetic algorithm (Man 1999), discrete particle swarm (Eberhardt 2001), and discrete differential evolution (Price 2005) algorithms provide excellent candidate algorithms for optimizing f.V and they can easily be compiled into f.score by common compilation techniques currently in the main stream. The f.V vector is optimized by scoring f, then altering the values in f.V, then repeating the process iteratively until an optimum NLSE is achieved. For instance, the regression champion agent in (E3) is optimized with:

- f.V == < 2, 4, 1, 6 >

Then the optimized regression champion agent in (E3) has a concrete conversion counterpart as follows:

- f = (log(**x2**)/sin(**x4***45.396))>**x1** ? tan(**x6**) : cos(**x2**)

Similarly, we can enhance our nonlinear regression system with the ability to optimize individual functions by adding abstract functions rules to our built-in algebraic expression grammar.

- **Abstract Functions**: f1, f2, and f10

Abstract functions represent placeholders for built-in functions which are to be optimized by the nonlinear regression system. To further optimize f we would alter the expression in (E2) as follows.

- (*E4*): f = (**f1**(x3)/**f2**(x2*45.3))>x4 ? **f3**(x6) : **f4**(x3)

The compiler adds a new integer vector, F, attribute to f such that f.F has as many elements as there are abstract features in (E4). Each integer element in the f.F vector is constrained between 1 and (number of built-in functions available in the expression grammar), and represents a choice of built-in function. Optimizing this version of f requires that the built-in "score" method compiled into f be changed from a single pass to a multiple pass algorithm in which the integer values in the abstract function vector, f.F, are iterated until the expression in (E4) produces an optimized NLSE. This new score method has the side effect that executing f.score(X,Y) also alters the abstract function vector, f.F, to integer choices selecting optimal built-in functions. Clearly the genetic algorithm (Man et al., 1999), discrete particle swarm (Eberhart et al., 2001), and discrete differential evolution (Price et al., 2005) algorithms provide excellent candidate algorithms for optimizing f.F and they can easily be compiled into f.score by common compilation techniques currently in the main stream. Summarizing, we have a new grammar term, f1, which is an indirect function reference thru to the 1st element of the integer vector, f.F (in C language syntax f1 == funtionList[f.F[1]]). The f.F vector is optimized by scoring f, then altering the values in f.F, then repeating the process iteratively until an optimum NLSE is achieved. For instance, if the valid function list in the expression grammar is

- f.functionList = < log, sin, cos, tan, max, min, avg, cube, sqrt >

And the regression champion agent in (E4) is optimized with:

- f.F = < 1, 8, 2, 4 >

Then the optimized regression champion agent in (E4) has a concrete conversion counterpart as follows:

- $f = (\log(x3)/\mathbf{cube}(x2*45.3))){>}x4 \; ? \; \mathbf{sin}(x6) : \mathbf{tan}(x3)$

The built-in function argument arity issue is easily resolved by having each built-in function ignore any excess arguments and substitute defaults for any missing arguments.

Finally, we can enhance our nonlinear regression system with the ability to optimize either features or constants by adding abstract term rules to our built-in algebraic expression grammar.

- **Abstract Terms**: t1, t2, and t10

Abstract terms represent placeholders for either abstract features or constants which are to be optimized by the nonlinear regression system. To further optimize f we would alter the expression in (E2) as follows.

- *(E5)*: $f = (\log(\mathbf{t0})/\sin(\mathbf{t1*t2})){>}\mathbf{t3} \; ? \; \tan(\mathbf{t4}) : \cos(\mathbf{t5})$

The compiler adds a new binary vector, T, attribute to f such that f.T has as many elements as there are abstract terms in (E5). Each binary element in the f.T vector is either 0 or 1, and represents a choice of abstract feature or abstract constant. Adding abstract terms allows the sytem to construct a universal formula containing all possible concrete formulas. Additional details on Abstract Expression Grammars can be found in (Korns, 2009).

4.   Universal Abstract Expressions

A general nonlinear regression system accepts an input matrix, X, of N rows and M columns and a dependent variable vector, Y, of length N. The dependent vector Y is related to X thru the (quite possibly nonlinear) transformation function, Q, as follows: $Y[n] = Q(X[n])$. The nonlinear transformation function, Q, can be related to linear regression systems, without loss of generality, as follows. Given an N rows by M columns matrix X (independent variables), an N vector Y (dependent variable), and a K+1 vector of coefficients, the nonlinear transformation, Q, is a system of K transformations, $Q_k : (R_1 x R_2 x ... R_M){-}{>} R$, such that $y = C_0 + (C_1 * Q_1(X)) + ...(C_K * Q_K(X)){+}err$ minimizes the normalized least squared error.

Obviously, in this formalization, a nonlinear regression system is a linear regression system which searches for a set of K suitable transformations which minimize the normalized least squared error. If K is equal to M, then Q is *dimensional*, and Q is *covering* if, for every m in M, there is at least one instance of X_m in at least one term Q_k.

With reference to our system architecture, what is needed to implement general nonlinear regression, in this formalization, is a method of constructing a universal goal expression which contains all possible nonlinear transformations up to a pre-specified complexity level. Such a method exists and is described as follows.

Given any concrete expression grammar, suitable for nonlinear regression, we can construct a universal abstract goal expression, of an arbitrary grammar node depth level, which contains all possible concrete instance expressions within any one of the K transformations in Q. For instance, the universal abstract expression, U_0, of all Q_k of depth level 0 is **t0**. Remember that t0 is either v0 or c0. The universal abstract expression, U_1, of all Q_k of depth level 1 is f0(t0,t1). In general we have the following.

- U_0: t0
- U_1: f0(t0,t1)
- U_2: f0(f1(t0,t1),f2(t2,t3))
- U_3: f0(f1(f2(t0,t1),f3(t2,t3)),f4(f5(t4,t5),f6(t6,t7)))
- U_k: f0(U_{k-1}, U_{k-1})

Given any suitable functional grammar with features, constants, and operators, we add a special operator, **noop**, which simply returns its first argument. This allows any universal expression to contain all smaller concrete expressions. For instance, if f0 = noop, then f0(t0,t1) = **t0**. We solve the arity problem for unary operators by altering them to ignore the rightmost arguments, for binary operators by altering them to substitute default arguments for missing rightmost arguments, and for N-ary operators by wrapping the additional arguments onto lower levels of the binary expression using appropriate context sensitive grammar rules. For example, let's see how we can wrap the 4-ary conditional function(operator) **?** onto multiple grammar node levels using context sensitive constraints.

- y = **f0**(**f1**(*expr,expr*),**f2**(*expr,expr*))

Clearly if, during evolution in any concrete solution, the abstract function **f0** were to represent the **?** conditional function, then the abstract function **f1** would be restricted to one of the relational functions(operators), and the abstract function **f2** would be restricted to only the colon function(operator). Therefore one would have any number of possible solutions to the goal expression, but some of the possible solutions would violate these context sensitive constraints and would be unreasonable. The assertion that certain possible solutions are *unreasonable* depends upon the violation of context sensitive constraints implicit with each operator as follows.

- y = **f0**(**f1**(*expr,expr*),**f2**(*expr,expr*)) (goal expression)
- y = **?**(**<**(*expr,expr*),**:**(*expr,expr*)) (reasonable solution)
- y = **?**(**max**(*expr,expr*),**mod**(*expr,expr*)) (unreasonable solution)
- y = **?**(**+**(*expr,expr*),**:**(*expr,expr*)) (unreasonable solution)
- y = **+**(**mod**(*expr,expr*),**/**(*expr,expr*)) (reasonable solution)
- y = **+**(**mod**(*expr,expr*),**:**(*expr,expr*)) (unreasonable solution)

Applying our system architecture to solve the problem of general nonlinear regression absolutely requires the implementation of context sensitive grammar rules to keep the various concrete solutions *reasonable* during the evolution process. This unavoidable mathematical property of unrestricted nonlinear regression transformations requires us to extend the genome to include context sensitive contraints. Since the genome must be extended to include context sensitive constraints, we use this opportunity to extend the genome to give much greater implicit and explicit user control of the search process.

In our new system architecture, the genome is extended such that each genome has both epigenetic and constraint wrapper vectors which, in addition to enforcing appropriate context sensitive grammar rules, can be promoted to give the user much greater implicit and explicit control of the search space. Control of the search space will become a very important aspect of future nonlinear regression systems and will be discussed in detail later in this chapter.

5.   Constraints

In order to perform general symbolic regression with a universal abstract goal expression, the genome must be context sensitive. This implies that for some solutions of the abstract goal expression, certain choices of concrete features, concrete real numbers, or concrete functions are unreasonable. Consider the following goal expression: y = **f0**(**f1**(*expr,expr*),**f2**(*expr,expr*)). If we have no additional information about any particular solution to this goal expression, then we must assume that the constraints for abstract functions f0, f1, and f2 are as follows (i.e. unconstrained).

- *constraints*: **f0**(+ * / % max min mod sqrt square cube abs sign sigmoid cos sin tan tanh log exp < <= == ! = >= > ? : noop)
- *constraints*: **f1**(+ * / % max min mod sqrt square cube abs sign sigmoid cos sin tan tanh log exp < <= == ! = >= > ? : noop)
- *constraints*: **f2**(+ * / % max min mod sqrt square cube abs sign sigmoid cos sin tan tanh log exp < <= == ! = >= > ? : noop)

However if we know that a particular solution has selected **f0** to be the operator **?**, then we must implicitly assume that the constraints for abstract functions f0, f1, and f2, *with respect to that solution* are as follows.

- *constraints*: **f0**(?)

- *constraints*: **f1**($< <= == ! = >= >$)
- *constraints*: **f2**(:)

In the goal expression genome, **f0** is a single gene located in position zero in the chromosome for abstract functions. The constraints are wrapped around each chomosome and are a vector of *reasonable* choices for each gene. In a context insensitive genome, chosing any specific value for gene f0 or gene v6, etc. has no effect on the contraint wrappers in the genome. However, in a context sensitive genome, chosing any specific value for gene f0 or gene v6, etc. may have an effect on the contraint wrappers in the genome. Furthermore, we are not limited to implicit control of the genome's contraint wrappers. We can extend control of the genome's contraints to the user in an effort to allow greater control of the search space. For instance, if the user wanted to perform a univariate regression on a problem with ten features but desired only logrithmic transforms in the output, the following abstract goal expression would be appropriate.

- $y = $ **f0**(**v0**) where f0(cos sin tan tanh)

Publishing the genome's contraints for explicit user guidance is an attempt to explore greater user control of the search space during the evolutionary process.

6.   Epigenome

In order to perform symbolic regression with a single abstract goal expression, all of the individual solutions must have the same shape genome. In a context insensitive architecture with only one population island performing only a general search strategy, this is not an issue. However, if we wish to perform symbolic regression, with a single abstract goal expression, on multiple population islands each searching a different part of the problem space, then we have to be more sophisticated in our approach.

We have already seen how constraints can be used to control, both implicitly and explicitly, evolutionary choices within a single gene. But what if we wish to influence which genes are chosen for exploration during the evolutionary process? Then we must provide some mechanism for choosing which genes are to be chosen and which genes are not to be chosen for exploration.

Purely arbitrarily and in the sole interest of keeping faith with the original biological motivation of genetic algorithms, we choose to call genes which are chosen for exploration during evolution as *expressed* and genes which are chosen NOT to be explored during evolution as *unexpressed*. Furthermore, the wrapper around each chomosome, which determines which genes are and are not expressed, we call the **epigenome**.

Once again, consider the following goal expression.

- **regress(f0(f1**(*expr*,*expr*),**f2**(*expr*,*expr*)))** where f0(?)

Since we know that the user has requsted only solutions where **f0** has selected to be the operator **?**, then we must implicitly assume that the constraints and epigenome for abstract functions f0, f1, and f2, *with respect to any solution* are as follows.

- *constraints*: **f0**(?)
- *constraints*: **f1**($<$ $<=$ $==$! $=$ $>=$ $>$)
- *constraints*: **f2**(:)
- *epigenome*: **ef**(f1)

We can assume the epigenome is limited to function f1 because, with both gene f0 and gene f2 constrained to a single choice each, f0 and f2 are implicitly no longer allowed to vary during evolution, *with respect to any solution*. Effectively both f0 and f2 are *unexpressed*.

In the goal expression genome, **ef** is the epigenome associated with the chromosome for abstract functions. The epigenomes are wrapped around each chomosome and are a vector of *expressed* genes. In a context insensitive genome, chosing any specific value for gene f0 or gene v6, etc. has no effect on the contraint wrappers or the epigenome. However, in a context sensitive genome, chosing any specific value for gene f0 or gene v6, etc. may have an effect on the contraint wrappers and the epigenome. Of course, we are not limited to implicit control of the epigenome. We can extend control of the epigenome to the user in an effort to allow greater control of the search space. For instance, the following goal expression is an example of a user specified epigenome.

- (*E6*): **regress**(f0(f1(f2(v0,v1),f3(v2,v3)),f4(f5(v4,v5),f6(v6,v7))))
- (*E6.1*): **where** {}
- (*E6.2*): **where** {ff(noop) f2(cos sin tan tanh) ef(f2) ev(v0)}

Obviously expression (E6) has only one genome; however, the two **where** clauses request two distinct simultaneous search strategies. The first where clause (E6.1) tells the system to perform an unconstrained general search of all possible solutions. The second where clause (E6.2) tells the system to simultaneously perform a more complex search among a limited set of possible solutions as follows. The *ff(noop)* condition tells the system to initialize all functions to noop unless otherwise specified. The *f2(cos sin tan tanh)* condition tells the system to restrict abstract function f2 to only the trigonometric functions starting with cos. The *ef(f2)* epigenome tells the system that only f2 will participate in the evolutionary process. The *ev(v0)* epigenome tells the system that only v0 will participate in the evolutionary process. Therefore, (E6.2) causes the system to evolve only solutions of a single trignonometric function on a single feature i.e. tan(x4), cos(x0), etc. These two distinct search strategies are explored simultaneously. The resulting champion will be the winning (*optimal*) solution across all simultaneous search strategies.

7.   Control

The user community is increasingly demanding better control of the search space and better control of the output from symbolic regression systems. In search of a control paradigm for symbolic regression, we have chosen to notice the relationship of SQL to database searches. Originally database searches where highly constrained and heavily dictated by the choice of storage mechanism. With the advent of relational databases, searches became increasingly under user control to the point that modern SQL is amazingly flexible.

An unanswered research question is how much user control of the symbolic regression process can be reasonably achieved? Our system architecture allows us to use abstract goal expressions to better explore the possibilities for user control. Given the immense value of search space reduction and search specialization, the symbolic regression system can benefit greatly if the epigenome and the constraints are made available to the user. This allows the user to specify goal formulas and candidate individuals which are tailored to specific applications. For instance, the following univariate abstract goal expression is a case in point.

- (*E7*): **regress**(f0(f1(f2(v0,v1),f3(v2,v3)),f4(f5(v4,v5),f6(v6,v7))))
- (*E7.1*): **where** {}
- (*E7.2*): **where** {ff(noop) f2(cos sin tan tanh) ef(f2) ev(v0)}
- (*E7.3*): **where** {ff(noop) f1(noop,*) f2(*) ef(f1) ev(v0,v1,v2)}
- (*E7.4*): **where** {ff(noop) f0(cos sin tan tanh) f1(noop,*) f2(*) ef(f0,f1) ev(v0,v1,v2)}
- (*E7.5*): **where** {f0(?) f4(:)}

Expression (E7) has only one genome and can be entered as a single goal expression requesting five distinct simultaneous search strategies. Borrowing a term from chess playing programs, we can create an *opening book* by adding where clauses like (E7.2), (E7.3), (E7.4), and (E7.5).

The first where clause (E7.1) tells the system to perform an unconstrained general search of all possible solutions.

The second where clause (E7.2) tells the system to evolve only solutions of a single trignonometric function on a single feature i.e. tan(x4), cos(x0), etc.

In the third where clause (E7.3), the *f1(noop,*)* condition tells the system to restrict abstract function f1 to only the noop and * starting with noop. The *f2(*)* condition tells the system to restrict abstract function f2 to only the * function. The *ef(f1)* epigenome tells the system that only f1 will participate in the evolutionary process. The *ev(v0,v1,v2)* epigenome tells the system that only v0, v1, and v2 will participate in the evolutionary process. Therefore, (E7.3) causes the system to evolve champions of a pair or a triple cross correlations only i.e. (x3*x1) or (x1*x4*x2).

In the fourth where clause (E7.4), the *ff(noop)* condition tells the system to initialize all functions to noop unless otherwise specified. The *f0(cos sin tan tanh)* condition tells the system to restrict abstract function f0 to only the trigonometric functions starting with cos. The *f1(noop, *)* condition tells the system to restrict abstract function f1 to only the noop and * starting with noop. The *f2(*)* condition tells the system to restrict abstract function f2 to only the * function. The *ef(f0,f1)* epigenome tells the system that only f0 and f1 will participate in the evolutionary process. The *ev(v0,v1,v2)* epigenome tells the system that only v0, v1, and v2 will participate in the evolutionary process. Therefore, (E7.4) causes the system to evolve champions of a single trignonometric function operating on a pair or triple cross correlation only i.e. cos(x3*x1) or tan(x1*x4*x2).

In the fifth where clause (E7.5), causes the system to evolve only conditional champions i.e. ((x3*x1)<cos(x5)) ? tan(x1*x4) : log(x0).

These five distinct search strategies are explored simultaneously. The resulting champion will be the winning (*optimal*) solution across all simultaneous search strategies.

Of course (E7) alone, with no where clauses, can guide a thorough symbolic regression run; however, assuming there are five features in the problem (x0,x1,x2,x3, and x4) and the twenty-eight operators of our basic grammar, then (E7.1) is searching a space of $(5^8 * 28^7) = 5.27E+15$ discrete points. Whereas (E7.2) is searching through only $(5*4) = 20$ discrete points. Expression (E7.3) is searching through only $(5^3 * 2) = 250$ discrete points. Expression (E7.4) is searching through only $(5^3 * 2)^4) = 3.90625E9$ discrete points. Allowing user specified constraints and epigenomes can greatly reduce the search space in cases where the application warrants.

Our current abstract regression system supports user specified constraints and epigenomes. For general regression problems, with no user specified where clauses, the system supports an implicit opening book looking for linear, square, cube, and trignonmetric unary functions on single features plus all possible pair or triple cross correlations.

We believe that it should be possible to develop libraries of where clauses useful in specific application areas. Such libaries could be developed, published, and shared between user communities. We believe that we have just scratched the surface on understanding the benefits possible with context sensitive constraints, epigenomes, and opening books.

8.   Enhanced Results on Nine Base Problems

We used a feature-terminated universal expression, of depth level three, for both problem sets as shown below. In all cases the system was told to halt when an NLSE of less than .15 was achieved at the end of an epoch. The feature-

Table 7-3. Result For 10K rows by 5 columns no Random Noise.

Test	Minutes	Train-NLSE	Train-TCE	Test-NLSE	Test-TCE
linear	1	0.00	0.00	0.00	0.00
cubic	1	0.00	0.00	0.00	0.00
cross	9	0.00	0.00	0.00	0.00
elipse	1	0.00	0.00	0.00	0.00
hidden	1	0.00	0.00	0.00	0.00
cyclic	1	0.00	0.00	0.00	0.00
hyper	1	0.03	0.00	0.03	0.00
mixed	35	0.87	0.26	0.88	0.27
ratio	34	0.87	0.26	0.88	0.27

terminated universal expression, V_3, is specified as shown below. Note that V_3 and U_3 are identical except for their terminators.

- V_3: f0(f1(f2(v0,v1),f3(v2,v3)),f4(f5(v4,v5),f6(v6,v7)))
- U_3: f0(f1(f2(t0,t1),f3(t2,t3)),f4(f5(t4,t5),f6(t6,t7)))

For the five column no noise problems, with twenty-eight operators, five features, and five universal transforms of type V_3 to choose from, there are $(5^8 * 28^7)^5 = 4.06753E + 78$ discrete points in the search space. With twenty-eight operators and twenty features to choose from, the magnitude of the search space for the twenty column problems cannot be expressed in our 64bit computer. It is essentially $(20^8 * 28^7)^{20}$. Of course this still does not take into account the difficulties arising from the 40% added noise.

The enhanced results of training on the nine base training models on 10,000 rows and five columns with no random noise and only 20 generations allowed, are shown in Table 7-3 in order of difficulty.

The enhanced results of training on the nine base training models on 10,000 rows and twenty columns with 40% random noise and only 20 generations allowed, are shown in Table 7-4 in order as shown above.

Clearly, in time-constrained training (only 20 generations), the enhanced symbolic regression system is an improvement over the previously published results. While the enhanced system performs poorly on the two test cases *mixed* and *ratio* with conditional target expressions, the performance on all other nine base test cases is acceptable. In addition, the testing TCE scores indicate that we can perform some useful classification even in the difficult conditional problems with noise added.

Taken together with the absence of bloat and increased user control of the search space, these results portray a symbolic regression system which is ready to handle many industrial strength problems.

Table 7-4. Result for 10K rows by 20 columns with 40% Random Noise.

Test	Minutes	Train-NLSE	Train-TCE	Test-NLSE	Test-TCE
linear	1	0.11	0.00	0.11	0.00
cubic	1	0.11	0.00	0.11	0.00
cross	49	0.83	0.21	0.81	0.20
elipse	1	0.12	0.00	0.12	0.00
hidden	1	0.11	0.02	0.11	0.02
cyclic	1	0.14	0.00	0.14	0.00
hyper	1	0.12	0.00	0.12	0.00
mixed	56	0.90	0.29	0.90	0.30
ratio	59	0.90	0.29	0.90	0.30

9.   Summary

The use of abstract grammars in symbolic regression moves the entire discipline much closer to *industrial ready* for many applications.

First, we have a formalization which clearly emphasizes our value added as a search algorithm for finding nonlinear transformations. We are no longer cast in a competitive role against univariate regression, multivariate regression, support vector regression, etc. In fact we enhance these regression techniques with our nonlinear search capabilities. For instance, this formalization gives us the opportunity to partner with regression professionals, who have a large body of well thought out statistics for choosing one multivariate model over another. The situation is similar with the support vector community. I believe that these opportunities for cross disciplinary work should be encouraged.

Second, we no longer have a bloat problem of any kind. Further experimentation with context sensitive constraints and epigenomes will improve the symbolic regression process from the user's perspective. Effectively, with bloat, symbolic regression is a black box tool because the resulting expression is practically unreadable by users. However, with user specified goal expressions, constraints, and epigenomes, the symbolic regression process can become effectively white box. From an industrial perspective, a white box tool is far preferable to a black box tool.

Third, we now have a much greater degree of user control over the search space and over the form of the output. We have the potential to specify symbolic regression problems in terms the user can understand which are specific to the application. Furthermore, using multiple where clauses, the user can be much more sophisticated in specifying search strategy. Opening books of where clauses, useful in specific application areas, can be developed, published, and shared between users.

Financial institutional interest in the field is growing while pure research continues at an aggressive pace. Further applied research in this field is absolutely warranted. We are using our nonlinear regression system in the financial domain. But as new techniques are added and current ones improved, we believe that the system has evolved to be a domain-independent tool that can provide superior regression and classification results for industrial scale nonlinear regression problems.

Clearly we need to experiment with even more techniques which will improve our understanding of constraints and epigenetics. Primary areas for future research should include: experimenting with statistical and other types of analysis to help build conditional WFFs for difficult conditional problems with large amounts of noise; experimenting with opening books for general regression problems, and parallelizing the system on a cloud environment.

References

Eberhart, Russell, Shi, Yuhui, and Kennedy, James (2001). *Swarm Intelligence.* Morgan Kaufmann, New York.

Hornby, Gregory S. (2006). ALPS: the age-layered population structure for reducing the problem of premature convergence. In *etal., Maarten Keijzer, editor,* GECCO 2006: Proceedings of the 8th annual conference on Genetic and evolutionary computation, *volume 1, pages 815–822, Seattle, Washington, USA. ACM Press.*

Korns, Michael F. (2006). Large-scale, time-constrained symbolic regression. In Riolo, Rick L., Soule, Terence, and Worzel, Bill, editors, Genetic Programming Theory and Practice IV, *volume 5 of* Genetic and Evolutionary Computation, *chapter 16, pages –. Springer, Ann Arbor.*

Korns, Michael F. (2007). Large-scale, time-constrained symbolic regression-classification. In Riolo, Rick L., Soule, Terence, and Worzel, Bill, editors, Genetic Programming Theory and Practice V, *Genetic and Evolutionary Computation, chapter 4, pages 53–68. Springer, Ann Arbor.*

Korns, Michael F. (2009). Symbolic regression of conditional target expressions. In Riolo, Rick L., O'Reilly, Una-May, and McConaghy, Trent, editors, Genetic Programming Theory and Practice VII, *Genetic and Evolutionary Computation, chapter 13, pages 211–228. Springer, Ann Arbor.*

Korns, Michael F. and Nunez, Loryfel (2008). Profiling symbolic regression-classification. In Riolo, Rick L., Soule, Terence, and Worzel, Bill, editors, Genetic Programming Theory and Practice VI, *Genetic and Evolutionary Computation, chapter 14, pages 215–229. Springer, Ann Arbor.*

Man, Kim-Fung, Tang, Kit-Sang, and Kwong, Sam (1999). Genetic Algorithms. *Springer, New York.*

Price, Kenneth, Storn, Rainer, and Lampinen, Jouni (2005). Differential Evolution: A Practical Approach to Global Optimization. *Springer, New York.*

Chapter 8

AGE-FITNESS PARETO OPTIMIZATION

Michael Schmidt[1] and Hod Lipson[2,3]

[1]*Computational Biology, Cornell University, Ithaca, NY 14853, USA;* [2]*School of Mechanical and Aerospace Engineering, Cornell. University, Ithaca NY 14853, USA;* [3]*Computing and Information Science, Cornell University, Ithaca, NY 14853, USA.*

Abstract   We propose a multi-objective method, inspired by the Age Layered Population Structure algorithm, for avoiding premature convergence in evolutionary algorithms, and demonstrate a three-fold performance improvement over comparable methods. Previous research has shown that partitioning an evolving population into age groups can greatly improve the ability to identify global optima and avoid converging to local optima. Here, we propose that treating age as an explicit optimization criterion can increase performance even further, with fewer algorithm implementation parameters. The proposed method evolves a population on the two-dimensional Pareto front comprising (a) how long the genotype has been in the population (age); and (b) its performance (fitness). We compare this approach with previous approaches on the Symbolic Regression problem, sweeping the problem difficulty over a range of solution complexities and number of variables. Our results indicate that the multi-objective approach identifies the exact target solution more often than the age-layered population and standard population methods. The multi-objective method also performs better on higher complexity problems and higher dimensional datasets - finding global optima with less computational effort.

Keywords: Symbolic Regression, Age, Fitness, Multi-objective

1.   Introduction

A common problem in many applications of evolutionary algorithms is when the progress of the algorithm stagnates and solutions stop improving (Murphy and Ryan, 2007). Expending additional computational effort in the evolution often fails to make any substantial progress. This problem is known as premature convergence (Ryan, 1996; Louis and Rawlins, 1993).

A common method for dealing with premature convergence is to perform many evolutionary searches, randomizing and restarting the search multiple times (Auger and Hansen, 2005; Jansen, 2002). This approach can be wasteful however, as the entire population is repeatedly thrown out. There is also the difficulty of deciding when to restart, and the possibility that the converged population could continue improving with additional diversity.

One of the best performing methods in the genetic programming literature for addressing premature convergence is the Age-Layered Population Structure (ALPS) method (Hornby, 2006; Hornby, 2009a; Hornby, 2009b). ALPS uses a special notion of age - how long genotypic material has existed in the population - in order to partition the evolving population into age layers (Figure 8-1). Random individuals are constantly inserted into the youngest population layer, and layers evolve independently of others. As a result, the youngest layers, tend to be very diverse, and are allowed to evolve and mature before competing against the oldest and most fit solutions. This improves upon random restarts in that the best solutions are never thrown out and new solutions maintain diversity as they propagate up the layers. Implementation of the ALPS algorithm, however, requires new parameters, such as how to pick age layer cutoffs and how many solutions to keep in each layer, etc.

In this paper, we consider using the ALPS concept of age as a fundamental property in the evolutionary optimization. Rather than using age to partition the population into layers, we use age as an independent dimension in a multi-objective Pareto front optimization. In this context, a solution is selected for if it has both higher fitness and lower genotypic age than other solutions.

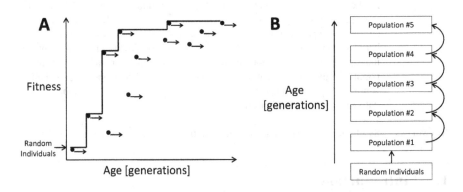

Figure 8-1. The two primary optimization methods compared. The Age-Fitness Pareto Population algorithm (A) considers a single population of individuals moving in a two-dimensional Age-Fitness Pareto space. Individuals are selected for if they simultaneously have higher fitnesses and lower age than other individuals. Ages increase every generation, or are inherited during crossover, and new random individuals are added with zero age. In the Age-Layered Population Structure (ALPS) algorithm, there are several layers of populations for each age group. New individuals are added to the youngest population, and individuals migrate to older populations as their age increases.

As in the ALPS method, random individuals are added into the population at each generation. Rather than flowing up the age layers, they flow through a two-dimensional space of fitness and age (Figure 8-1). Young solutions exist in the same population as the oldest and most fit, but persist because they are non-dominated in the two-dimensional objective space.

A key benefit of the proposed approach is that it does not require a population partitioning or structuring. For example it does not constrain intermediate layer sizes, the number of total layers, or layer partitions. These variations all exist within the larger Pareto space of the search, allowing the age-fitness distributions to vary dynamically.

Like ALPS, this approach makes no assumptions about the underlying solution representation. Therefore, it can be applied to nearly any evolutionary search problem to improve the optimization performance. In the next sections, we provide broader background on the premature convergence problem and describe the Age-Fitness Pareto Algorithm. We then describe our experiments and results, before concluding with discussion and final remarks.

2. Background

An essential component for avoiding premature convergence is maintaining diversity in the population throughout evolution. A deceptively-simple way to increase diversity in an evolutionary algorithm is to increase the mutation rate. Increasing the mutation rate however also increases the rate of deleterious mutations. Effectively, high mutation rate increases diversity but greatly inhibits the search performance. Instead, recent research has focused on alternative methods for maintaining diversity without heavily sacrificing the evolution performance.

One way to maintain diversity is using similarity-sensitive selection methods, such as fitness-sharing and crowding methods. Fitness-sharing penalizes solutions that are similar to existing solutions, whereas crowding methods replace existing solutions with similar ones. For example, in deterministic crowding (Mahfoud, 1995), individuals in the population are only removed from the population when replaced by direct similar descendent. In effect, these methods sustain multiple partially-independent evolutionary trajectories in one population simultaneously.

Another approach is to prevent the population from converging entirely. In Hierarchical Fair Competition (HFC) (Hu et al., 2002; Hu et al., 2005), the algorithm maintains sub-populations of various fitness ranges. Therefore, the algorithm always contains several individuals at different fitness values to enforce diversity.

A common technique to deal with premature convergence in practice is to simply perform many evolutionary searches (Auger and Hansen, 2005; Jansen,

2002), accepting that nearly all runs converge to local optima. In effect, each random restart explores a new set of evolutionary trajectories, starting from new random individuals.

All of these methods are known to reduce premature convergence and increase the chance of identifying global optima using existing evolutionary algorithm machinery (mutation, selection, fitness, etc).

Other research has looked at tracking solution age. Most notably is the Age-Layered Population Structure (ALPS) mentioned earlier (Hornby, 2006; Hornby, 2009a; Hornby, 2009b). Similar to HFC, the algorithm maintains sub-populations of individuals, but splits these sub-populations by the genotypic age of the solution. Therefore, very young solutions are not selected out by old and optimized solutions in the population.

Similar to random restarts, ALPS adds new random solutions into the lowest layer throughout evolution. As the evolution continues, the solutions age and are promoted to the next age group. In effect, ALPS performs many random restarts in parallel.

3.   Algorithm

In this section we describe the details and reasoning behind the multi-objective Age-Fitness Pareto optimization algorithm.

Genotypic Age

Interestingly, the concept of genotypic age as used in ALPS has shown to be one of the best approaches for avoiding premature convergence and improving results (Hornby, 2006). Our goal in this paper is to develop this idea further by utilizing genotypic age as a fundamental search trait.

The age of a solution is generally measured in generations, or alternatively computational effort measured in fitness evaluations for steady-state algorithms (Hornby, 2009a; Hornby, 2009b).

All randomly initialized individuals start with age of one. With each successive generation that an individual exists in the population, the age is incremented by one. This alone measures the amount of time an individual has existed in the population. However, we are more interested in the age of the genotype.

To measure the age of the genotype, we need to pass on ages during crossover and mutation events. There are several options, such as taking the age of the most similar parent, taking the average age of the parents, etc. The best method reported in the literature (Hornby, 2009b), and the method we use, is to inherit the maximum age of the parents.

Therefore, the age is a measure of how long the oldest part of the genotype has existed in the population.

Age-Fitness Pareto Population

The Age-Fitness Pareto Population method uses a single population, in contrast to the population layers in the ALPS algorithm. The algorithm tracks the fitness of each individual as in a normal evolutionary algorithm, and also the maximum genotypic age described in the previous section.

The individuals in the population can be thought of as lying on a two-dimensional plane of age and fitness, as in Figure 8-1. The multi-objective optimization task is to identify the non-dominated Pareto front of the problem domain (Deb, 2001); here, the objectives are to maximize the fitness with minimum age.

The age is a special objective however. Age is constantly increasing for all individuals in each generation, either through staying in the population for multiple generations, or inheriting older genotypes in crossover. Like in the ALPS algorithm, new random individuals are added to the population every generation. We add a single new random individual each generation. More than one can be added per generation; however, one of these is likely to dominate the others in fitness, making it equivalent to adding this most dominant random individual each generation.

The age objective effectively protects young, low fit individuals from being replaced by old, high-fit individuals. Since the Pareto front identifies non-dominated solutions, each solution on the front can only be replaced or removed by the occurrence of a younger and fitter solution

Individuals that evolve to a local optimum and become trapped there are likely to stay there for many generations. In this case, new random individuals may converge to different optima with potentially higher fitnesses, thereby dominating and eventually replacing the older stagnant individual.

Pareto Tournament Selection

There are a number of ways to implement multi-objective evolution (Deb, 2001). In this paper, we use the simple random mating with tournament selection method (Kotanchek et al., 2009).

Each generation, we select random pairs of individuals, cross and mutate them probabilistically, and add them to the current population. Additionally, a new random individual is added to the population.

We specify a target population size - analogous to the population size in a traditional evolutionary algorithm. The goal of the selection is to remove dominated individuals from the population until the target population size is reached.

It is possible that the non-dominated set - the age-fitness Pareto front of the population - is larger than the target population size. In this case, our selection method does not remove any further individuals, and the population size may remain larger than the target size. However, in our experiments, this was never the case. The population size always reached the target size.

The Pareto tournament selection method we used selects groups of k individuals randomly from the population. It then forms the Pareto front among those individuals, and discards any dominated individuals from the tournament. This is repeated until the population is less than or equal to the target population size again, or until the population is entirely non-dominated.

This selection method allows for the possibility for dominated solutions to persist in the population through successive generations. They simply need to survive by being non-dominated in smaller random Pareto tournaments. In our experiments we used a tournament size of two.

4.   Experiments

In this section we detail our experimental methods to test the impact of treating age as a fundamental search optimization criterion.

We perform identical experiments on three algorithms: (1) the ALPS algorithm (Hornby, 2006), (2) the proposed Age-Fitness Pareto algorithm, and (3) the Deterministic Crowding algorithm (Mahfoud, 1995), a well established diversity-maintenance method.

We experimented on the Symbolic Regression problem. Symbolic regression (Koza, 1992) is the problem of identifying the simplest equation (Grunwald, 1999) that most accurately fits a given set of data. Symbolic regression has a wide range of applications, such as prediction (Korns, 2009), classifi-

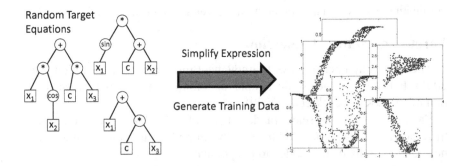

Figure 8-2. The generation of random test problems for symbolic regression. We start by picking a random number of inputs, between one and ten. We then generate a random equation using these inputs and simplify the equation before measuring its complexity (the number of nodes in the binary tree). We then generate a random training data set by sampling the input variables around the origin and evaluating the target equation on these data points. We then generate a validation data set in a similar fashion, but with a wider range around the origin to test if the solutions extrapolate to the exact solution.

cation (Doucette et al., 2009), modeling, and system identification. Recently, symbolic regression has been used to detect conserved quantities in data representing physical laws of nature (Schmidt and Lipson, 2009), as well as infer the differential equations underlying dynamical systems (Bongard and Lipson, ress).

We chose the Symbolic Regression problem because it is a common benchmark of genetic programming (Koza, 1992). Additionally, we can easily vary the problem complexity and the problem dimensionality in order to study and compare how the proposed method scales with problem complexity.

Symbolic Regression

Symbolic regression (Koza, 1992) is the problem, and classic application of genetic programming, of searching a space of symbolic expressions computationally to minimizing various error metrics for a particular data set. Both the parameters and the form of the equation are subject to search. In symbolic regression, many initially random symbolic equations compete to model experimental data in the most parsimonious way. It forms new equations by recombining previous equations and probabilistically varying their sub-expressions. The algorithm retains equations that model the experimental data well while abandoning unpromising solutions. After an equation reaches a desired level of accuracy, the algorithm terminates, returning the most parsimonious equations that may correspond to the intrinsic mechanisms of the observed system.

In symbolic regression, the genotype or encoding represents symbolic expressions in computer memory. Often, the genotype is a binary tree of algebraic operations with numerical constants and symbolic variables at its leaves (McKay et al., 1995; de Jong and Pollack, 2003). Other encodings include acyclic graphs (Schmidt and Lipson, 2007) and tree-adjunct grammars (Hoai et al., 2002). The fitness of a particular genotype (a candidate equation) is a numerical measure of how well it fits the data, such as the equation's correlation or squared-error with respect to the experimental data.

A point mutation can randomly change the type of the floating-point operation (for example, flipping an add operation to a multiply or an add to a system variable), or randomly change the parameter constant associated with that operation (if it is used). The crossover operation recombines two existing equations to form a new equation. To perform crossover, we select a random location in the genotype, and copy all operation and parameter values to the left of this point from the first parent and remaining operations and parameters to the right from the second parent.

Generating Test Problems

We measured the performance of each algorithm on randomly generated test problems. To generate a random problem in symbolic regression, we simply need a random target equation to find and a set of data corresponding to that equation for the fitness error metric.

We experimented by varying two characteristics of the random symbolic regression problems: (1) the dimensionality of the data (i.e. the number of variables in the data set, and (2) the complexity of the target function (i.e. the size of the equation's binary parse tree). Both of these characteristics factor in to the problem's difficulty. Increasing dimensionality increases the base set of possible variables the equation may use, while increasing complexity increases the chances of coupled nonlinear features.

The first step in our random test problem generation is to randomly sample the dimensionality of the problem. We picked a random number of variables ranging between one and ten.

Next, we generated a random equation which can use any of these variables. We generated a random equation in the same fashion that we generate random individuals in the evolutionary algorithm.

Many randomly generated equations may have compressible terms. For example, $f(x) = 4.211 + 0.93x^2 + 1.23$ is equivalent to $f(x) = 0.93x^2 + 5.441$. Therefore, we perform a symbolic simplification on the randomly generated equation in order to get an accurate measure of the target equation's complexity. We measure complexity of the problem as the total number of nodes in the binary tree representation of the equation. For example, the complexity of the equation mentioned above is seven.

We repeated this step as necessary in order to get a uniform distribution of problem complexities. We continued generating and simplifying equations in order to uniformly cover the problem complexities ranging between 1 and 32.

Next, we randomly sampled the input values of the equation 500 times. These variables were sampled from a normal distribution around the origin, with standard deviation of two. The equation was then evaluated on these variables in order to get the target output value. Several examples of training data are shown in Figure 8-2.

Finally, we also generated a separate validation data set of 500 points. The validation data set was created in the same fashion as the training data set, however the input variables were sampled with a standard deviation of three. By using a broader input sampling, we can use the validation dataset to test whether solutions extrapolate in their predictions to unseen data.

We also use this to measure the percent of times the algorithms find the exact solution - if the algorithm achieves near zero error on the extrapolated validation dataset. Since we are not adding any noise to the dataset, we expect the algorithms to reach zero error on the generated data, if the exact solution is in fact found.

Measuring Performance

We tested each algorithm on 1000 randomly-generated symbolic regression problems. Each evolutionary search was performed on a single quad-core computer.

Evolution was stopped if the algorithm identified a zero error solution on the validation data set (i.e. less than $10 \sup -3$ normalized mean absolute error), or when the algorithm reached one million generations. Throughout each search, we log the best equation, its fitness (i.e. normalized mean absolute error) on the training and validation sets, its complexity, and the total computational effort. We measure computational effort as the total equation evaluations performed in fitness calculations.

The fitness of the normalized mean absolute error is normalized using the standard deviation of the target output values. The normalized fitness allows comparing fitnesses between evolution runs and detecting convergence to the exact target solution more easily. In all figures, we show the fitness on the validation data set (i.e. the normalized mean absolute error on the validation data).

Algorithm Settings

We used the symbolic regression algorithm described in (Schmidt and Lipson, 2006; Schmidt and Lipson, 2008) as the basis for our implementation. We simply swap out the population representation and selection for the three compared algorithms.

In the ALPS algorithm we use exponential scaling of the layer limits, with a base multiplier of 20. The maximum age for a layer i is given by the equation $20 * 2i$. This was chosen such that there could be up to a maximum of 16 layers should the evolution reach the maximum of one million generations.

We performed selection in the ALPS populations using Deterministic Crowding (Mahfoud, 1995). The number of individuals in each layer was calculated as the target population size of 256 divided by the current number of layers. One new individual was added to the first layer each generation. The Age-Fitness Pareto algorithm used a target population size of 256. One new random individual was added to the population each generation. Finally, the deterministic crowding method uses a population size of 256. One new random individual is added to the population each generation by replacing the worst ranked solution. For all algorithms, crossover probability was 0.75 and mutation probability was 0.01.

5.   Results

This section summarizes the experimental results comparing the three algorithms: (1) the ALPS algorithm, (2) Age-Fitness Pareto algorithm, and (3) the Deterministic Crowding algorithm with randomized individuals.

Fitness and Convergence

Our first observation is that the fitness versus the computational effort of each algorithm are similar (Figure 8-3). On average, the ALPS algorithm has the lowest error early on while the Age-Fitness Pareto algorithm has the highest error. This difference, however, does not appear to be significant due to the overlapping standard errors.

Later into the evolutionary search, all algorithms converge to similar fitness values. This suggests that the algorithms are reaching common local optima. The deterministic crowding method does perform worse here as it is the last to converge on to this trend. Near the end however, the average fitnesses are very similar, as most runs for all algorithms do converge to the exact solution.

Figure 8-3 also shows the rate that each algorithm identifies the exact target solution. Here we have differences and non-overlapping standard errors for each algorithm.

The ALPS algorithm again has the highest exact solution rate early on in evolution. All algorithms show the standard s-shaped convergence rates where computational effort increases greatly for the hardest of the test problems.

Late in the searches, the algorithms begin to plateau at different rates of finding the exact solution. The Age-Fitness Pareto algorithm performed the best, finding the exact solution approximately 5% more often than the ALPS algorithm.

Importantly, Figure 8-3(a) further demonstrates that the hardest problems solved by ALPS were solved by the Age-Fitness Pareto algorithm using a third of the computational effort.

The deterministic crowding algorithm, with the added randomized individual per generation, performed worst of the three algorithms. Here, deterministic crowding identified the exact target solution approximately 5% less often than the ALPS algorithm, and approximately 10% less often than the Age-Fitness Pareto algorithm.

Computational Effort

We also compared the total computational effort each algorithm required to find the exact target solution. Here, we look at the computational effort versus the complexity of the target solution, and the dimensionality of the datasets for each evolutionary search (Figure 8-4).

In the computational effort versus the target solution complexity, we notice that ALPS performs the best for the simplest test problems, requiring the least computational effort to identify the exact solution. As the complexity and

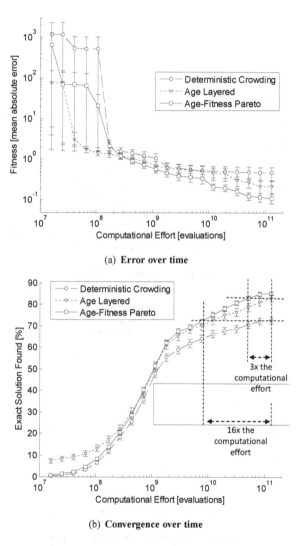

(a) **Error over time**

(b) **Convergence over time**

Figure 8-3. The fitness and convergence rate to the exact solution of the compared algorithms versus the total computational effort of the evolutionary search. The fitness plotted (a) is the normalized mean absolute error on the validation data set. Fitness is normalized by the standard deviation of the output values. Convergence to the exact solution (b) is percent of the trials which reach epsilon error on the validation data set. The error bars indicate the standard error.

difficulty of the problem increases, the computational effort approaches the Age-Fitness computational effort.

Deterministic crowding required the most computational effort for the simplest test problems. Interestingly, deterministic crowding does better relatively as the solution complexity increases. This is likely due to the fact that it is not

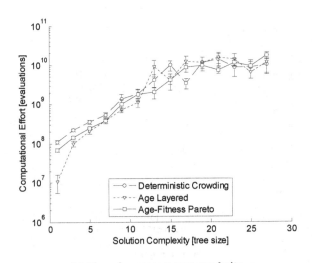

(a) **Time of convegence over complexity**

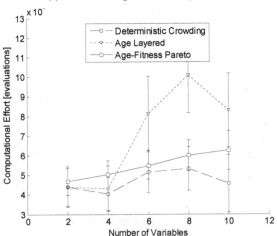

(b) **Time of convergence over number of inputs**

Figure 8-4. The computational effort required when the exact solution was found versus the target equation complexity (a) and the number of variables in the dataset (b). Each algorithm found the exact solution with different frequencies; these plots show the computation effort for when the algorithms did find the exact solution. The error bars indicate the standard error.

finding the exact solution as much as the other algorithms. In effect, it is only finding the exact solution for the easiest of the high complexity target solutions.

This same effect may also arise for the ALPS trends with complexity. The Age-Fitness Pareto algorithm holds the middle amount of computational effort to find the exact solution across almost all solution complexities. However, it also found the exact target solution most often as found in Figure 8-3.

When looking at the computational effort used to find the exact solution versus the number of variables in the data set, we can see a similar trend. These values are most-likely dominated by the most difficult target solutions.

Therefore, ALPS showed the most computational effort but still found the exact solution with a similar rate to the Age-Fitness Pareto algorithm. Deterministic crowding required less computational effort, but identified the exact solution much less often.

It is also interesting to note that there was a much stronger dependence on the target solution complexity than the number of variables in the dataset.

Solution Bloat

Finally, we looked at the amount of solution bloat experienced by each algorithm over the course of the evolutionary searches in Figure 8-5.

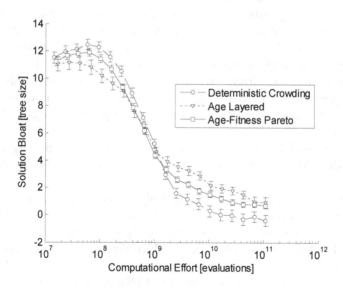

Figure 8-5. Solution bloat over the course of the evolutionary search. Solution bloat is defined as the binary tree size of the best individual in the population minus the binary tree size of the target solution. The error bars indicate the standard error.

We define bloat as the binary tree size of the best solution in the population minus the binary tree size of the target solution. Therefore, the most bloated solutions have positive bloat values, and overly simple solutions have negative bloat values.

In these results, all algorithms started with high amount of bloated solutions early on in the evolutionary searches. On average, the bloat decreased as the search progressed, and the algorithm converged toward exact solutions. Our only method of bloat control comes from coevolution (Schmidt and Lipson, 2008), where changing fitness biases the search toward simpler solutions.

Interestingly, the deterministic crowding algorithm dropped the most in solution bloat. This suggests that the algorithm is under-fitting - it is stagnating at simple local optima.

In contrast, the ALPS and Age-Fitness Pareto algorithms have similar, more-complex solutions on average, which converge toward slightly bloated solutions.

On average, ALPS was the least bloated early on in the evolutionary searches, but bloated the most as the searches progressed.

6.   Discussion

The results in the previous section show several interesting differences and similarities between the three compared algorithms.

Primarily, we found that the Age-Fitness Pareto algorithm performed best overall, identifying the exact target solution most often and earlier (Figure 8-3). The ALPS algorithm was close behind, and the deterministic crowding algorithm performed the worse, finding the exact solution least often.

The deterministic crowding algorithm used a randomized individual each generation, similar to the Age-Fitness Pareto and ALPS algorithms. However, it still performed significantly worse than the other algorithms. This suggests that the performance improvement is not coming solely from increased diversity through random individuals. Therefore, the genotypic age is playing an important role.

We also found that the performance was most affected by the target solution complexity. The performance trend with the number of variables was much weaker.

On average, the deterministic crowding algorithm experienced the least bloat, suggesting that it could be under-fitting, stagnating at low complexity local optima. The ALPS and Age-Fitness Pareto algorithms instead tended toward slightly bloated solutions on average, which may reflect their higher performance overall.

Another trend we noticed was that the ALPS algorithm found the exact solution with the least computational effort on the simplest test problems, and found the exact solutions most often early in the evolutionary search. One possible explanation is that ALPS gets the most benefit from its very first population layers. However, the computational efficiency declines as more and more age layers are maintained. In contrast, the Age-Fitness Pareto algorithm can discard entire ranges of ages should a low age and fit solution arise in the population.

There is also the possibility that the layer sizes and partitions could be optimized further for the random target test problems. However, it is unclear if this could affect the longer term trends on the most difficult and complex test problems.

One final difference of the Age-Fitness Pareto algorithm is that it does not introduce any new evolutionary parameters to the algorithm or addition of multiple population structures. Instead, it simply adds an additional search objective.

7. Conclusion

In summary, we proposed a multi-objective algorithm inspired by the ALPS algorithm (Hornby, 2006) for addressing premature convergence in evolutionary algorithms - a common problem experienced in evolutionary computation where the evolutionary search stagnates at local optima solutions.

Previous research has shown that genotypic age can be used to substantially improve performance in genetic programming by preventing high-fitness and old genotypes from defeating newer and more diverse genotypes. The Age-Fitness Pareto algorithm considers this concept of genotypic age as a fundamental trait in the evolutionary search which can be optimized as an additional objective. Selection favors non-dominated solutions with high fitness and low genotypic age.

Results on randomly generated symbolic regression problems indicate that this approach finds the exact target solution more often than previous methods over a range of target problem complexities and dataset dimensions.

Finally, this approach can be readily incorporated into other evolutionary algorithms, as it makes no assumptions about the problem or solution representations. Additionally, it does not require structuring the multiple sub-populations. It simply adds an additional search objective of genotypic age.

Acknowledgment

This research is supported by the U.S. National Science Foundation (NSF) Graduate Research Fellowship Program, NSF Grant ECCS 0941561 on Cyber-enabled Discovery and Innovation (CDI), and the U.S. Defense Threat Reduction Agency (DTRA) grant HDTRA 1-09-1-0013.

References

Auger, Anne and Hansen, Nikolaus (2005). A restart CMA evolution strategy with increasing population size. In *IEEE Congress on Evolutionary Computation*, pages 1769–1776. IEEE.

Bongard, J. and Lipson, H. (in press). Automated reverse engineering of nonlinear dynamical systems. *Proceedings of the National Academy of Sciences of the United States of America*.

de Jong, Edwin D. and Pollack, Jordan B. (2003). Multi-objective methods for tree size control. *Genetic Programming and Evolvable Machines*, 4(3):211–233.

Deb, Kalyanmoy (2001). *Multi-Objective Optimization Using Evolutionary Algorithms*. Wiley, Chichester, UK.

Doucette, John, Lichodzijewski, Peter, and Heywood, Malcolm (2009). Evolving coevolutionary classifiers under large attribute spaces. In Riolo, Rick L., O'Reilly, Una-May, and McConaghy, Trent, editors, *Genetic Programming Theory and Practice VII*, Genetic and Evolutionary Computation, chapter 3, pages 37–54. Springer, Ann Arbor.

Grunwald, P. (1999). Model selection based on minimum description length.

Hoai, N. X., McKay, R. I., Essam, D., and Chau, R. (2002). Solving the symbolic regression problem with tree-adjunct grammar guided genetic programming: The comparative results. In Fogel, David B., El-Sharkawi, Mohamed A., Yao, Xin, Greenwood, Garry, Iba, Hitoshi, Marrow, Paul, and Shackleton, Mark, editors, *Proceedings of the 2002 Congress on Evolutionary Computation CEC2002*, pages 1326–1331. IEEE Press.

Hornby, Gregory (2006). ALPS: the age-layered population structure for reducing the problem of premature convergence. In Cattolico, Mike, editor, *Genetic and Evolutionary Computation Conference, GECCO 2006, Proceedings, Seattle, Washington, USA, July 8-12, 2006*, pages 815–822. ACM.

Hornby, Gregory S. (2009a). Steady-state ALPS for real-valued problems. In Rothlauf, Franz, editor, *Genetic and Evolutionary Computation Conference, GECCO 2009, Proceedings, Montreal, Québec, Canada, July 8-12, 2009*, pages 795–802. ACM.

Hornby, Gregory S. (2009b). A steady-state version of the age-layered population structure EA. In Riolo, Rick L., O'Reilly, Una-May, and McConaghy, Trent, editors, *Genetic Programming Theory and Practice VII*, Genetic and Evolutionary Computation, chapter 6, pages 87–102. Springer, Ann Arbor.

Hu, Jianjun, Goodman, Erik D., Seo, Kisung, Fan, Zhun, and Rosenberg, Rondal (2005). The hierarchical fair competition (HFC) framework for sustainable evolutionary algorithms. *Evolutionary Computation*, 13(2):241–277.

Hu, Jianjun, Goodman, Erik D., Seo, Kisung, and Pei, Min (2002). Adaptive hierarchical fair competition (AHFC) model for parallel evolutionary algorithms. In Langdon, W. B., Cantú-Paz, E., Mathias, K., Roy, R., Davis, D., Poli, R., Balakrishnan, K., Honavar, V., Rudolph, G., Wegener, J., Bull, L., Potter, M. A., Schultz, A. C., Miller, J. F., Burke, E., and Jonoska, N., editors, *GECCO 2002: Proceedings of the Genetic and Evolutionary Computation Conference*, pages 772–779, New York. Morgan Kaufmann Publishers.

Jansen, Thomas (2002). On the analysis of dynamic restart strategies for evolutionary algorithms. In Merelo Guervós, Juan Julián, Adamidis, Panagiotis, Beyer, Hans-Georg, Fernández-Villacañas, José-Luis, and Schwefel, Hans-Paul, editors, *Parallel Problem Solving from Nature - PPSN VII*, pages 33–43, Berlin. Springer.

Korns, Michael F. (2009). Symbolic regression of conditional target expressions. In Riolo, Rick L., O'Reilly, Una-May, and McConaghy, Trent, editors, *Genetic Programming Theory and Practice VII*, Genetic and Evolutionary Computation, chapter 13, pages 211–228. Springer, Ann Arbor.

Kotanchek, Mark E., Vladislavleva, Ekaterina Y., and Smits, Guido F. (2009). Symbolic regression via GP as a discovery engine: Insights on outliers and prototypes. In Riolo, Rick L., O'Reilly, Una-May, and McConaghy, Trent, editors, *Genetic Programming Theory and Practice VII*, Genetic and Evolutionary Computation, chapter 4, pages 55–72. Springer, Ann Arbor.

Koza, John R. (1992). *Genetic Programming: On the Programming of Computers by Means of Natural Selection*. MIT Press, Cambridge, MA, USA.

Louis, Sushil J. and Rawlins, Gregory J. E. (1993). Syntactic analysis of convergence in genetic algorithms. In Whitley, L. Darrell, editor, *Foundations of Genetic Algorithms 2*, pages 141–151, San Mateo. Morgan Kaufmann.

Mahfoud, Samir W. (1995). *Niching methods for genetic algorithms*. PhD thesis, Champaign, IL, USA.

McKay, Ben, Willis, Mark J., and Barton, Geoffrey W. (1995). Using a tree structured genetic algorithm to perform symbolic regression. In Zalzala, A. M. S., editor, *First International Conference on Genetic Algorithms in Engineering Systems: Innovations and Applications, GALESIA*, volume 414, pages 487–492, Sheffield, UK. IEE.

Murphy, Gearoid and Ryan, Conor (2007). Manipulation of convergence in evolutionary systems. In Riolo, Rick L., Soule, Terence, and Worzel, Bill, editors, *Genetic Programming Theory and Practice V*, Genetic and Evolutionary Computation, chapter 3, pages 33–52. Springer, Ann Arbor.

Ryan, Conor (1996). *Reducing Premature Convergence in Evolutionary Algorithms*. PhD thesis, University College, Cork, Ireland.

Schmidt, Michael and Lipson, Hod (2007). Comparison of tree and graph encodings as function of problem complexity. In Thierens, Dirk, Beyer, Hans-Georg, Bongard, Josh, Branke, Jurgen, Clark, John Andrew, Cliff, Dave, Congdon, Clare Bates, Deb, Kalyanmoy, Doerr, Benjamin, Kovacs, Tim, Kumar, Sanjeev, Miller, Julian F., Moore, Jason, Neumann, Frank, Pelikan, Martin,

Poli, Riccardo, Sastry, Kumara, Stanley, Kenneth Owen, Stutzle, Thomas, Watson, Richard A, and Wegener, Ingo, editors, *GECCO '07: Proceedings of the 9th annual conference on Genetic and evolutionary computation*, volume 2, pages 1674–1679, London. ACM Press.

Schmidt, Michael and Lipson, Hod (2009). Distilling free-form natural laws from experimental data. *Science*, 324(5923):81–85.

Schmidt, Michael D. and Lipson, Hod (2006). Co-evolving fitness predictors for accelerating and reducing evaluations. In Riolo, Rick L., Soule, Terence, and Worzel, Bill, editors, *Genetic Programming Theory and Practice IV*, volume 5 of *Genetic and Evolutionary Computation*, chapter 17, pages –. Springer, Ann Arbor.

Schmidt, Michael D. and Lipson, Hod (2008). Coevolution of fitness predictors. *IEEE Transactions on Evolutionary Computation*, 12(6):736–749.

Chapter 9

SCALABLE SYMBOLIC REGRESSION BY CONTINUOUS EVOLUTION WITH VERY SMALL POPULATIONS

Guido F. Smits[1], Ekaterina Vladislavleva[2] and Mark E. Kotanchek[3]

[1]*Dow Benelux B.V., Terneuzen, the Netherlands;* [2]*University of Antwerp, Antwerp, Belgium.*
[3]*Evolved-Analytics, LLC, Midland, MI, USA.*

Abstract   The future of computing is one of massive parallelism. To exploit this and generate maximum performance it will be inevitable that more co-design between hardware and software takes place. Many software algorithms need rethinking to expose all the possible concurrency, increase locality and have built-in fault tolerance. Evolutionary algorithms are naturally parallel and should as such have an edge in exploiting these hardware features.

In this paper we try to rethink the way we implement symbolic regression via genetic programming with the aim to obtain maximum scalability to architectures with a very large number of processors. Working with very small populations might be an important feature to obtain a better locality of the computations. We show that quite reasonable results can be obtained with single chromosome crawlers and a diverse set of mutation-only operators. Next we show that it is possible to introduce a mechanism for constant innovation using very small population sizes. By introducing a computation, with competition for cpu-cycles based on the fitness and the activity of an individual, we can get continuous evolution within the same cpu-budget as the single chromosome crawlers. These results are obtained on a real life industrial dataset with composition data from a distillation tower with 23 potential inputs and 5000 records.

Keywords:

symbolic regression, genetic programming, continuous evolution, parallel computing, evolvability

1.   Introduction

Future computer systems are anticipated to be massively parallel with hundreds of cores per chip (Sarkar et al., 2009; Heroux, 2009; Agerwala, 2008). The use of these so-called Extreme Scale systems will pose significant challenges in terms of software design and will most probably require more software-hardware co-design to maximize their performance.

The three main features that will dominate the software design are first, the need for orders of magnitude more concurrency in applications compared to current systems, second the need for much more locality i.e co-location of tasks and data to meet the energy requirements of these future systems. There will be much less memory available per core and moving data around on a chip will be quite expensive in terms of power consumption. The last feature that will need to be addressed is the fact that Extreme Scale systems will be subject to frequent faults and failures so software will need to be designed such that it is maximally resilient and fault-tolerant.

Evolutionary computation is inherently parallel and should be able to benefit greatly from these new hardware architectures. Some powerful examples show what is possible by exploiting the architecture of graphics processing units (Langdon, 2010; Harding and Banzhaf, 2009). In GPUs parallelism is exploited by executing the same instruction on multiple data (SIMD). In principle this is a straightforward way to exploit data parallelism but things get more complicated quickly as soon as branching starts to cause so-called divergence in execution threads. Using sub-machine code GP together with a reverse polish interpreter and randomized sub selection from a test suite, impressive speeds of over 250 billion GP operations per second have been achieved on a Tesla T10 192 core GPU, (Langdon, 2010). In these experiments the fitness evaluation was performed on the GPU while the rest of the work (mutation, crossover) was still executed on a CPU.

In this paper we would like to explore what we can do generically and how we can increase both the concurrency as well as the locality for Symbolic Regression via GP to obtain a long-term scalability to large numbers of processors.

Typical population sizes in GP are quite large, typically from a few hundred to thousands of individuals. Since large population sizes decrease locality, our current research is focussing on the use of very small GP populations together with a new approach to obtain continuous evolution. We use a variable-length, linear representation which can be compiled to a reverse polish expression via a stack in a single pass. The different positions in the variable size stack are used to encode multiple equations in the same chromosome.

At one extreme, a population can be collapsed to a single individual that is evolved via an extensive set of mutation operators. The idea here is that one individual is assigned to one processor and evolves independently of all the others. This kind of evolution would occur though mutation only and without any communication between individual chromosomes.

Another approach that is explored here uses populations of very small size where individuals compete for a batch of evaluation cycles. The activity during this batch of evaluations, where evolution occurs in a mutation-only mode, is considered to be a measure for the potential to evolve. The more actual improvements in fitness and near-neutral moves that can be made during the batch of evaluation cycles the higher to potential to evolve even further is considered to be. This activity, together with the fitness, is combined in a Pareto front which is used to tag individuals for replacement, crossover and/or new evaluation cycles. This mechanism is shown to be quite effective in allowing continuous evolution despite the very small population sizes being used. Experiments are performed on a real world dataset (Smits and Vladislavleva, 2006). The Tower problem is an industrial data set of a gas chromatography measurement of the composition of a distillation tower. The underlying data set contains 5000 records with noise and 23 potential input variables.

2. Genome Representation

The Symbolic Regression system used for our experiments is based on linear genomes of variable length n. Every element in this genome consists of 3 elements $[e1, e2, e3]$ so the total genome can be represented by a $n \times 3$ matrix. For every row the first element is used to decide how the second element needs to be decoded and and can take any value from the list [-2,-1,0,1,2]. The specific meaning of these values is the following:

- 2: the second element is interpreted as a reference to an arity-2 operator. The actual operator is determined by mod(e2,number of arity-2 operators).

- 1: the second element is interpreted as a reference to an arity-1 operator. The actual operator is determined by mod(e2,number of arity-1 operators).

- 0: the second element is determined as a reference to a terminal. Whether the terminal is a variable or a constant depends on the current value of a state variable which is modified each time a value e1 is encountered with the value -2. In this way entire regions in the genome will point to constants or variables as terminals. The actual variable is determined by mod(e2,number of variables). In case the terminal points to a constant the value in e3 is used.

- -1: this is interpreted as a *noop* (no operation) and is simply skipped during the compilation phase.

- -2: this controls the state variable mentioned earlier that is used to decide whether a terminal is pointing to a variable or a constant.

A genome is initialized by picking random values for [e1,e2,e3] within their allowed ranges. The range for e2 is all integers between one and the product of

Table 9-1. This table illustrates the encoding of multiple equations in a single genome $[x_1, x_2, x_3, *, \sin, x_4]$ as well as the effect of a changing maximum stack depth between 1 and 4. The first column contains the decoded genome and the other columns show the contents of the stack when the genome is evaluated from the top to the bottom. All the equation that are present on the stack at the end of the evaluation are considered as separate equations.

Depth	1	2	3	4
x_1	x_1	x_1	x_1	x_1
x_2	x_1	$x_1; x_2$	$x_1; x_2$	$x_1; x_2$
x_3	x_1	$x_1; x_2;$	$x_1; x_2; x_3$	$x_1; x_2; x_3$
$*$	x_1	$x_1 * x_2;$	$x_1; x_2 * x_3$	$x_1; x_2 * x_3$
$\sin$	$\sin x_1$	$\sin x_1 * x_2;$	$x_1; \sin x_2 * x_3$	$x_1; \sin x_2 * x_3$
x_4	$\sin x_1$	$\sin x_1 * x_2; x_4$	$x_1; \sin x_2 * x_3; x_4$	$x_1; \sin x_2 * x_3; x_4$

the number of variables, the number of arity-1 operators, the number of arity-2 operators and the number of states that are possible (constant or variable).

The genome can be either compiled or evaluated in a single pass by starting at the end and working backward to the beginning of the genome until a termination point is reached. This termination point is a property of the specific genome and can also vary during the evolution. A stack is used to hold intermediate values during evaluation. Also the maximum stack depth that can be used is a property of the specific genome that can be varied during evolution. By modifying this maximum stack-depth the interpretation of a genome will change and can actually encode multiple equations since every value that is still on the stack will be interpreted is the result of a separate formula (see table 9-1). Any operation that is not feasible e.g. applying an operator when no variables are on the stack or trying to push another variable on the stack when the maximum stack-depth is reached all result in a *noop* and are simply skipped.

Finally, the fitness of the genome is considered to be the maximum correlation coefficient of the predicted vs. actual data for all formulas that are part of the genome.

While this is not the topic of the current paper, it is also possible to calculate different complexity metrics as well as dimensionality and variable presence in a single pass during the compilation of the genome. The current representation is found to be very effective and can be evaluated extremely fast.

3.   Single Chromosome Crawler

In this approach we let a single chromosome evolve independently by applying mutation operators only. We accept any moves (mutations) that do not result in a lower fitness within a certain dynamic tolerance limit. This means we accept any move that improves the fitness of the chromosome. We also accept all neutral moves i.e. changes that leave the fitness unaffected. Lastly we even accept moves that lower the fitness slightly - in the spirit of simulated annealing - as long as the decrease in fitness falls within the selected tolerance limit. We define a lower bound on acceptable fitness as a moving average of the current fitness and the previous fitness (OR the previous tolerance limit) of all the accepted moves e.g.

$$fitness_{MA} = 0.8 fitness_{MA} + 0.2 fitness,$$

where *fitness* is individual's fitness at the current step provided the move is accepted. The initial value of the moving average $fitness_{MA}$ at the first generation is equal to the actual *fitness* of the individual, and from generation *two* it is always smaller than the current *fitness*. Any move that generates a fitness which is lower than the current value of $fitness_{MA}$ is rejected. In practice, this minimal acceptable fitness threshold is relatively large in the beginning of an evolution but gets gradually smaller and smaller as the evolution progresses (i.e. larger drops in fitness are allowed at the beginning, but only smaller drops are tolerated towards the end of the run).

The list of mutation operators that can be selected in our implementation is:

- **Delete** a tuple $[a, g, c]$ at the selected location and reinitialize the tuple at the first position;

- **Insert Arity 1 item** $[1, g, c]$ at the selected location and reinitialize the tuple at the first position;

- **Insert Arity 2 TAG item** $[[2, g, c], [0, g, c]]$ at the selected location and reinitialize the tuples at the first and second position;

- **Insert Arity 2 item** $[2, g, c]$ at the selected location and reinitialize the tuple at the first position;

- **Reinitialise item** $[a, g, c]$ at the selected position;

- **Shift**: Change the constant at the selected location according to:

$$c = c + randn * (1 - fitness),$$

where $randn$ is a random number with a gaussian distribution;

- **Scale**: Change the constant at the selected location according to:

$$c = c * randn * (1 - fitness),$$

where $randn$ is a random number with a gaussian distribution;

- **ReinitializeTop**: Reinitialize all tuples from position 1 to the selected location:

$$[1 : location, :] = new;$$

- **ReInitializeBottom**: Reinitialize all tuples from the selected location to the last position:

$$[location : end, :] = new;$$

- **CycleUp**: The first $[a, g, c]$ tuple is moved to the last position and all the others are moving up one place;

- **CycleDown**: The last $[a, g, c]$ tuple is moved to the first position and all the others are moving down one place;

- **CycleRandom**: CycleUp or Down N times;

- **Reinitialize Maximum Stackdepth**;

- **Reinitialize Effective chromosome length**.

We evaluated the performance of these single-chromosome crawlers on the Tower dataset. If we examine the fitness versus the number of iterations (every iteration is a random mutation from the above list followed by a reevaluation; see Figure 9-1) we see that (even for a single chromosome) evolution is quite fast and has a reasonable reproducibility. We do see however, that stagnation does occur occasionally. While some evolutionary runs make it to the expected fitness of 0.95 (Smits and Vladislavleva, 2006), a number of runs level off slightly lower, around a fitness of 0.9.

These results are not surprising since no crossover or reinitialization is occurring at any stage. Still, in a context of having the possibility of having many of these single-chromosome evolutions in parallel in future systems, this may a very effective approach. There is little communication overhead and any of these individual runs can be implemented such that they are extremely efficient e.g. the entire evaluation stack could be cached and depending on the mutation operator being applied significant parts of the evaluation could be reused.

In the next section we investigate the use of small populations of e.g. 8-32 individuals where the locality is still quite high. This permits the introduction of a mechanism to continually introduce new genetic material as well as crossover leading to much more reproducible results for the same cpu-budget.

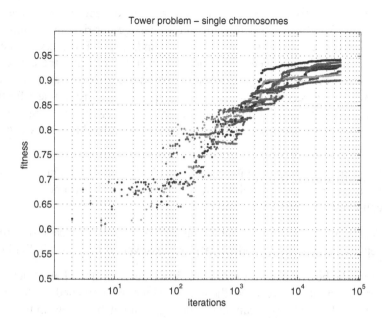

Figure 9-1. Fitness traces for ten individual runs of a single chromosome crawler for the Tower problem. While some runs achieve very high fitnesses, stagnation can be observed as well.

4. Continuous Symbolic Regression with Small Populations

In the previous sections we saw that a reasonable convergence can be achieved by evolving single chromosomes using mutation only. An issue with this approach is a dependence on the starting point that sometimes results in stagnation of a run. To eliminate this problem and get more consistency, we can work with very small populations of chromosomes, e.g. between 8 and 32 individuals. This still preserves the locality and consequently the scalability to large numbers of processors. We also assume that the same cpu budget is available to the population as for the single chromosome crawlers.

We start by assigning a batch of iterations (e.g. 100) using mutation-only to every individual. After this initialization stage, every chromosome in the population will have achieved a certain fitness and will have shown a certain degree of 'activity'. This activity is defined as the sum of the number of moves that either improved the fitness or neutral moves that resulted in either no change in fitness or a change that was less than a given (dynamic) tolerance limit as discussed in the previous section. Some graphs of this activity vs fitness is shown in Figure 9-2. Higher fitness for a chromosome is better but we also consider higher activity to be better in the sense that high activity is a measure for a larger 'potential to improve'. The converse i.e. low activity is a measure of stagnation. We can use this information to manage our risk and assign the next batch of cpu-cycles to the most promising individual. For every problem there is a relationship between the fitness of an individual and the expected activity. As the evolution progresses fitness will increase but activity will tend to decrease - it will become more difficult to improve the current fitness for the individual. The natural solution is to work with the Pareto-fronts of fitness vs activity. From these we will extract three candidate individuals for a certain action:

1. From the top Pareto front i.e the individuals with the highest activity for a given fitness, we select a random candidate to get a new batch of cpu-cycles on the next iteration.

2. Also from the top Pareto front we can also select a random candidate (except the highest fitness individual) for crossover with the best individual.

3. From the bottom Pareto front .e. the individuals with the lowest activity for a given fitness we select the individual that is dominated by the most other individuals as a candidate for replacement by a new individual. This new individual can either be generated from scratch or can be the result of cross-over.

At every cycle we choose an action at random which can be:

- Update current candidate for cpu-cycles by executing the predetermined number of mutation-only iterations.

- Reinitialize current candidate for replacement and executing the predetermined number of mutation-only iterations.

- Crossover current candidate for crossover with the best individual and execute the predetermined number of mutation-only iterations.

In Figure 9-2 we illustrate the first four steps of this process. In every subplot we show the current candidate for replacement, updating or crossover as labeled squares. The larger square is used to denote the action that was actually chosen and which individual was assigned 100 iterations of mutation-only evolution. The arrow in the next subplot then indicates the new position of that individual in the fitness vs activity chart.

Since any individual on the top Pareto front has an equal chance of being assigned cpu-cycles there is constant innovation possible with new genetic material irrespective of the actual fitness of the individuals and despite the very small population size (16 individuals in this particular case).

Figure 9-3 illustrates the consistent progress by showing snapshots of fitness vs. activity at steps 1, 10, 100 and 1000 for the Tower problem. Notice that

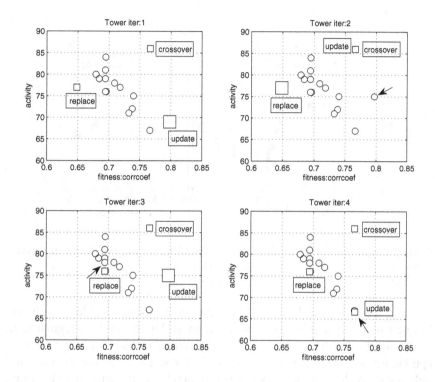

Figure 9-2. This figure illustrates the first four steps of the evolution process of the Tower problem. In every subplot we show the current candidate for replacement, updating or crossover as labeled squares. The larger square is used to denote the candidate and the action that was actually chosen. Subsequently, this individual was assigned 100 iterations of mutation-only evolution. The arrow in the next subplot then indicates the new position of that individual in the fitness vs activity chart. Notice that the successive actions in this particular case were Update-Replace-Update

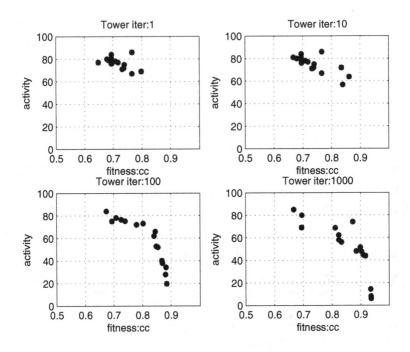

Figure 9-3. Snapshots of fitness vs. activity at steps 1, 10, 100 and 1000. Every step consists of 100 mutation-only iterations for a single individual

convergence is indicated by the presence of high fitness individuals with very low activity but even then new individuals are still introduced at a regular pace.

Despite the fact that we are working with a (small) population, notice that our cpu-budget is still virtually the same as with the single chromosome runs since only one individual gets the execute a given number of mutation-only iterations at the time. The fact that these iterations are mutation-only also makes this an operation with very high locality. Figure 9-4 shows a typical cpu-budget allocation process. Every black line segment denotes a batch of 100 mutation-only evolutions that are allocated to that particular individual. The overall effort is spread quite nicely over all individuals.

Figure 9-5 shows the overall convergence for the Tower problem with a population size of 16. Overall convergence is now steady and more reproducible compared to the single chromosome runs - see Figure 9-1. In Figure 9-6 we show the same convergence plot (the x-axis is now no longer on a log scale) but with the emphasis on the individual fitness profile of one of the chromosomes. This chromosome turns out to have the best fitness at the end of the run. Notice however that this individual was replaced and had to start over on multiple occasions. The notion of 'activity' as a proxy for 'potential to improve' clearly

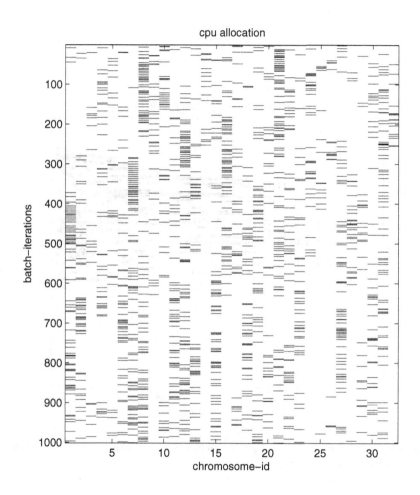

Figure 9-4. Graphical representation of a typical cpu-budget allocation process. Every black line segment denotes a batch of 100 mutation-only iterations that are allocated to that particular individual. The overall effort is spread quite nicely over all individuals.

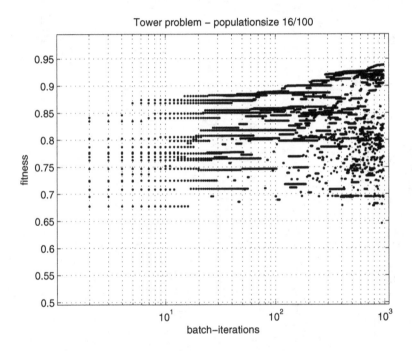

Figure 9-5. Overall convergence for the Tower problem with a population size of 16. Steady progress is observed during the run.

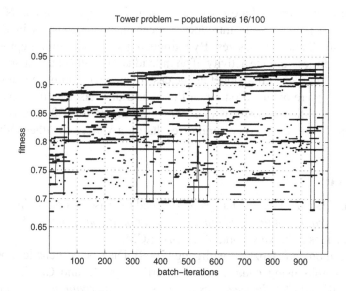

Figure 9-6. Overall convergence for the Tower problem with a population size of 16.with emphasis on the individual fitness profile of the chromosomes with maximum fitness at the end of the run. Notice the multiple restarts that occurred for this individual.

allows newly introduced individuals to effectively compete with other high fitness individuals in the population.

In all runs with no exceptions we observed the constant renewal process of chromosomes in the population, when the lower fitness chromosomes replaced the higher fitness chromosomes that already evolved for a while but could no longer compete based on their activity. Such renewal process is happening all the time and virtually eliminates any chance for permanent stagnation of a run.

5. Discussion and Conclusions

The future of computing is one of massive parallelism. To exploit this and generate maximum performance it will be inevitable that we co-design software with new hardware. Many software algorithms need rethinking to expose all the possible concurrency, increase locality and have built-in fault tolerance. Evolutionary algorithms are naturally parallel and should as such have an edge in exploiting these hardware features.

In this paper we try to rethink the way we implement symbolic regression via genetic programming with the aim to obtain maximum scalability to architectures with a very large number of processors. Working with very small populations might be an important feature to obtain a better locality of the computations. We showed that quite reasonable results can be obtained with single chromosome crawlers and a diverse set of mutation-only operators. Next we showed that it is possible to introduce a mechanism for constant innovation using very small population sizes. By introducing a competition for cpu-cycles based on the fitness and the activity of an individual we can get continuous evolution within the same cpu-budget as the case of single chromosome crawlers. These results were obtained on a real life industrial dataset with composition data from a distillation tower with 23 potential inputs and 5000 records (reported here). We obtain very similar results on a variety of other industrial datasets.

References

Agerwala, Tilak (2008). Challenges on the road to exascale computing. In *ICS '08: Proceedings of the 22nd annual international conference on Supercomputing*, pages 2–2, New York, NY, USA. ACM.

Harding, Simon and Banzhaf, Wolfgang (2009). Distributed genetic programming on gpus using cuda. In Risco-Mart'n, Jos^ L. and Garnica, Oscar, editors, *WPABA'09: Proceedings of the Second International Workshop on Parallel Architectures and Bioinspired Algorithms (WPABA 2009)*, pages 1–10, Raleigh, NC, USA. Universidad Complutense de Madrid.

Heroux, Michael A. (2009). Software challenges for extreme scale computing: Going from petascale to exascale systems. *Int. J. High Perform. Comput. Appl.*, 23(4):437–439.

Langdon, W. B. (2010). A many threaded CUDA interpreter for genetic programming. In Esparcia-Alcazar, Anna Isabel, Ekart, Aniko, Silva, Sara, Dignum, Stephen, and Uyar, A. Sima, editors, *Proceedings of the 13th European Conference on Genetic Programming, EuroGP 2010*, volume 6021 of *LNCS*, pages 146–158, Istanbul. Springer.

Sarkar, Vivek, Harrod, William, and Snavely, Allan E (2009). Software challenges in extreme scale systems. *Journal of Physics: Conference Series*, 180(1):012045.

Smits, Guido and Vladislavleva, Ekaterina (2006). Ordinal Pareto Genetic Programming. In *2006 IEEE Congress on Evolutionary Computation (CEC'2006)*, pages 10471–10477, Vancouver, BC, Canada. IEEE.

Chapter 10

SYMBOLIC DENSITY MODELS OF ONE-IN-A-BILLION STATISTICAL TAILS VIA IMPORTANCE SAMPLING AND GENETIC PROGRAMMING

Trent McConaghy[1]

[1]*Solido Design Automation Inc., Canada.*

Abstract

This paper explores the application of symbolic regression for building models of probability distributions in which the accuracy at the distributions' *tails* is critical. The problem is of importance to cutting-edge industrial integrated circuit design, such as designing SRAM memory components (bitcells, sense amps) where each component has extremely low probability of failure. A naive approach is infeasible because it would require billions of Monte Carlo circuit simulations. This paper demonstrates a flow that efficiently generates samples at the tails using *importance sampling*, then builds genetic programming symbolic regression models in a space that captures the tails – the normal quantile space. These symbolic density models allow the circuit designers to analyze the tradeoff between high-sigma yields and circuit performance. The flow is validated on two modern industrial problems: a bitcell circuit on a 45nm TSMC process, and a sense amp circuit on a 28nm TSMC process.

Keywords: symbolic regression, density estimation, importance sampling, Monte Carlo methods, memory, SRAM, integrated circuits, extreme-value statistics

1. Introduction

In many types of industrial designs, random factors during the manufacturing process affect the performance of the final product. This is certainly the case in modern integrated circuits, where shrinking transistors have led to large process variations and therefore large performance variations. This in turn hurts chip yields, affecting time-to-market and profitability of semiconductor vendors.

Memory chips are among the circuits most affected in modern semiconductor design; effective solutions are of critical importance to memory vendors. While statistical effects can be simulated in a flow that incorporates a circuit simulator (e.g. SPICE) with a Monte Carlo analysis, that's not enough for memory design. Memory building block like bitcells are replicated millions of times or more on a chip; this means that for overall yields to be reasonable (e.g. >90%), each bitcell must have yields with failure rates millions of times lower than the overall chip. That is, they need yields up to 99.9999998% (6 sigma[1]).

For effective analysis, the memory circuit designer needs to analyze the tradeoff between such high-sigma yields and circuit performance. Equivalently, he or she needs accurate models of the extreme tails of the distribution.

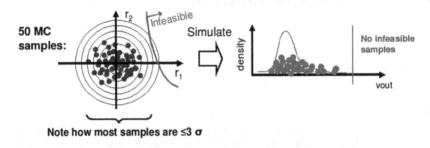

Figure 10-1. Monte Carlo sampling. Process point samples are drawn from a distribution (left), then simulated (middle), to get corresponding output values (right). A sample is "feasible" if all outputs' specifications are met. Here, a sample is feasible if $v_{out} \leq v_{out_{thr}}$, where $v_{out_{thr}}$ is represented by the vertical bar in the output space (right), which maps to the nonlinear "infeasible" boundary in the process-variation space (left). Yield is the expected percentage of samples that are feasible. The challenge is: when the yield is extremely high, a small number of Monte Carlo samples will almost never have a failure, so yield cannot be accurately estimated.

This problem is challenging on several counts. Consider modeling a circuit where one in a million samples fail. Figure 10-1 shows the case if one draws a small number of Monte Carlo samples in process-variation space, and simulates them to get circuit performances (e.g. v_{out}). No samples will even be close to failure, so any subsequent modeling on top of it would be useless. To get just one failure, one would expect to run 1 million simulations, and 10 failures would take on average 10 million simulations. Figure 10-2 illustrates this case. One million simulations, even on a fast-simulating circuit and with a compute cluster, still typically takes a full day. So ten million is ten days, and 10 billion is 3 years.

---

[1]Sigma is another unit for yield: yield is the area under a Gaussian curve in the range -sigma to +sigma. Therefore 6 sigma is yield of 99.9999998%, or probability of failure 1.973e-9, which is about 2 in a billion.

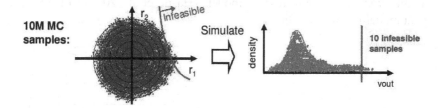

Figure 10-2. Monte Carlo sampling with many samples can capture the tails, but is computationally expensive.

A normal Monte Carlo run draws process points directly from the process variation distribution. As seen, far too many samples are needed in order to get (rare-event) failures in the design. A key insight is that we do not need to draw samples directly from the distribution. Instead, we can create samples that are infeasible more often, so that decent information is available at the tails. Importance Sampling (IS)(Hesterberg, 1988) is a well-known approach for rare event simulation, where the sampling distribution is shifted towards rare infeasible samples, as Figure 10-3 illustrates. Each sample has a weight that relates its density on the sampling pdf to the true pdf.

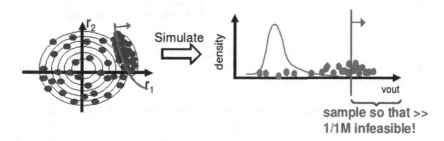

Figure 10-3. Importance sampling takes more samples at the tails of the distribution. But how do we build (symbolic) models from that data?

Given that we can efficiently take samples at the tails, how can we construct symbolic density models? This paper explores a practical flow using genetic programming (GP)(Koza, 1992). Specifically, GP symbolic regression models the distributions accurately even at the tails, by working from the importance-sampled data points, rescaled into the normal quantile space. Figure 10-4 right illustrates.

For reference, we show the naive Monte Carlo-based flow in Figure 10-4 left. As discussed, it is impractical because it requires too many simulations. Also, the high sample count is too computationally expensive for classical density estimation techniques such as kernel density estimation or expectation-maximization of gaussian mixture models (Hastie et al., 2001). Finally, the output model is not symbolic.

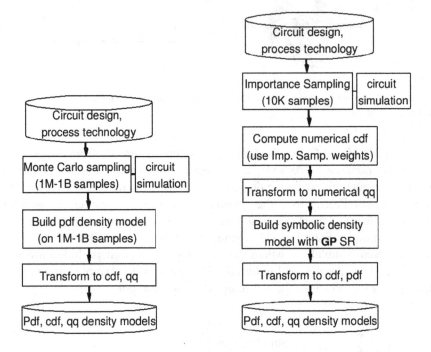

Figure 10-4. Left: Naive Monte Carlo based extraction of pdf, cdf, and nq density models needs too many samples for accuracy at the tails. Right: Proposed flow returns symbolic density models that are accurate even at the one-in-a-billion tails.

Working with importance-sampled data is not straightforward, because not every sample is equal; in fact some samples can have orders of magnitude more weight than others. This constraint renders most traditional density estimation techniques useless. Fortunately, we have a starting point: a numerical cdf (cumulative density function) can be computed from the raw importance-sampled data, where the y-values are dependent on the relative weights of samples.

One could consider a regression-style approach to build a density model in the cdf space, but that has problems. First, it underemphasizes the importance of the tails. Second, the search imposes difficult constraints: the cdf function must be monotonically increasing left-to-right, start at y=0.0 and end at y=1.0. To handle such constraints, one might use guaranteed-monotonic functions such as mixture-of-sigmoids (which is restrictive), or do numerical analysis of chosen functions (which is expensive and provides no guarantees). One could also consider transforming the data into pdf space (probability densities, the derivative of cdf); but this is even more difficult because pdf models must be guaranteed to integrate to 1.0 across their whole input range. It is possible, but unpalatable: one must do numerical integration (which is computationally expensive), symbolic integration by linking to symbolic math software (which is complex), or use easy-to-analyze functional forms such as mixture of gaussians (which is restrictive). Further, doing regression on pdfs also underemphasizes the importance of the tails.

Rather than building models in cdf or pdf space, this paper proposes to build models in the *normal quantile* (nq) space, wherein raw cdf values are transformed based on the Gaussian function. A major benefit is that the closer a distribution is to Gaussian, the more linear the nq model is; this is quite unlike the highly nonlinear curves in cdf and pdf space. The only constraint for nq space is monotonicity, which is easy to meet by simply rejecting models that fail; because models are near-linear, most easily pass this constraint. Once models are built in nq space, they can be subsequently transformed to cdf and pdf space. The final challenge is how to make the regression-style nq models to be human-interpretable equations. This is the role of symbolic regression (SR) – the automated extraction of static whitebox models that map input variables to output variables. To ensure the models are human-interpretable, we use SR with canonical-form functions constrained by a grammar; that is, CAFFEINE (McConaghy and Gielen, 2006; McConaghy and Gielen, 2009). Figure 10-4 shows these steps of building symbolic density models in nq space, and transformation to cdf and pdf.

The rest of this paper is organized as follows. Section 2 reviews related work in GP. Section 3 describes the importance sampling approach, section 4 describes regression-style density modeling from importance samples, and section 5 describes symbolic regression-style density modeling. Section 6 gives the experimental setup, and section 7 presents experimental results. Section 8 concludes.

2.   Related Work in GP

With a thorough search of the GP literature, we found just one set of work doing density estimation (Defoin Platel et al., 2007)[1]. However, that work could not model the crucial data – the tails – because it worked directly from Monte Carlo samples, and with just MC samples there are no samples at the high-sigma tails. One cannot model a region if one has no data for that region. In contrast,our approach explicitly samples at the tails, and avoids artificially underemphasize the importance of the tails by modeling in normal quantile space.

---

[1] While (Whigham, 2000) had "density model" in its title, it did not actually model pdfs/cdfs.

3.   Optimal Importance Sampling

Importance Sampling (IS) (Hesterberg, 1988) is a well-known approach for rare event simulation. In IS, samples are drawn from a sampling distribution $g(r)$ that is different than the true distribution $p(r)$. The sampling distribution has a greater bias towards the tails, e.g. towards the rare infeasible samples. To make statistical estimates (e.g. mean, yield) from importance sampled data, a weight w is assigned to each sample r: $w(r) = p(r)/g(r)$.

There are few theoretical constraints on the choice of sampling distribution, except that $g(r) > 0$ for all r that $p(r) > 0$. In practice, choosing g is more of a challenge when the random variables r have dimensionalty >10; we have 50-150 random variables. The challenge is to choose a $g(r)$ such that samples are infeasible often, yet the samples are sufficiently probable in $p(r)$ such that the weights $w(r)$ are not negligible. A pragmatic technique is to compute "centers", which are subsequently used as the means of Gaussian distributions for $g(r)$. Rather than heuristically choose centers as in (Kanj et al., 2006), we can cast the problem into an optimization problem:

$$\begin{aligned} r^* &= argmax\{p(r)\} \\ s.t. \quad &feasible(r) = True \end{aligned} \qquad (10.1)$$

where r is a random point in process variation space. r^*, the optimal r, is found by maximizing its density $p(r)$, subject to violating at least one performance value specification during simulation. If the true pdf has normal, independent and identically-distributed (NIID) random variables with mean equal to zero and no correlations, then maximizing density(r) is equivalent to minimizing $\|r\|$.

Then, finding good centers amounts to solving the optimization problem, using an appropriate solver. We solve the optimization problem via (a) higher standard deviation random sampling and simulation until a minimum number of infeasible samples are found, then (b) applying a small-population evolutionary programming algorithm (Yao et al., 1999), with SPICE simulation in the loop, to locally optimize the most-probable infeasible samples. Once the centers are found, $g(r)$ is defined as a mixture of (a) 25% samples from a mean equal to zero pdf with higher standard deviation, and (b) 75% samples are drawn from the centers with standard deviation=1.0. The sampling of Figure 10-3 follows this sampling. Importance sampling proceeds using this distribution until a stopping criteria is met; we stop when 10,000 samples have been taken. We dub this overall approach Optimal Importance Sampling.

The key output of importance sampling is a tuple for each sample i, where each tuple contains the process point r_i, its weight $w_i = w(r_i)$, and its SPICE-simulated performance value $m_i = simulate(r_i)$[1].

4. Density Modeling from Importance Samples

This section describes how density models can be computed from importance sampling data.

A typical (non-IS) density modeling problem is: given a set of performance values $\{m_1, m_2, \ldots, m_N\}$, compute a distribution $p(m)$ in terms of density, cumulative density, or normal quantiles (nq). This is usually treated as an unsupervised learning problem, and solved with e.g. kernel density estimation or Gaussian mixture models (Hastie et al., 2001).

Working with importance-sampled data is not straightforward, because not every sample is equal – they have weights. If we were to ignore the weights and compute the density, the density values in the tail regions would be far too large. However, we can apply a regression-style approach in nq space. Its steps are:

1. : Sort performance values in ascending order $m_1 <= m_2 <= \ldots < m_N$, keeping corresponding weights aligned.

2. : Compute numerical cdfs as $cdf_i = \sum_{j=1}^{i} w_j$. These make the y-values in the numerical cdf, and the x-values are the corresponding m_i values.

3. : Compute numerical nq with the inverse-normal transformation $nq_i = erf^{-1}(2*cdf_i - 1)*\sqrt{2}$, where $erf(x) = 2/\sqrt{\pi} \int_0^x e^{-t^2} dt$. These make the y-values in the numerical nq, and the x-values are the corresponding m_i values.

4. : Build a model $\widehat{nq}$ that maps $m \to nq$, i.e. a density model in nq space, using the training data $\{m_i, nq_i\}\forall i, i = 1..N$. This is performed with a 1-D regression method that minimizes the sum-squared prediction error across all possible input data, such as least-squares linear regression, quadratic regression, or more complex approaches.

5. : The model $\widehat{cdf}$ is the normal transformation from nq to cdf: $\widehat{cdf} = (1 + erf(\widehat{nq}/\sqrt{2}))/2$. This transformation can be performed symbolically or numerically.

---

[1]For simplicity, we will focus on just one performance value at a time. This is a reasonable simplification for memory problems.

6. : The model $\widehat{pdf}$ is the derivative of the cdf model: $\widehat{pdf} = d\widehat{cdf}/dm$. This transformation can be performed symbolically (e.g. with automatic differentiation) or numerically (e.g. with finite element models).

5. Symbolic Density Modeling with CAFFEINE

The last section described how to make regression-based density models from importance-sampled data. To make *symbolic* density models, the key is to use symbolic regression (SR) in the last section's model-building step (step 4). We use CAFFEINE (McConaghy and Gielen, 2006; McConaghy and Gielen, 2009), but any almost GP-based SR system would do here since the problem is a simple 1-D mapping. CAFFEINE's advantage is that it uses a grammar to constrain its search to the space of human-interpretable expressions, which ensures human readability and implicitly prevents bloat. We used CAFFEINE off-the-shelf, without changing any parameters compared to (McConaghy and Gielen, 2009). Population size was 100, running for 100 generations. This includes the CAFFEINE's multi-objective search: minimize error, and minimize model complexity, to return a set of nondominated models.

To speed up runtime[1], prior to CAFFEINE, we pruned each training dataset down to 50 points in a two-step flow. In the first step, the samples were sorted and every n^{th} sample was taken, such that just 250 samples remained. In the second step, we applied the SMITS balancing procedure of (Vladislavleva, 2008) to prune down to 50 samples. In each iteration of the SMITS algorithm, the weights of all samples are computed and the lowest-weighted sample is removed. The weights are based on "local deviation from linearity": at each point, its $k = 8$ closest neighbors in input space (m) are selected, a linear model from m to nq is constructed; then the weight is the absolute distance from the point to the linear model (plane in 2-d space). This weighting procedure naturally focuses the samples towards those with high information content, i.e. at the nonlinear "bends" in the training data.

The multi-objective approach taken in CAFFEINE used nondominated-sorting layers (NSGA-II) (Deb et al., 2002). An issue with NSGA-II is that the final nondominated set can be over-represented in some regions. So, we apply bottom-up clustering (hierarchical agglomerative clustering) to the 2-D Pareto Front.

6. Experimental Setup

We use two test circuits, a bitcell and a sense amp, as shown in Figure 10-5. These are the two major building blocks in designing memory circuits.

---

[1]Note: the speedups are not *needed*, they just help to get results in real-time.

The bitcell has 6 devices, and the sense amp 12. Each circuit's device sizes were set to have "reasonable" values by a memory circuit designer, leading to "reasonable" performance values. For the bitcell, the circuit performance of interest is v_{out}, focusing accuracy in the specification region of $v_{out} > 17$ mV. For the sense amp, it is -22 mV $\leq v_{offset} \leq 22$ mV.

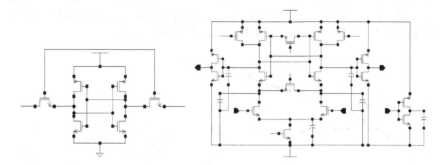

Figure 10-5. Circuit schematics. Left: bitcell. Right: sense amp

The variations in the circuit performance due to manufacturing imprecision can be modeled as a joint probability density function (jpdf). We use the well-known model (Drennan and McAndrew, 1999) where the random variables are "process variables" which model quantities like "substrate doping concentration". Variations in these quantities affect the electrical behavior of the circuit, and therefore its performances. In this model, there are about 10 normal independent identically-distributed (NIID) random variables per transistor. In total, the bitcell had 55 process variables, and the sense amp 125. In a Monte Carlo run, random points are drawn directly from the jpdf describing the process variations; and in importance sampling, random points are drawn from a sampling jpdf. Via simulation, the process-variation distribution maps to the performance distribution.

At each random point, we simulate the circuit at pre-specified environmental conditions. The bitcell's environmental conditions were temp=25degC, power supply voltage V_{dd}=1.0 V, and V_{cn}=0.0 V. The sense amp's environmental conditions were: load capacitance C_l=1e-15 F, temp=25degC, and V_{dd}=1.0 V. The simulator was was HSPICE^{TM}. The technology for the bitcell was TSMC 45nm CMOS, and for the sense amp 28nm CMOS.

7.   Experimental Results

This section describes the results to validate the importance sampling plus SR flow on the bitcell and the sense amp.

First, we aimed to ensure that importance sampling could faithfully sample a broad range of the distribution. For "golden" results (results that we can use as a reference for comparison), we ran 1M Monte Carlo samples for the bitcell and 100K for the sense amp. For IS results, we ran 10K importance samples. Then, we constructed a numerical nq plot for each set of results, using steps 2 and 3 in section 4 (in MC, all the weights are equal). The results are plotted in Figure 10-6. Note how the normal quantile values for the IS data line up nicely with the MC data, even in the tails (e.g. where normal quantile <-3 and >3). The discrete steps for the IS data are due to some samples having larger weights, which in turn influences the cdf and nq values more.

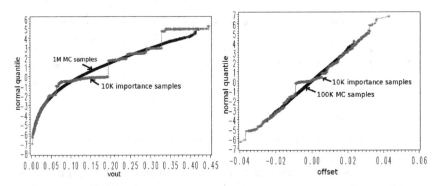

Figure 10-6. Importance Sampling results verified against "golden" Monte Carlo samples. Left: bitcell. Right: sense amp

These curves on their own have value to provide insight to the designer – information about the tails that we would not normally get with a limited sample MC run. In the sense amp, the linearity of the curves indicate that the sense amp's offset is Gaussian-distributed even into the tails, and that the mapping from process variables to offset is linear. In contrast, the bitcell's v_{out} curve bends towards the bottom left, indicating a strong nonlinearity. Such information is valuable to gain insight into the nature of the tails of the distribution, and to understand the tradeoff between specifications and yield. From here on, we will focus on the bitcell results because, being nonlinear, they are the most interesting. (CAFFEINE solved the linear sense amp problem trivially.)

The next step was to build symbolic density models from the IS nq data, and to examine the results in nq, cdf, and pdf space. Given the $\{m,nq\}$ training data, the models were built according to section 5. Both steps of pruning took about 3 s total; CAFFEINE took about 30 s to run, and return its Pareto-optimal models. The models were pruned from 31 to 6 models. The Pareto-optimal models' output is plotted against the nq training data in Figure 10-7 top. The simplest CAFFEINE model was linear (note how its straight line misses the nonlinearity in the bottom left).

The other models had similar performance, and successfully captured the nonlinearity. The cdf and pdf curves for the lowest-error model were computed

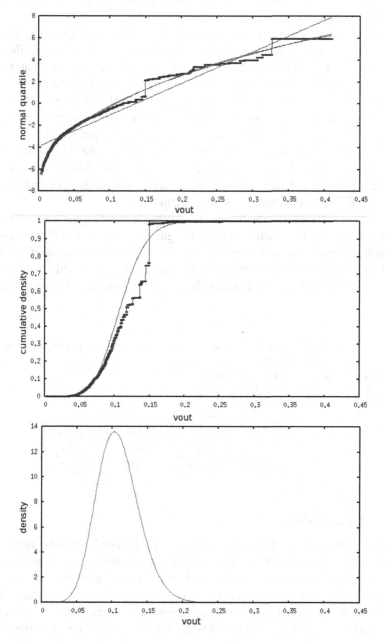

Figure 10-7. CAFFEINE results and training data in nq space (top), cdf space (middle), and pdf space (bottom). In the nq space, all nondominated models are shown. In the other spaces, just the lowest-error model is shown.

numerically according to the flow in section 4; they are shown in Figure 10-7 middle and bottom.

Notice how the cdf curve naturally starts at a value of exactly 0.0, and monotonically increases to finish at exactly 1.0. This would have been difficult or expensive to do if doing symbolic regression in cdf space, but was natural and simple by transforming from nq to cdf space. Also, with an "eyeball" check we can see that the pdf curve roughly integrates to 1.0. Once again, this would have been difficult or expensive if doing symbolic regression in the pdf space, but was natural and simple by transforming from cdf to pdf space.

The results in the three spaces are complementary: the nq illuminates the tails the most, the cdf allows one to quickly assess the tradeoff between yield (equivalent to the cdf value or 1-cdf value, depending on the spec), and the pdf gives intuition about where the samples tend to focus.

The output symbolic models have high value to the designer, as he can manually manipulate the equation. For high-sigma memory design, the nq space is actually the most natural, so the CAFFEINE models can be used directly. Table 10-1 shows some of CAFFEINE-output models. Note how readily-interpretable they are, while accurately capturing the mapping from v_{out} to normal quantile nq.

Table 10-1. CAFFEINE-generated models mapping v_{out} to normal quantile nq, in order of decreasing error and increasing complexity.

Train error (%)	nq Expression
26.3	$-3.903 + 28.90 * v_{out}$
11.42	$-7.358 - 3.736 * v_{out} + 23.89 * \sqrt{v_{out}}$
11.01	$368.1 - 46.482 * v_{out} + 170.959 * \sqrt{v_{out}}$ $+41.0435 * log10(1.07285e - 7 * \sqrt{v_{out}})$ $-0.002472/\sqrt{max(0, 1.562e - 10/\sqrt{v_{out}})}$

8.   Conclusion

This paper described a new challenge for GP-based symbolic regression: building density models that are accurate at the extreme tails of the distribution. This challenge matters for the real-world problem of variation-aware memory circuit design. This paper discussed how a naive approach using plain Monte Carlo would fail in handling such rare-event tails. Then, this paper described a flow to extract extreme-value symbolic density models: optimal importance sampling, symbolic regression in the normal quantile space, and transformation to cdf and pdf space. The flow was validated on two industrial problems: a bitcell circuit on a 45nm TSMC process, and a sense amp circuit on a 28nm TSMC process.

9. Acknowledgment

Funding for the reported research results is acknowledged from Solido Design Automation Inc.

References

Deb, Kalyanmoy, Pratap, Amrit, Agarwal, Sameer, and Meyarivan, T. (2002). A fast and elitist multiobjective genetic algorithm: Nsga-ii. *IEEE Transactions on Evolutionary Computation*, 6:182–197.

Defoin Platel, Michael, Verel, Sébastien, Clergue, Manuel, and Chami, Malik (2007). Density estimation with genetic programming for inverse problem solving. In et al., Marc Ebner, editor, *Proc. European Conference on Genetic Programming*, volume 4445 of *Lecture Notes in Computer Science*, pages 45–54. Springer.

Drennan, P. and McAndrew, C. (1999). A comprehensive mosfet mismatch model. In *Proc. International Electron Devices Meeting*.

Hastie, T., Tibshirani, R., and Friedman, J.H. (2001). *The Elements of Statistical Learning*. Springer.

Hesterberg, T.C. (1988). *Advances in importance sampling*. PhD thesis, Statistics Department, Stanford University.

Kanj, R., Joshi, R.V., and Nassif, S.R. (2006). Mixture importance sampling and its application to the analysis of sram designs in the presence of rare failure events. In *Proc. Design Automation Conference*, pages 69–72.

Koza, John R. (1992). *Genetic Programming: On the Programming of Computers by Means of Natural Selection*. MIT Press, Cambridge, MA, USA.

McConaghy, T. and Gielen, G.G.E. (2006). Canonical form functions as a simple means for genetic programming to evolve human-interpretable functions. In *Proc. Genetic and Evolutionary Computation Conference*, pages 855–862.

McConaghy, T. and Gielen, G.G.E. (2009). Template-free symbolic performance modeling of analog circuits via canonical form functions and genetic programming. *IEEE Trans. Comput.-Aided Design of Integr. Circuits and Systems*, 28(8):1162–1175.

Vladislavleva, E. (2008). *Model-based Problem Solving through Symbolic Regression via Pareto Genetic Programming*. PhD thesis, Tilburg University.

Whigham, P. A. (2000). Induction of a marsupial density model using genetic programming and spatial relationships. *Ecological Modelling*, 131(2-3):299–317.

Yao, Xin, Member, Senior, Liu, Yong, Member, Student, and Lin, Guangming (1999). Evolutionary programming made faster. *IEEE Transactions on Evolutionary Computation*, 3:82–102.

Chapter 11

GENETIC PROGRAMMING TRANSFORMS IN LINEAR REGRESSION SITUATIONS

Flor Castillo[1], Arthur Kordon[1] and Carlos Villa[1]
[1] *The Dow Chemical Company.*

Abstract   The chapter summarizes the use of Genetic Programming (GP) in Multiple Linear Regression (MLR) to address multicollinearity and Lack of Fit (LOF). The basis of the proposed method is applying appropriate input transforms (model respecification) that deal with these issues while preserving the information content of the original variables. The transforms are selected from symbolic regression models with optimal trade-off between accuracy of prediction and expressional complexity, generated by multiobjective Pareto-front GP. The chapter includes a comparative study of the GP-generated transforms with Ridge Regression, a variant of ordinary Multiple Linear Regression, which has been a useful and commonly employed approach for reducing multicollinearity. The advantages of GP-generated model respecification are clearly defined and demonstrated. Some recommendations for transforms selection are given as well. The application benefits of the proposed approach are illustrated with a real industrial application in one of the broadest empirical modeling areas in manufacturing - robust inferential sensors.   The chapter contributes to increasing the awareness of the potential of GP in statistical model building by MLR.

Keywords: Genetic Programming, Multiple Linear Regression, multicollinearity, soft sensor

1.   Introduction and Considerations of Transform selection

In general, the MLR model with p regressors or predictor (input) variables and one response (output variable) can be represented by:

$$y = \beta_0 + \beta_1 x_1 + \beta_2 x_2 + \ldots + \beta_k x_p + \varepsilon \qquad (11.1)$$

β_i are the regression coefficients estimated from the data by Ordinary Least Squares (OLS). OLS estimators are Best, Linear, and Unbiased Estimators (BLUE). Best refers to the property of having least variance among all other linear estimators. OLS estimators are also a linear function of the observations and are unbiased. That is, the expected value of β_i is the true value. ε is a random error component. The errors (residuals) are assumed to be uncorrelated with zero mean and constant variance, IID $N(0,\sigma^2)$. The constant variance assumption can be checked with plot of residuals, which should not contain any pattern. If the assumption of constant variance is not satisfied, a variance-stabilizing transformation, such as a power transformation of the response, can be considered (Box and Cox, 1964). In this case the response variable is raised to some power λ according to:

$$y^\lambda = \begin{cases} \frac{y^\lambda - 1}{\lambda \dot{y}^{\lambda-1}} & \text{if } \lambda \neq 0 \\ \dot{y}\ln(y) & \text{if } \lambda = 0 \end{cases} \tag{11.2}$$

$\dot{y}$ is the geometric mean and λ is chosen as the value that minimizes the sum squares of the differences between actual output and predicted output (SSE).

On the other hand, if the assumption of uncorrelated errors is not satisfied, OLS is no longer appropriate. This is because the presence of correlated errors causes the least squares estimator of the regression coefficients to be inefficient (they no longer have minimum variance) and produces biased estimates of the standard errors of the regression coefficients. This bias can lead to incorrect hypothesis tests and incorrect conclusions.

Autocorrelation can be detected by a plot of the sample autocorrelation function. When autocorrelation is suspected, the sources underlying the correlation need to be investigated. There are several causes of autocorrelation. One of them may be the omission of important regressors that are correlated with the response. In this situation, identifying and including the omitted inputs will solve autocorrelation. In other cases, autocorrelation occurs because variables are measured in a sequential order in very close proximity; in other words data may be collected at too frequent a time interval. Often manufacturing data sampled in minute time interval are in this category. If autocorrelation can not be resolved, then models that incorporate the correlation structure need to be considered. These models occur often in economics and business and in some engineering applications. The reader is referred to Greene (2002), Mackenzie and McAleer (1994), Harvey and Phillips (1979) and Judge et al. (1985) for a discussion of MLR with correlated errors in Economics literature. For methods of incorporating correlation structure including time series modeling, see Box and Jenkins (2008). Such models require special parameter estimation techniques and are out of the scope of this discussion. Provided that the IID $N(0,\sigma^2)$ assumptions are satisfied MLR can be used. Models may include interactions and non-linear terms in the inputs as presented in equations (11.3) and (11.4).

$$y = \beta_0 + \beta_1 x_1 + \beta_2 x_2 + \beta_{12} x_1 x_2 + \varepsilon \qquad (11.3)$$

$$y = \beta_0 + \beta_1 x_1 + \beta_2 x_1^2 + \varepsilon \qquad (11.4)$$

Thus MLR models are linear with respect to the coefficients regardless of the nonlinearity in the inputs. The use of GP transforms in Multiple Linear Regression addresses two very important issues commonly found in industrial applications: Multicollinearity and Lack of Fit. Successful applications can be found in Castillo (2004, 2006).

Multicollinearity occurs when the predictor variables are highly correlated to each other. This can seriously affect the precision of the estimated regression coefficients, making them sensitive to the data collected and producing large confidence intervals for these coefficients. In this case it is difficult, and even misleading, to assess the relative importance of the regressors in explaining the variation observed in the response. In fact, variables would often show as non-significant even though they may be important.

GP transforms can help to alleviate the issue of multicollinearity by model respecification. One form of model respecification includes finding a functional form that encompasses the relationship among the regressors. For example, if x_1, x_2, x_3 are correlated inputs, it may be possible to find a function such as $x = (x_1 * x_2)/x_3$ or other functional form that preserves the information of the regressors but reduces multicollinearity (Koza, 1992). One limitation of this technique is that the functional relationship among the predictors is often unknown. Here the use of genetic programming (GP) symbolic regression offers a unique opportunity to explore functional forms for model respecification. A second form of respecification may involve transformation of individual predictors. The MLR model with transformed predictor may show less multicollinearity than the model with the original regressors. The third, and perhaps most obvious form of respecification, involves elimination of variables or terms in the MLR equation. This is effective provided that the eliminated variable has no significant impact on the response. Unfortunately, multicollinearity may cause variables to become not significant after other explanatory variables have been accounted for or incorporated in the model. Thus the contribution of variables for variable selection may become difficult.

The second issue in which GP transforms can be helpful is Lack of Fit situations. LOF may be detected by scatter diagrams or residual plots or by a formal LOF test which requires replicated observations (Draper and Smith, 1998). In general, LOF indicates that the functional form being considered is not adequate to fit the data. The reason for LOF needs to be carefully investigated. It may be that a nonlinear relationship with the inputs, such (x^2 or x^{-1}) needs to be considered. In Design of Experiments (DOE) cases, LOF is commonly addressed by collection of additional experimental runs to fit a higher order, often second order, polynomial function that is able to adequately fit the data. In LOF cases GP transforms may help by pointing out a possible transformation that may uncover an underlying relationship between the regressor and the response (i.e. reciprocal, exponential), which accounts for the observed LOF. This may be particularly useful in DOE cases when second order models have already been considered and LOF is still significant.

This chapter is divided into three main cases, Case one, (sections 2-5) provides guidelines about transform selection and includes a comparative study of the GP-generated transforms with the Ridge Regression, a commonly employed approach for reducing multicollinearity. Case two, (section 6) presents a case study using GP transforms to solve Lack of Fit by identifying multiple populations of data. Case three, (section 7) includes an application of GP transforms in a robust inferential sensor design.

2. Case 1. Transform selection

Even though GP transforms show potential in the situations already mentioned, there is little guidance on the choice of transformations from the GP generated models. This is a new field of study and much remains to be done to optimize the transforms via GP. The following are some proposed guidelines:

1. Start with simple transforms (i.e. $1/x$) to facilitate model interpretation. Recall that in a MLR model of the form specified in equation (11.1), the regression coefficients, β, can be interpreted as the amount the response variable y changes when the corresponding regressor changes 1 unit after adjusting for all other regressors. This interpretation is simple and quite helpful and can be used with simple transforms such as:

$$y = \beta_0 + \beta_1(1/x_1) + \beta_2 x_2 + ... + \beta_k x_p + \varepsilon \qquad (11.5)$$

When the model includes interaction terms, such as in equation (11.3), the interpretation is more complicated because the impact of one variable is not the same through the different values of the second variable. In these cases the interpretation of the interaction among two variables x_i and x_j is facilitated by selecting specific levels of one of the variables and observing the impact of changes in the second variable. It is important to note that when transformations are used with MLR, the estimates of the regression coefficients have least square properties with respect to the transformed data and not to the original data. Also the assumptions of IID $N(0,\sigma^2)$ must be verified.

2. If simple transforms are not effective, especially in cases of multicollinearity, more elaborate transforms may be considered since the functional relationships among the regressors such as $x = x_1/x_2$ or $x = x_1 * x_2 * x_3$ may be suggested by GP models. However, keep in mind that transformations involv-

ing two and three variables are difficult to interpret. In special situations when the input variables x_i involve *sizes* and *dimensions*, some transformations may be interpreted to represent *volumes* or *areas*. On the other hand, when ratios of variables are the suggested transforms, interpretation may be simplified by taking the log of each variable instead of the ratio itself. In general, interpretation of transforms involving three or more variables is very challenging and often requires input from mechanistic modelers. These transformations may involve variables such us density, viscosity, velocity etc, which may result in dimensionless quantities (i.e. Reynolds number) which can only be verified and correctly interpreted with first principles.

3. Check for the scientific context of the effect the transformation has on the data. For instance, does the transform split the data in groups such that at least one of the groups has most of the observations belonging to the same group? This may indicate the presence of distinctive populations and thus the need for more than one model. If the log transformation is suggested, the modeler must consider the fundamental effect of this transform. This is especially important with variables exhibiting wide ranges. For example, suppose the following values for the variable x_1 were obtained: 2.75, 7.55, 20.34, and 56.6. The natural log transform will produce: 1, 2, 3, and 4. Although that may be a promising transform, the modeler must investigate if it makes sense to allow the difference between 2.75 and 7.55, which is 1 in the natural log scale, to be the *same* as the difference between 20.34 and 56.6 which is also 1 in the natural log scale. Depending on the variable considered this transform may or may not be suitable.

4. Automatic selection of transformations is not recommended; instead what is preferable is to try to build a model using transforms but incorporating some theory. It is recommended to check the proper physical dimensionality as well (Keijzer and Babovic, 1999). Fundamental knowledge can be incorporated by working together with the experts, verifying the model makes sense. In the next sections we present three case studies of using GP transformations in MLR.

3. Model Respecification Using Genetic Programming and Ridge RegressionRidge Regression

Several methods have been proposed to deal with multicollinearity. One alternative is Ridge Regression (Hoerl and Kennard, 1970). This method decreases multicollinearity by introducing a bias in the parameters estimates. A Ridge parameter estimate is obtained by adding a constant, k, to the least squares estimators and determining the value of k for which the decrease in multicollinearity is more than the increase in the bias. We consider a case study with a data set with large multicollinearity and compare the Ridge Regression method with the approach of model respecification using GP. The data set used consisted of 38 observations of an industrial process with three input variables ($x_1 - x_3$) and one response (y). For details of the data the reader may contact the authors. Because the data had been collected as undesigned data, there was no obvious model structure that linked the data to the model. The following first order MLR model was considered:

$$y = \beta_0 + \beta_1 x_1 + \beta_2 x_2 + \beta_3 x_3 + \beta_{12} x_1 x_2 \beta_{13} x_1 x_3 + \beta_{23} x_2 x_3 \qquad (11.6)$$

where the β_i coefficients are the model parameters estimated by the method of least squares and x_i are coded variables between -1, and 1. The corresponding parameter estimates at 5% significance level are shown in Table 11-1. All analysis were completed using JMP®.

Table 11-1. Parameter estimates case 1.

Term	Estimate	Std Error	t Ratio	Prob>|t|	VIF
Intercept	-0.29	0.35	-0.82	0.42	
x_1	0.68	0.58	1.19	0.24	7.84
x_2	-6.09	1.38	-4.43	<0.001	80.37
x_3	4.30	1.32	3.25	<0.001	73.17
$x_1 * x_2$	5.10	1.59	3.21	<0.001	25.08
$x_1 * x_3$	-4.14	1.89	-2.20	0.04	27.71
$x_2 * x_3$	1.72	0.58	2.97	0.01	1.74

This model has a R^2 of 0.89 and adjusted R^2 of 0.87 but shows significant multicollinearity as evidenced by the large Variance Inflation Factors (VIF). The VIF is $1/(1 - R_j^2)$ where R_j^2 is found by regression of each jth input on the remaining set of regressors included in the model under consideration. Thus for independent inputs R_j^2 is zero and VIF=1. In general, VIF greater than 10 indicates large multicollinearity.

4. The Ridge Regression Method

The Ridge Regression method provides a biased estimator of the regression coefficient which has a smaller variance than the unbiased estimator found by least squares. This biased estimator can be found by solving the following, modified version of the normal equations used by least squares to estimate the regression coefficients:

$$\hat{\beta}_R = (X'X + \kappa I)^{-1} X'y \qquad (11.7)$$

where k is a constant, y is an $n \times 1$ vector of responses; X is an $n \times p$ matrix of the regressor variables, $\hat{\beta}_R$ is the ridge estimator, a $p \times 1$ vector of unknown

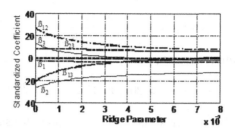

Figure 11-1. Ridge Trace Plot.

constants. The data is standardized to have a zero mean and a variance of 1. Thus $X'X$ and $X'y$ are in correlation form and $\hat{\beta}_R$ are standardized regression coefficients. When $k=0$, the ridge estimator is the least squares estimator. The Mean Square Error (MSE) of the ridge estimator is defined by:

$$MSE(\hat{\beta}_R) = \sigma^2 Tr[(X'X+\kappa I)^{-1}X'X(X'X+\kappa I)^{-1}]+\kappa^2\beta'(X'X+\kappa I)^{-2}\beta$$
(11.8)

The first right hand term of equation (11.8) is the sum of the variances and the second term is the square of the bias. The objective is to select a value of k such that the reduction in the variance term is greater than the increase in squared bias. Several methods were considered to estimate the value of k. The first method was the inspection of the ridge trace (Hoerl and Kennard, 1970b). In this method, standardized regression coefficients for different values of k are calculated and k is selected as the value that stabilizes these coefficients. Figure 11-1 shows the ridge trace for the model considered in equation (11.6). The MATLAB (Statistics Toolbox) Ridge function was used to produce the Ridge trace.

As the value of k increases, some of the ridge estimates change drastically showing the instability of the regression coefficients. From Figure 11-1, an estimate of the value of k that stabilizes the ridge estimates is approximately in the region between 0.005 and 0.007. A more precise value of k was obtained by an analytical solution (Hoerl et al., 1975). In this iterative method the calculated Ridge Regression coefficients, $\hat{\beta}_R$, are used to estimate a new value of k. Starting with k_o, which is the least squares solution: $(k = 0)$.

$$k_0 = \frac{p\hat{\sigma}^2}{\hat{\beta}'\hat{\beta}}$$
(11.9)

$$k_1 = \frac{p\hat{\sigma}^2}{\hat{\beta}'_R(ko)\hat{\beta}'_R(ko)}$$
(11.10)

$$k_1 = \frac{p\hat{\sigma}^2}{\hat{\beta}'_R(k_{j-1})\hat{\beta}'_R(k_{j-1})} \qquad (11.11)$$

The algorithm terminates when;

$$\frac{k_{j-1} - k_j}{k_j} > 20(Tr(X'X)^{-1}/p)^{-1.3} \qquad (11.12)$$

where p is the number of regressors. Table 11-2 shows the standardized coefficients for several values of k. The iterative estimation method produced a value of 0.0061. Table 11-2 also shows the R^2 and the MSE for each ridge model.

Table 11-2. Standardized Coefficients at various values of k.

	k = 0.0000	k = 0.0021	k = 0.0035	k = 0.0046	k = 0.0054	k = 0.0061
$\beta1$	-2.26	-2.99	-3.12	-3.18	-3.21	-3.22
$\beta2$	-26.89	-17.56	-15.52	-14.41	-13.80	-13.36
$\beta3$	13.29	3.14	1.10	0.07	-0.46	-0.82
$\beta12$	26.94	14.33	11.66	10.25	9.50	8.95
$\beta13$	-20.88	-6.47	-3.49	-1.95	-1.13	-0.56
$\beta23$	8.69	7.84	7.54	7.32	7.18	7.07
R2	0.8927	0.8652	0.8547	0.8489	0.8451	0.8424
MSE	0.0034	0.0034	0.0036	0.0037	0.0037	0.0038

The corresponding VIF values for the various values of k are presented in Table 11-3.

Table 11-3. VIF for the various values of k.

	k = 0.0000	k = 0.0021	k = 0.0035	k = 0.0046	k = 0.0054	k = 0.0061
$\beta1$	7.84	6.90	6.46	6.19	6.00	5.86
$\beta2$	80.37	60.84	52.40	47.43	44.08	41.63
$\beta3$	73.17	55.42	47.75	43.24	40.20	37.97
$\beta12$	25.08	22.60	21.21	20.27	19.58	19.03
$\beta13$	27.71	24.69	23.06	21.99	21.19	20.58
$\beta23$	1.74	1.65	1.61	1.59	1.57	1.56

A comparison between the least squares estimator (k=0) with the ridge estimator for the chosen value of k=0.0061, first and last columns of Table 11-2, shows no significant increase in the MSE or loss of R^2. There is however a considerable improvement (decrease) in the maximum VIF from 80.37 for the least squares fit to 41.63 for Ridge Regression fit with k=0.0061 (first and lasts column in Table 11-3). Although a 50% improvement (decrease) in the maximum VIF is being achieved by Ridge Regression, significant multicollinearity is still present.

5.   Model Respecification Using GP

The alternative of redefining the regressors by considering transformation of the inputs was considered. The appropriate choice of inputs transformation is found by using genetic programming (GP) symbolic regression (Koza, 1992). The multiplicity of models provided by GP offers a rich set of possible transformations, otherwise unknown, which have the potential to minimize multicollinearity. The GP algorithm was implemented as a toolbox in MATLAB. The proposed procedure can be found in Castillo et al (2004, 2006) and is briefly discussed here for convenience: In step 1 of the procedure, a set of alternative candidate models in terms of the original variables is produced through GP-generated symbolic regression. Equations are chosen from symbolic regression models with optimal trade-off between accuracy of prediction and expressional complexity, generated by multi-objective Pareto-front GP. In step 2, the relationship between the variables is observed and the original variables are transformed according to the functional form of the relationship revealed by GP-generated models. Then in step 3, a MLR model is fitted to the transformed variables. In step 4 the resulting model is assessed in terms of R^2 and the error structure is evaluated to check the IIDN$(0,\sigma^2)$ assumption needed for least squares estimation. If the assumption of constant variance is violated (see an example in Figure 11-2), a variance-stabilizing power transformation of the response (y) such as a Box- and Cox transformation may be performed (Figure 11-3). In step 5 the error structure is re-evaluated. If the error assumptions are correct, the VIF are checked to ensure that no severe multicollinearity is observed.

The method previously described was applied to the original data. In step 1 the following equation produced by GP was selected:

$$y = 0.17364 + 2.8234e^{x_1}x_2^2 \qquad (11.13)$$

The GP symbolic regression generation takes 20 runs with 500 as the population size, 100 as the number of generations and 4 reproductions per generation. The equation generated by GP indicates an exponential relationship with x_1, and a quadratic relationship with x_2. Table 11-4 shows the transformations applied to the input variables as supplied by the GP function.

Table 11-4.   Input transformations uncovered by GP.

Original Value	Transformed Variable
x_1	$z_1 = exp(x_1)$
x_2	$z_2 = x_2^2$
x_3	$z_3 = x_3$

The MLR model presented in equation (6) was then fitted taking into account the transformed variables (z) presented in Table 11-4. This produced a model with R^2 of 0.90 and adjusted R^2 of 0.88. Table 11-5 shows the parameter estimates of this model. Analyse were performed at the 5% significance level. In Table 11-5, the significant terms have Prob>|t| less than 0.05.

Table 11-5. Parameter estimates for model in transformed inputs.

Term	Estimate	Std Error	Prob>|t|	VIF
Intercept	1.10	0.21	<0.001	
x_3	-0.30	0.22	0.17	2.22
z_1	-1.54	0.32	<0.001	2.32
z_2	0.58	0.33	<0.001	2.68
$x_3 * z_1$	1.37	0.63	0.04	2.34
$x_3 * z_2$	2.18	0.72	<0.001	4.20
$z_1 * z_2$	-3.66	0.63	<0.001	4.70

Note that x_3 is not significant but is involved in significant interactions with z_1 and z_2. According to the procedure, the error structure of this transformed model was evaluated. The corresponding residual plot is presented in 11-2.

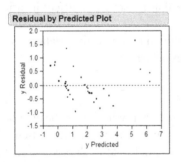

Figure 11-2. Residual plot for FRM model.   *Figure 11-3.* Box-Cox Transformations

Inspection of the residual plot suggests a violation of the assumption of constant variance required by the least-squares method (curve patter observed in Figure 11-2. In this case, a variance stabilizing transformation was performed. The Box and Cox variance stabilizing transformation was considered. A plot λ versus the error sum of squares (SSE) is shown in Figure 11-3. The value of $\lambda=0.2$ was selected as the value that minimizes the SSE. Using $y^{0.2}$ as the response variable according to equation (11.2), the model presented in

Table 11-6. Parameter estimate with $y^{\lambda} = y^{0.2}$.

Term	Estimate	Std Error	t Ratio	Prob>|t|	VIF
Intercept	-0.19	0.12	-1.56	0.13	
x_3	-0.75	0.13	-5.87	<0.001	2.22
z_1	-0.91	0.19	-4.81	<0.001	2.32
z_2	0.13	0.19	0.70	0.49	2.68
$x_3 * z_1$	0.99	0.37	2.70	0.01	2.34
$x_3 * z_2$	0.97	0.42	2.32	0.03	4.19
$z_1 * z_2$	-1.56	0.37	-4.19	<0.001	4.7

equation (11.6) was fit to the data. The parameter estimates are presented in Table 11-6.

The assumption of IID $N(0,\sigma^2)$ was re-evaluated and no violation in this assumption was detected. Lastly, multicollinearity was evaluated using VIF values which are shown in the last column of 11-6. Note that none of the VIF values was greater than 10. The maximum VIF is 4.7. Recall that the maximum VIF for the least squares estimation was 80.37 and 41.63 for the Ridge estimator with k=0.0061. Thus compared with the Ridge Regression estimates, the VIF has been greatly improved by model respecification considering the input transformations found by GP and no indication of severe multicollinearity exists at this point. The advantage of this approach is the potential to alleviate multicollinearity without introducing bias in the parameter estimates.

6. Case 2. GP transform in LOF: Detecting Multiple Populations of Data in Experimental Design Situations

In Design of Experiments (DOE) situations, the variables and their levels are selected in such way to produce orthogonal regressors so multicollinearity is avoided and the effect of the variables and interactions can be quantified. A MLR model is fit to the data and the capability of the model to represent the data can be assessed through a formal Lack of Fit (LOF) test when experimental replicates are available. Significant LOF indicates that the functional form of the model initially considered is not appropriate. A more adequate model may be found by adding experimental runs and fitting a polynomial of higher order. Specialized designs such as the Central Composite Design are available for this purpose (Box and Draper, 1987). In some cases however, even the higher order polynomial does not resolve LOF. Sometimes the reason for LOF is the presence of multiple populations in the response variable. This can be the case for example, in systems with multiple steady states (Villa et al., 2004) or systems where product characteristics change for a set of experimental runs. Unfortunately, this situation is often unknown before hand. Being able to detect the situation is of critical importance for proper analysis and interpretation of the available data. In this case study, GP transforms were used as an alternative to solve LOF in a second order polynomial. The GP transforms alleviate LOF by uncovering the existence of multiple populations of data in the response variable. This study is presented in Castillo (2008). The data set consisted of a 2^4 factorial design with three center points that was set up to explore and quantify the effects of four input variables (x_1, x_2, x_3, x_4) on a response variable (y). A total of 19 experiments were performed. The 2^4 design with three center points is shown in Table 11-7 (runs 1-19). The factors were coded to a value of -1 at the low level, +1 at the high level, and 0 at the center point.

Table 11-7. Experimental Data.

Run	x_1	x_2	x_3	x_4	y	Run	x_1	x_2	x_3	x_4	y
1	1	-1	1	-1	23.3	15	1	-1	1	1	8.44
2	-1	1	1	1	2.48	16	0	0	0	0	8.68
3	-1	-1	1	-1	3.76	17	1	-1	1	-1	8.04
4	1	1	1	-1	35.3	18	-1	1	1	-1	8.04
5	-1	1	1	1	7.88	19	1	-1	1	1	4.72
6	-1	-1	1	-1	8.93	20	0	0	1	0	6.75
7	1	1	1	1	15.0	21	0	0	0	1	2.21
8	0	0	0	0	6.81	22	0	0	1	0	13.5
9	-1	-1	1	1	4.32	23	1	0	0	0	8.86
10	-1	-1	1	1	5.24	24	0	0	0	-1	na
11	1	1	1	-1	29.4	25	-1	0	0	0	6.68
12	0	0	0	0	7.88	26	0	-1	0	0	4.09
13	-1	1	1	-1	45.7	27	0	1	0	0	17.3
14	1	1	1	1	6.13						

Using the data from the 2^4 design, the response variable (y) was fit to the following first-order MLR model: All analysis were performed with 5% significance level.

$$y = \beta_0 + \sum_{i=1}^{k} \beta_i x_i + \sum \sum_{i<j} \beta_{ij} x_i x_j \qquad (11.14)$$

The model obtained had an adjusted R^2 of 0.67 and exhibited significant LOF (p=0.0140). In order to address the Lack of Fit, additional experiments were planned to complete a Central Composite Design. These additional experimental runs correspond to runs 20-27 in Table 11-7. With these additional runs the following second-order polynomial model was fit by MLR.

$$y = \beta_0 + \sum_{i=1}^{k} \beta_i x_i + \sum \beta_{ii} x_i^2 + \sum \sum_{i<j} \beta_{ij} x_i x_j \qquad (11.15)$$

This second-order model obtained using the complete Central Composite Design had an adjusted R^2 of 0.76. However, it still exhibited significant Lack of Fit (p=0.0258). Removal of LOF in this situation is particularly challenging because a second-order model had already been considered. The alternative of adding experiments to fit a third-order polynomial is not feasible because it is costly, may require experiments at unfeasible experimental conditions, introduces correlations among the model parameters, and cannot guarantee that the resulting model will not have significant LOF. In this situation GP transforms were considered. The GP symbolic regression generation takes 20 runs with 500 as the population size, 100 as the number of generations and 4 reproductions per generation. Many equations were generated. Among the multiple equations generated, the expressions shown in Table 11-8 were the most often encountered.

Table 11-8. Expression most often encountered in GP-generated symbolic regression.

Original Term	Expression
x_4	$\lvert \ln(x_4) \rvert$
x_2	$\sqrt{x_2}$

The expression for x_2 presented in Table 11-8 indicates a non-linear relationship in this input. However, the $\ln(x_4)$ expression called special attention since input x_4 corresponded to the concentration of a particular species in which the low level of concentration encountered was zero (equivalent to-1 in the coded form presented in Table 11-7). By taking the $\ln(x_4)$ the GP algorithm eliminated the observations where x_4 was zero and produced equations with high fitness in the remaining data. This transform split the data into distinctive groups suggesting the presence of two separate groups of data previously unknown: one for x_4 equal to zero (-1 in the coded from shown in Table 11-7), and one for values of x_4 greater than zero.

Additional investigation revealed that when x_4 was equal to zero, a product with very different characteristics was obtained. This is a significant finding and explains why the addition of experimental runs to fit a second-order polynomial was not enough to remove Lack of Fit.

The two populations or groups of data were separated and a model was fit for values of x_4 greater than zero. This includes 18 observations from Table 11-

7 which provided enough degrees of freedom to fit a model in the four input variables. This model considers the linear and interaction effects of the four input variables and the quadratic effect of input x_2. The analysis revealed a very significant regression equation (p=0.0002) with no Lack of Fit (p=0.2405) and an adjusted R^2 of 0.85. The corresponding parameter estimates are presented in Table 11-9.

Table 11-9. Parameter Estimates Model with $x_4 > 0$.

Term	Estimate	Std Error	t Ratio	Prob>|t|	VIF
Intercept	8.26	0.59	14.01	<0.0001	
x_1	1.66	0.51	3.22	0.0092	1
x_2	6.61	1.15	5.74	<0.001	5
x_3	-2.57	0.51	-4.99	<0.001	1
x_4	-4.74	1.03	-4.58	0.001	1.8
$x_2 * x_3$	-1.20	0.58	-2.09	0.063	1
$x_2 * x_4$	-5.51	1.29	-4.28	0.002	5
$x_2 * x_2$	3.09	1.04	2.97	0.014	1.8

The error structure from the model was evaluated to check the IIDN(0,σ^2) assumption. The residual plot (not shown) did not suggest violation in these assumptions. Finally, multicollinearity was evaluated using Variance Inflation Factors (VIF). This was necessary because the separation of the groups reduced the data available for model fitting which could induce multicollinearity. The VIF values presented in the last column of Table 11-9 indicate no real concerns regarding multicollinearity.

In this study the use of GP transforms aided in alleviating LOF by identifying two populations of data. Being able to detect this situation is of critical importance for the proper statistical analysis of data and removal of LOF. The study illustrates the importance of investigating the reasons for LOF beyond just the application of higher order terms or nonlinear transforms. Further research is necessary especially in cases where more that two populations are identified.

7.   Case 3. GP Transforms in Inferential Sensors Applications

One of the first application areas of GP in industry is inferential sensors (Kordon et al., 2003). Inferential or soft sensors are empirical models that infer expensive quality measurements from cheap process sensors, such as temperature, pressure, and flow. At the basis of inferential sensors is the underlying assumption that there is a relationship between the inputs and the outputs. It is desirable to approximate this relationship by a MLR model. This is due to the nice properties of OLS estimators. Process engineers prefer the symbolic regression-type inferential sensors over the commercially available neural network-based solutions due to their explicit mathematical form and potential for physical interpretation. Recently, the demand for GP-based inferential sensors is growing. However, the issues of handling multicollinearity in the data and offering reliable confidence limits of the estimated parameters are critical for successful scale-up of the technology. An example of using GP transforms in resolving these issues is shown in this section.

Multicollineary of the data from a manufacturing process is more a rule than an exception. Very often the cause of multicollinearity is based on the laws of physics, as is the case of different temperatures in a chemical reactor. Additionally, observations from these processes are likely to be autocorrelated. As mentioned before, autocorrelation hinders statistical analysis with OLS.

When autocorrelation is suspected, the sources underlying this are investigated. In some cases, autocorrelation occurs because variables are measured in a sequential order at too small time interval. Efforts to reduce the autocorrelation in this situation may include decreasing the frequency of data collection. This approach is used in Statistical Process Control (Psydek ,1992) and other applications (Swihart and Slade, 1985). Observations are more likely to be independent the further away they are in time. However it is important to note that information may be missing by decreasing too much the sample frequency. Another approach to deal with autocorrelation, often used with simulation models, includes averaging during specified periods of time (Thesen and Travis, 1992).

When deciding about data collection frequency, it is critical to consider the goal of the study since the data must be representative of the circumstances for which it is intended to be used. While statistical independence may be critical for some analysis (low frequency data), high frequency data may be necessary for other analysis as is the case of patterns. Thus depending on the application it may or may not make sense to sample at lower frequencies. Furthermore, if the autocorrelation between data points that are close to each other cannot be ignored, a time series approach, with models that incorporate the autocorrelation structure should be used. This case study is based on a real-world application of an inferential sensor for a chemical property based on six process measurements. The original data included 696 observations with a sampling time of 10 minutes. The autocorrelation function using JMP®shows high autocorrelation up to lag 13. This was likely due to a very frequent data collection. In an attempt to produce independent observations, the sample interval was incremented. After taking every 15th sample, the autocorrelation was eliminated and the final data set includes six input variables and 46 independent observations. A MLR model of type 11-1 was then developed with R^2 of 0.91 and its estimated parameters are given in Table 11-10. All analysis were at 5% significance level (input 2 is removed as statistically insignificant).

Table 11-10. Parameter estimates of inferential sensor MLR.

Term	Estimate	Std Error	t Ratio	Prob>|t|	VIF
Intercept	-145.50	159.65	-0.91	0.37	
x_1	679.19	165.94	4.09	<0.001	852.64
x_3	9.30	0.82	11.34	<0.001	2.78
x_4	-662.17	163.49	-4.05	<0.001	15884.55
x_5	1.44	0.35	4.15	<0.001	11401.95
x_6	-8.93	1.72	-5.20	<0.0001	3.04

As it is shown in Table 11-10, the VIFs for x_1, x_4 and x_5 are very large and it is difficult to interpret the strength of the relationship between the inputs and the output. It is not recommended to be applied on-line.

The proposed approach of using GP-generated transforms to reduce multi-collinearity has been implemented. The transforms have been selected from models, generated by Pareto-front GP (Smits and Kotanchek, 2004) with the following key optimal settings, recommended by (Castillo et al., 2007): 20 runs, 25 cascades, 25 generations, and population size of 200. The Pareto front on the accuracy-complexity plane is shown in Figure 11-4, where the selected models with optimal trade-off between accuracy and complexity are shown with arrows.

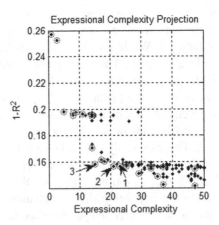

Figure 11-4. Pareto front of generated symbolic regression models for inferential sensorinferential sensor.

Note that all the three selected models have similar accuracy (R^2 is 0.85 - 0.86) and are with relatively low complexity (measured by the total number of nodes in all sub-expressions). In addition, these three models offer different transforms, described below.

GPModel1 is the following equation with R^2 of 0.86:

$$y_{GPModel1} = -53.0537 + 0.03215 * (x_5 + x_3^2 - x_6^2) \qquad (11.16)$$

The following transforms have been defined:

$$z_1 = x_3^2 \qquad (11.17)$$

$$z_2 = x_6^2 \qquad (11.18)$$

The parameters of the corresponding MLR model of type (1) are shown in Table 11-11.

Table 11-11. Parameter estimates of inferential sensor MLR model1.

Term	Estimate	Std Error	t Ratio	Prob>|t|	VIF
Intercept	-112.98	82.75	-1.37	0.18	
x_5	0.03	0.01	5.66	<0.0001	2.5
z_1	0.03	0.00	9.60	<0.0001	1.7
z_2	-0.03	0.01	-3.26	0.002	2.4

As it is seen from Table 11-11, the VIF has been significantly reduced and the interpretability of the estimates is very clear. Note the opposite impact of z_1 and z_2 (associated with x_3 and x_6). The residual plot, not shown, does not indicate violations in the IID $N(0,\sigma^2)$ assumption.

GPModel2 is the following equation with R^2 of 0.86:

$$y_{GPModel2} = -8.1312 + 0.11664 * (\sqrt{x_5} * (x_3 + x_4 - x_6)) \qquad (11.19)$$

$$Z_3 = \sqrt{x_5} \qquad (11.20)$$

The parameters of the corresponding MLR model of type (11-1) are shown in Table 11-12.

As it is clearly seen from Table 11-12, the VIF has been significantly reduced. However two VIF exceed 20 showing large multicollinearity for x_4 and z_3.

The third interesting model on the Pareto front is the following equation with R^2 of 0.85:

$$y_{GPModel3} = -423.6894 + 3.408 * (x_5 + (x_3/x_6)^2) \qquad (11.21)$$

The following obvious transform can be defined:

Table 11-12. Parameter estimates of inferential sensor MLR model2.

Term	Estimate	Std Error	t Ratio	Prob>|t|	VIF
Intercept	-239.51	207.19	-1.16	0.25	
x_3	7.23	0.77	9.36	<0.0001	1.76
x_4	7.42	8.39	0.88	0.382	29.89
x_6	-6.40	1.89	-3.38	0.002	2.64
z_3	2.20	2.53	0.87	0.390	26.98

$$z_4 = (x_3/x_6)^2 \qquad (11.22)$$

It is a valid transform and the corresponding MLR equation3 (not shown) eliminates multicollinearity. However, since the ratio of the variables is the suggested transform rather than the variables themselves, a transform based on the logarithms is suggested as specified by the generic recommendations given previously.

$$z_5 = \ln(x_3) \qquad (11.23)$$

$$z_6 = \ln(x_6) \qquad (11.24)$$

The parameters estimates of the corresponding MLR model of type (11-1) are shown in Table 11-13.

Table 11-13. Parameter estimates of inferential sensor MLR model4.

Term	Estimate	Std Error	t Ratio	Prob>|t|	VIF
Intercept	-1008.34	911.53	-1.11	0.275	
x_5	0.03	0.01	5.67	<0.0001	2.51
z_5	881.63	89.80	9.82	<0.0001	1.74
z_6	-680.93	201.73	-3.38	0.002	2.46

As it is seen from Table 11-13, the VIF has been significantly reduced and with the last two transforms the interpretability of the estimates is very clear. Note again the opposite impact of x_6 and x_3 (z_5 and z_6) The error structure, not shown, did not violate the IID $N(0,\sigma^2)$ assumptions . The suggested transforms in the first and third models significantly reduced multicollinearity and the resulting MLR models are with similar performance as the original MLR model but with stable behavior. As such, they can be implemented for on-line operation. One key advantage of the proposed MLR models is their capability

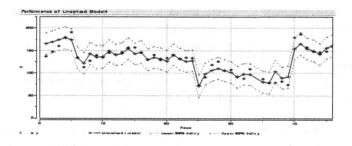

Figure 11-5. Inferential sensor predictions with confidence limits based on MLR model 4.

to show the confidence limits of the predictions, which is critical for inferential sensors with infrequent real measurements (Kordon et al., 2006). An example of inferential sensor predictions with confidence limits, based on MLR model 4 is shown in Figure 11-5.

8. Summary

Symbolic regression based on Pareto Front GP is a key approach for generating transforms and relationships among variables otherwise unknown which can be used in MLR situations. The results from implementing GP transforms show the potential of this approach in MLR, especially in solving problems with multicollinearity and LOF. Automatic selection of transforms is not recommended. Transform selection is only successful if it can be interpreted with fundamental knowledge. Much remains to be done in this field. Specifically the use of the transforms when autocorrelation cannot be ignored and OLS cannot be used.

Acknowledgements: Helpful suggestions by the reviewers is gratefully acknowledged.

References

Box, G.E.P. and Cox, D.R. (1964). An analysis of transformations. *J. R. Stat. Soc. Series B*, 26:211–243.

Box, G.E.P and Draper, N. R. (1987). John Wiley and Sons, New York.

Castillo, F., Kordon, A., and Smits, G. (2007). *Robust Pareto Front Genetic Programming Parameter Selection Based on Design of Experiments and Industrial Data*, pages 149–166. Springer, New York.

Draper, N. R. and Smith, H. (1998). *Applied Regression Analysis*. Wiley, New York.

Hoerl, A. E., Kennard, R.W., and Baldwin, K. F. (1975). Ridge regression: Some simulation. *Commun. Statis.*, 4:105–123.

Hoerl, Arthur E. and Kennard, Robert W. (1970). Ridge regression: Biased estimation for nonorthogonal problems. *Technometrics*, 12(1):55–67.

Keijzer, M. and Babovic, V. (1999). Dimensionally aware genetic programming. In *Proceedings of the Genetic and Evolutionary Computation Conference*, volume 2, pages 1069–1076, Orlando, FL, USA.

Kordon, A., Smits, G., Jordaan, E., Kalos, A., and Chiang, L. (2006). Empirical models with self-assessment capabilities for on-line industrial applications. In *Proceedings of CEC 2006*, pages 10463–10470, Vancouver.

Kordon, A., Smits, G., Kalos, A., and Jordaan, E. (2003). *Robust Soft Sensor Development Using Genetic Programming*, pages 69–108. Elsevier, Amsterdam.

Koza, J. (1992). *Genetic Programming: On the Programming of Computers by Means of Natural Selection*. MIT Press, Cambridge, MA.

Smits, G. and Kotanchek, M. (2004). *Pareto-front exploitation in symbolic regression*. Springer, New York.

Swihart, R.K. and Slade, N.A. (1985). Testing for independence of observations in animal movements. *Ecology*, 66:1176–1184.

Thesen, A. and Travis, L.E. (1992). *Simulation for Decision Making*. West Publishing Company.

Villa, C.M., Mazy, J.P, Castillo, F., Thompson, L.H., and Weston, J.W. (2004). Model validation in chemical process with multiple steady states. In *Proceedings of the Fourth International Conference on Sensitivity Analysis of Modeling Output*.

Chapter 12

EXPLOITING EXPERT KNOWLEDGE OF PROTEIN-PROTEIN INTERACTIONS IN A COMPUTATIONAL EVOLUTION SYSTEM FOR DETECTING EPISTASIS

Kristine A. Pattin[†], Joshua L. Payne[†], Douglas P. Hill, Thomas Caldwell, Jonathan M. Fisher, and Jason H. Moore
Dartmouth Medical Scool, One Medical Center Drive, HB7937, Lebanon, NH 03756 USA
[†] *These authors contributed equally to this work.*

Abstract   The etiology of common human disease often involves a complex genetic architecture, where numerous points of genetic variation interact to influence disease susceptibility. Automating the detection of such epistatic genetic risk factors poses a major computational challenge, as the number of possible gene-gene interactions increases combinatorially with the number of sequence variations. Previously, we addressed this challenge with the development of a computational evolution system (CES) that incorporates greater biological realism than traditional artificial evolution methods. Our results demonstrated that CES is capable of efficiently navigating these large and rugged epistatic landscapes toward the discovery of biologically meaningful genetic models of disease predisposition. Further, we have shown that the efficacy of CES is improved dramatically when the system is provided with statistical expert knowledge. We anticipate that biological expert knowledge, such as genetic regulatory or protein-protein interaction maps, will provide complementary information, and further improve the ability of CES to model the genetic architectures of common human disease. The goal of this study is to test this hypothesis, utilizing publicly available protein-protein interaction information. We show that by incorporating this source of expert knowledge, the system is able to identify functional interactions that represent more concise models of disease susceptibility with improved accuracy. Our ability to incorporate biological knowledge into learning algorithms is an essential step toward the routine use of methods such as CES for identifying genetic risk factors for common human diseases.

Keywords: Computational Evolution, , Genetic Epidemiology, , Epistasis, , Protein-Protein Interactions

1.   Introduction

Recent developments in high-throughput genotyping technologies have allowed for inexpensive and dense mappings of the human genome. These mappings often comprise single nucleotide polymorphisms (SNPs), which are single nucleotide pairs that vary among people. SNPs are of interest because they constitute the most abundant form of genetic variation in human populations, and thus offer the potential to act as reliable markers of disease-causing genetic variants. Genome-wide association studies (GWAS), measuring 10^6 or more SNPs per individual, are becoming a standard methodology for the detection of genetic risk factors of human disease. Though these studies have generated a wealth of data, few have successfully identified single sequence variants that are highly predictive of clinical endpoints. Moreover, recent analyses of the robustness and evolvability of regulatory and proteomic interaction networks (Albert et al., 2000; Aldana et al., 2007; Jeong et al., 2001) suggest that phenotypic aberrations, such as disease state, rarely result from single points of failure, but more often from the confluence of a number of interacting components. Taken together, these observations suggest that common human diseases possess complex genotype-phenotype maps, with multiple interacting genetic factors influencing disease susceptibility (Moore, 2003; Moore and Williams, 2009).

The development of computational methods that aid in the discovery and characterization of epistatic interactions in GWAS datasets is therefore of the utmost importance (Cordell, 2009; Moore and Williams, 2009; Moore et al., 2010). Specifically, there are two important computational challenges that need to be addressed (Moore et al., 2010). First, we need data mining, machine learning and computational intelligence algorithms that are capable of modeling nonlinear relationships between multiple SNPs and clinical endpoints such as disease susceptibility. Second, we need powerful search algorithms that are able to identify optimal nonlinear models in large, rugged fitness landscapes. Unfortunately, exhaustive methods that enumerate all possible SNP combinations are infeasible for this problem, because the number of possible combinations grows exponentially with the number of SNPs. For example, in an analysis of one million candidate SNPs, there are 5×10^{11} pair-wise combinations and 1.7×10^{17} three-way combinations to consider.

For the purpose of this study, we focus on machine learning and computational approaches to this problem. Notable examples of prior work include multifactor dimensionality reduction (Ritchie et al., 2001) and random chemistry (Eppstein et al., 2007). In addition, artificial evolution approaches, such as genetic programming (Moore and White, 2007), have been investigated. In their canonical form, these methods have demonstrated limited success, due to their reliance on the presence of building blocks. As the primary characteristic of an epistatic genetic architecture is the absence of individual genetic effects, these artificial evolution methods lack the critical components needed to piece together an effective solution. In an effort to provide these critical components, several studies have investigated the effect of including statistical expert knowledge (Greene et al., 2009c; Greene et al., 2009d; Moore and White, 2006; Moore and White, 2007), as derived from a family of machine learning techniques known as Relief (Kononenko, 1994). This expert knowledge consists of a population-level estimate of the probability with which a SNP is associated with disease status, via individual or interaction effects. These probabilities are then be used to bias variation operators (Greene et al., 2009c) or population initialization (Greene et al., 2009d) toward SNPs that are thought to be associated with disease, effectively seeding the population with the necessary building blocks.

While such statistical expert knowledge has improved the applicability of artificial evolution methods for epistasis analysis, it has been suggested (Banzhaf et al., 2006) that the incorporation of greater biological realism may offer further performance improvements. Specifically, Banzhaf et al. (2006) have called for the development of open-ended computational evolution systems (CES) that attempt to emulate, rather than ignore, the complexities of biological systems. Paying heed to this call, we have recently developed a hierarchical, spatially-explicit CES that allows for the evolution of arbitrarily complex solutions and solution operators, and includes population memory via archives, feedback loops between archives and solutions, and environmental sensing (Moore et al., 2008; Moore et al., 2009; Greene et al., 2009b; Payne et al., 2010). Analyses of this system have demonstrated its ability to identify complex disease-causing genetic architectures in simulated data, and to recognize and exploit useful sources of expert knowledge. Specifically, we have shown that statistical expert knowledge, in the form of ReliefF scores, can be incorporated via environmental sensing (Greene et al., 2009b) and population initialization (Payne et al., 2010) to improve system performance. In addition to the statistical expert knowledge provided by machine learning techniques, there are numerous sources of biological expert knowledge that could be used to improve the performance of CES. For example, information regarding biochemical pathways, regulatory networks, and protein-protein interactions (PPIs) could be used to bias CES toward pathways or gene combinations that are known to interact experimentally. Indeed, such an approach has already proven successful in other GWAS (Askland et al., 2009; Emily et al., 2009).

Here, we investigate the use of biological expert knowledge of PPIs, extracted from the Search Tool for the Retrieval of Interacting Genes/Proteins (STRING) database. To accommodate these data in CES, we extend two previously developed variation operators, so that solution construction is biased toward the inclusion of experimentally verified molecular interactions. We compare the performance of CES with and without this form of biological expert knowledge in the task of identifying an artificial two-locus epistatic genetic relationship in the background of real human genetic data.

2.   Conceptual Overview of the Problem

Since the structure of a protein interaction network is directly influenced by genetic variation, protein-protein interaction information may prove a valuable source of expert knowledge for CES. In Figure 12-1, we provide an overview of how we test this hypothesis in the current study. We evaluate the ability of CES to detect an artificial two-locus epistatic signal, generated from a genetic penetrance table (Fig 12-1A), that we placed in a real genetic bladder cancer background (Fig 12-1B). We selected two SNPs located in two separate genes (Fig 12-1C) to represent the epistatic signal such that this gene pair exhibited a validated protein-protein interaction (Fig 12-1D) in the STRING database (Fig 12-1E). Since we wish to understand the sensitivity of CES to PPI information, we generated data for interaction scenarios of varying strength, as described below.

3.   Methods

In this section, we first present our computational evolution system, highlighting the algorithmic adjustments made to accommodate protein-protein interaction information. We then discuss the database from which this biological expert knowledge was drawn, and the genetic data used for performance testing. Lastly, we present our experimental design.

Computational Evolution System

In Figure 12-2, we provide a graphical overview of CES, which is both hierarchically organized and spatially explicit. The bottom level of the hierarchy consists of a lattice of solutions (Fig. 12-2d), which compete with one another within spatially-localized, overlapping neighborhoods. The second layer of the hierarchy contains a lattice of arbitrarily complex solution operators (Fig. 12-2c), which operate on the solutions in the lower layer. The third layer of the hierarchy contains a lattice of mutation operators (Fig. 12-2b), which modify the solution operators in the second layer, and the highest layer of the hierarchy governs the rate at which the mutation operators are modified (Fig. 12-2a). CES includes environmental noise (Fig. 12-2h), which perturbs the attribute values of the solutions with probability p_{noise}, as they are read from the input data. Intermediate values of p_{noise} allow for the escape of local optima, and improve classification power (Greene et al., 2009a). In this study, $p_{noise} = 0.07$. CES also possesses an attribute archive (Fig. 12-2g), which stores the frequencies with which attributes are used. The solution operators can then exploit these

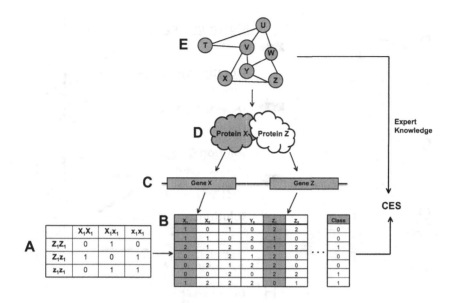

Figure 12-1. Overview of data generation and the integration of biological expert knowledge in CES. To assess the performance of CES on human data when provided with expert knowledge from protein-protein interactions, we merged an artificial two-locus epistatic signal with a real genetic dataset. This artificial signal was generated from a penetrance table (A) and represented by two SNPs selected from the bladder cancer dataset (B). Here, these SNPs are denoted X_1 and Z_1, and are located on different genes (C) whose protein products are a validated protein-protein interaction (D) in the STRING database (E).

data to bias the construction of solutions toward frequently utilized attributes. To conduct a more transparent analysis of the influence of biological expert knowledge on system performance, we prohibit the use of the archive in this study.

Solution Representation, Fitness Evaluation, and Selection

Each solution represents a classifier, which takes a set of SNPs as input and produces an output that can be used to assign diseased or healthy status. These solutions are represented as stacks, where each element in the stack consists of a function and two operands (Fig. 12-2). The function set contains $+, -, *, \%, <, \leq, >, \geq, ==, \neq$, where $\%$ denotes protected modulus (i.e., $x \% 0 = x$ (Langdon, 1998)). Operands are either SNPs, constants, or the output of another element in the stack (Fig. 12-2).

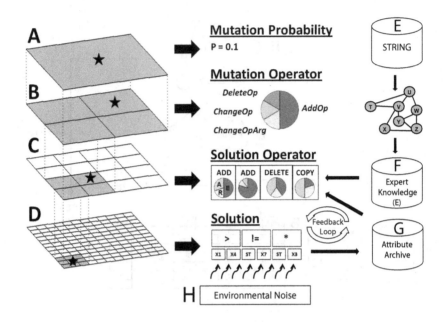

Figure 12-2. Visual overview of our computational evolution system for discovering symbolic discriminant functions that differentiate disease subjects from healthy subjects using information about single nucleotide polymorphisms (SNPs). The hierarchical structure is shown on the left while some specific examples at each level are shown in the middle. At the lowest level (D) is a grid of solutions. Each solution consists of a list of functions and their arguments (e.g. X1 is an attribute) that are evaluated using a stack (denoted by ST in the solution). The next level up (C) is a grid of solution operators that each consist of some combination of the ADD, ALTER, COPY, DELETE, and REPLACE functions and their respective set of probabilities that define whether expert knowledge (F) based on protein-protein interaction information from the STRING database (E) is used instead of a random generator (denoted by R in the probability pie). The attribute archive (G) is derived from the frequency with which each attribute occurs among solutions in the population. For this study, use of the attribute archive was prohibited. Finally, environmental noise (H) perturbs the data to prevent over fitting. The top two levels of the hierarchy (A and B) exist to generate variability in the operators that modify the solutions. A 12×12 grid is shown here as an example.

Each solution produces a discrete output S_i when applied to an individual i. Symbolic discriminant analysis (Moore et al., 2002) is then used to map this output to a classification rule, as follows. The solution is independently applied to the set of diseased and healthy individuals to obtain two separate distributions of outputs, $S^{diseased}$ and $S^{healthy}$, respectively. A classification threshold S_0 is then calculated as the arithmetic mean of these two distributions. The corresponding solution classifies individual i as diseased if $S_i > S_0$ and healthy otherwise. Solution accuracy is assessed through a comparison of predicted and actual clinical endpoints. Specifically, the number of true positives (TP), false positives (FP), true negatives (TN), and false negatives (FN) are used to calculate accuracy as

$$A = \frac{1}{2}\left(\frac{TP}{TP+FN} + \frac{TN}{TN+FP}\right). \tag{12.1}$$

Solution fitness is then given as a function of accuracy and solution length L

$$f = A + \frac{\alpha}{L}, \tag{12.2}$$

where α is a tunable parameter used to encourage parsimony (for all experiments reported here, $\alpha = 0.001$).

The population is organized on a two-dimensional lattice with periodic boundary conditions. Each solution occupies a single lattice site, and competes with the solutions occupying the eight spatially adjacent sites. Selection is both synchronous and elitist, such that the solution of highest fitness within a given neighborhood is always selected to repopulate the focal site of that neighborhood. Reproduction is either sexual or asexual, as dictated by the evolvable solution operators that reside in the next layer of the hierarchy.

The population is initialized by randomly generating solutions with one, three, and seven elements, in equal proportions. Functions are selected at random with uniform probability from the function set and SNP attributes are selected using an enumerative scheme. Specifically, SNPs are drawn with uniform probability and without replacement until all SNPs are represented. The attribute pool is then regenerated as a new random permutation of the SNPs, and the process is repeated, until the attribute requirements of all solutions are satisfied.

Solution Operators

CES allows for the evolution of arbitrarily complex variation operators. This is achieved by initializing the solution operator lattice (Fig. 12-2c) with a set of five basic building blocks (COPY, REPLACE, DELETE, ADD, ALTER), which can be recombined in any way to form new operators. The COPY operator inserts a random element of the focal solution stack into the stack of a randomly chosen neighboring solution. The REPLACE operator extracts a sequence of random length from a neighboring solution stack and overwrites a randomly chosen sequence of the focal solution stack with that information, and the DELETE operator removes an element from the focal solution stack.

In this study, the ADD and ALTER operators were modified to incorporate the biological expert knowledge of PPIs (Fig. 12-3). Specifically, the ADD operator (Fig. 12-3c) places a randomly chosen function and its arguments

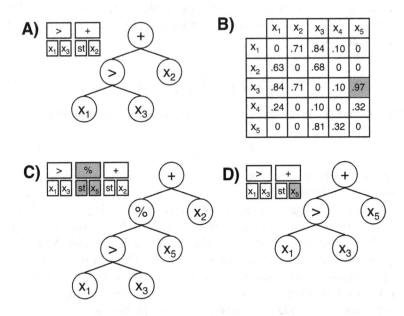

Figure 12-3. (A) In CES, solutions are represented using stacks, which naturally translate into the parse tree representations commonly used in genetic programming (Poli et al., 2008). To provide the variation operators with the biological expert knowledge of protein-protein interactions, we explicitly maintain an interaction matrix (B), where each element corresponds to the confidence score of that interaction. These scores are used to bias the selection of attributes in the solution operators, as illustrated for the (C) ADD and (D) ALTER operators. (C) The ADD operator chooses a random location in the stack and inserts a new element (shown in gray), which consists of a randomly generated function and two attributes. SNP attributes are selected by finding the nearest existing upstream SNP in the stack (x_3) and then choosing an interacting SNP from the PPI data (B) with probability proportional to the confidence score. In this case, x_5 is selected. (D) The ALTER operator chooses a random element in the stack and mutates its function, or one of its attributes. If a SNP is selected for mutation, then a new SNP is chosen in the same fashion as the ADD operator.

into an arbitrary location of the focal solution stack (Fig. 12-3a). The first argument is selected with uniform probability from three choices: stack output, constant, or attribute. If the argument is chosen to be an attribute, then the nearest upstream SNP in the list representation of the stack is identified. The PPI data for that SNP is then queried, and one of its interacting SNPs is selected (Fig. 12-3b). If the second argument is also chosen to be an attribute, then the PPI data corresponding to the first attribute is queried, and another interacting SNP is selected.

The ALTER operator (Fig. 12-3d) randomly chooses an element from the focal solution stack (Fig. 12-3a) and mutates either its function, or one of its input arguments. If the function is chosen for mutation, it is replaced by a randomly chosen function. If an input argument is selected for mutation, it can be replaced by the stack output, a constant, or an attribute. If the argument is chosen to be an attribute, then the corresponding SNP is selected in the same fashion as in the ADD operator.

In both the ADD and ALTER operators, SNPs were selected from the PPI data with probability proportional to their confidence scores. We used an exponential scaling function to increase the probability with which SNP pairings of high confidence were selected. Let $\vec{I}$ denote the vector of k SNPs with which SNP i interacts, and $\vec{S}$ denote the corresponding vector of confidence scores. The probability with which an interacting SNP $\vec{I}_j$ is selected is given by

$$p_{j|i} = \phi^z \tag{12.3}$$

where

$$z = \frac{(k-1)(\max(\vec{S}) - \vec{S}_j)}{(\max(\vec{S}) - \min(\vec{S}))}. \tag{12.4}$$

This mapping of raw confidence scores to selection probabilities has two main features: (i) selection probability decrease exponentially with decreasing confidence, and (ii) all probabilities fall in the range $(0, 1)$. The severity of the exponential decrease is controlled by ϕ. For all experiments considered herein, $\phi = 0.95$.

Solution operators possess evolvable probability vectors that determine the frequency with which functions and attributes are selected at random, from expert knowledge sources, or archives (Fig. 12-2). To highlight the influence of biological expert knowledge on system performance, functions were always chosen at random, and attributes were always selected based on the biological expert knowledge of PPIs, except for the control experiments, where attributes were selected at random.

The solution operators reside on a periodic, toroidal lattice of coarser granularity than the solution lattice (Fig. 12-2). Each site is occupied by a single solution operator, which is assigned to operate on 3x3 sub-grid of solutions. These operators compete with one another in a manner similar to the competition among solutions, and their selection probability is determined by the fitness changes they evoke in the solutions they control.

Mutation Operators

The third level of the hierarchy (Fig. 12-2b) contains the mutation operators, which are used to modify the solution operators. These reside on a toroidal lattice of even coarser granularity, and are assigned to modify a subset of the solution operators below. The mutation operators are represented as three-element vectors, where each element corresponds to the probability with which a specific mutation operator is used. These three mutation operators work as follows. The first (DeleteOp) deletes an element of a solution operator; the second (AddOp) adds an element to a solution operator, and the third (ChangeOp) mutates an existing element in a solution operator. The probabilities with which these mutation operators are used undergo mutation at a rate specified in the highest level of the hierarchy (Figure 12-2a).

STRING

There are a number of publicly available protein-protein interaction databases. For this study, we used the Search Tool for the Retrieval of Interacting Genes / Proteins (STRING) (Jenson et al., 2009), which incorporates PPI information from a number of widely used interaction databases, and currently contains over 2.5 million proteins from 630 different organisms. STRING is freely available, and provides a transparent application programming interface. Queries to the database require the specification of a protein identifier and return a list of all interaction partners, along with a numeric confidence score for each interaction. These confidence scores range from 0 to 1 and are based on a variety of factors, including experimental data and co-occurrence relationships found using text-mining applications. For a detailed description of the scoring methods, see (von Mering et al., 2005).

These confidence scores were maintained within CES as an interaction matrix (Fig. 12-3b). In the dataset considered herein, these scores were always symmetric, though this need not be the case in general. These scores were scaled and normalized by row to produce an attribute selection probability. The average number of interaction partners per SNP in our dataset (i.e., the average number of non-zero entries per row in the interaction matrix) was approximately 208, with a maximum of 811 and a minimum of 2. The average confidence score was 0.44, with a maximum of 0.99 and a minimum of 0.15.

Data Generation

In order to conduct controlled experiments that (i) highlight the sensitivity of our method to the strength of a PPI score, and (ii) allow for an assessment of system performance on human data, we merged an artificial two-locus epistatic signal with a real genetic dataset. These genetic data were originally collected in an effort to ascertain the genetic risk factors of bladder cancer (Andrew et al., 2008), and consist of 1,423 SNPs found in 394 genes across 491 cases and 791 controls. All of the 394 genes in this dataset were represented by multiple SNPs. However, we made the conservative assumption that the disease status associated with the two interacting genes was only associated with a single SNP on each gene (Fig. 12-1). In real data, it is probable that many, if not all, SNPs on these genes would be associated with disease status. This artificial, two-locus epistatic signal was generated from a penetrance table as described in (Culverhouse et al., 2002), with a minor allele frequency of 0.2 and a heritability of 0.4. The SNPs selected to exhibit this signal represented PPI scores of varying strength. Specifically, we considered four separate cases, with confidence scores ranging from 0.916 to 0.998. While these confidence scores are very close in absolute value, the latter score corresponds to an attribute selection probability that is approximately ten times that of the former. This results from the previously described exponential scaling function used for attribute selection.

Experimental Design

We investigated the effect of including biological expert knowledge of PPIs in CES through a direct comparison with two controls. In the first control, CES was not provided with expert knowledge of any form. In the second control, the two epistatic SNPs associated with disease status were chosen such that their corresponding gene products exhibited no functional interaction, i.e., the PPI associated with the two interacting SNPs did not exist in the STRING database.

For each interaction scenario, we generated 100 independent datasets, where the embedded epistatic signal was generated anew from the same penetrance function. The functionally interacting SNPs were therefore the same within each group of 100 datasets, but the individuals possessing the disease-state allele combination differed between these 100 datasets. This allowed for an assessment of the extent to which CES could identify the disease-causing genetic variants when associated with a variety of human genetic backgrounds. For each of the 100 datasets, we performed 100 independent replications. At the end of each of the 100 replications, we calculated the frequency with which all pairs of SNPs co-occurred in the best solution found by CES. We considered the system successful if the most common pairing was the embedded epistatic interaction.

4. Results

In all experiments, the results of the two controls were statistically indistinguishable. We therefore only report the data corresponding to the control where CES was not provided with the biological expert knowledge of PPIs. In this case, CES was unable to correctly identify the two functional SNPs for any confidence score. In contrast, when provided with biological expert knowledge, CES was able to correctly identify the two functional SNPs as the most frequent pair in the vast majority of the datasets considered (Table 12-1). For confidence scores greater than 0.96, CES found the correct SNPs in 100% of the datasets.

Table 12-1. Percentage of datasets in which CES successfully identified the correct SNP pairings as the most frequent, for the four confidence score scenarios considered.

Confidence Score of PPI	With Expert Knowledge	Control
0.998	100%	0%
0.963	100%	0%
0.933	96%	0%
0.916	80%	0%

For lower confidence scores, the percentage of successful trials decreased, but only to a minimum of 80%.

In Figure 12-4, we show the distributions of solution accuracy (A) and length (L) for those solutions that identified the two most frequent SNPs. These distributions were qualitatively similar for all confidence score scenarios, so we only depict the highest confidence case. For our controls, the most frequently identified SNP pairing was never the correct pair (Table 12-1), so these data correspond to incorrect models. However, the data corresponding to CES with biological expert knowledge pertain to models that successfully identified the correct SNP pair in the vast majority of cases. Within these cases, CES identified models of disease predisposition that were both more accurate and more concise (Figure 12-4).

Specifically, the average model accuracy of CES observed using the biological expert knowledge of PPIs was 0.79 while the average model accuracy without these data was only 0.64. The distribution of model accuracy for CES with expert knowledge was bimodal, with a smaller mode of less accurate solutions centered around an accuracy of 0.66. This mode corresponds to solutions that identified the correct two SNPs, but in a non-predictive model. For example, the model $x_1 \% z_1$ ($A = 0.64$) contained the correct SNPs but was unable to accurately predict disease status. The average number of replicates containing the most frequent SNP pair was much larger when CES used PPI data (27.48 models) than when it did not (13.18 models). This stems from the fact that the models identified by CES without expert knowledge were always incorrect and inaccurate. In these cases, the most frequent SNP pairing was determined by chance, and the number of replicates containing this pairing was therefore significantly reduced, relative to the case of CES with expert knowledge.

For both CES with and without expert knowledge, the distributions of solution length (L) were bimodal (Figure 12-4). However, the lower mode was much larger, and the higher mode much smaller, when CES used biological expert knowledge than when it did not. This results in an average solution length of 13.08 for CES with expert knowledge and an average solution length of 21.14 for CES without expert knowledge.

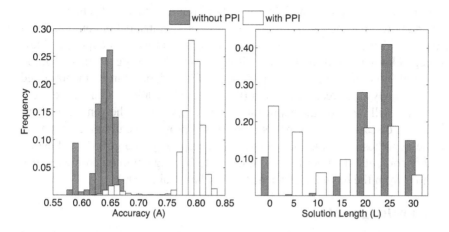

Figure 12-4. Frequency distributions of solution accuracy (left) and solution length (right), corresponding to the best final solutions found by CES with (white bars) and without (gray bars) the biological expert knowledge of protein-protein interactions. Data correspond only to those solutions that identified the most common SNP pairing of the 100 replications (see text). The bins are the same for both bar types, but are offset in the horizontal dimension for visual clarity.

5. Discussion

Our results demonstrate that CES exhibits the ability to identify simulated epistatic interactions in more concise models of disease susceptibility and with improved accuracy when using biological expert knowledge in the form of protein-protein interactions (PPI). In order to evaluate the influence of PPI confidence score strength on CES, we determined the frequency at which the system could identify our simulated two-locus interactions that represented a range of confidence scores. We found that CES achieved a success rate between 80% and 100% for low to high confidence scores. The genetic models discovered by CES with access to PPI information were significantly smaller and had significantly higher accuracies that those found by CES without expert knowledge. These results suggest that CES may be ready to tackle a wide range of real world data from studies designed to identify genetic predictors of susceptibility to common human diseases. Of course, real data brings its own unique challenges that will need to be addressed. These include low signal to noise ratio, noisy data due to laboratory errors, complex correlation structure and, of course, the challenge of providing a biological interpretation of CES models.

Although we focused exclusively on PPI as a source of biological knowledge in this study, the analysis of real world data will require giving CES access to other sources such as biochemical pathway information, gene ontology, and chromosomal location. In addition, it will be important to include other types of expert knowledge such as those derived from prior statistical or computational analyses. Our previous study showing that CES can learn to exploit a single source of knowledge from multiple different candidates suggests that a combination of biological and statistical sources of knowledge can be incorporated into the analysis of real world data (Greene et al., 2009b). Our future work with CES will focus on the application of this approach to the genetic analysis of human disease. Success in this domain will provide the ultimate validation of the hypothesis that the incorporation of complexity into genetic and evolutionary computation algorithms will facilitate solving complex problems such as those from the biomedical sciences (Banzhaf et al., 2006).

Acknowledgment

We would like to thank the participants of GPTP '09 for their insightful comments, many of which served to inspire the current study. This work was supported by NIH grants LM009012, LM010098 and AI59694.

References

Albert, R., Jeong, H., and Barabási, A.L. (2000). Error and attack tolerance of complex networks. *Nature*, 406:378–382.

Aldana, M., Balleza, E., Kauffman, S., and Resendiz, O. (2007). Robustness and evolvability in genetic regulatory networks. *Journal of Theoretical Biology*, 245:433–448.

Andrew, A.S., Karagas, M.R., Nelson, H.H., Guarrera, S., Polidoro, S., Gamberini, S., Sacerdote, C., Moore, J.H., Kelsey, K.T., Vineis, P., and Matullo, G. (2008). Assessment of multiple DNA repair gene polymorphisms and bladder cancer susceptibility in a joint italian and u.s. population: a comparison of alternative analytic approaches. *Human Heredity*, 65:105–118.

Askland, K., Read, C., and Moore, J.H. (2009). Pathway-based analyses of whole-genome association study data in bipolar disorder reveal genes mediating ion channel activity and synaptic neurotransmission. *Human Genetics*, 125:63–79.

Banzhaf, W., Beslon, G., Christensen, S., Foster, J.A., Képès, F., Lefort, V., Miller, J.F., Radman, M., and Ramsden, J.J. (2006). From artificial evolution to computational evolution: a research agenda. *Nature Reviews Genetics*, 7:729–735.

Cordell, H.J. (2009). Detecting gene-gene interactions that underlie human diseases. *Nature Reviews Genetics*, 10:392–404.

Culverhouse, R., Suarez, B.K., Lin, J., and Reich, T. (2002). A perspective on epistasis: limits of models displaying no main effect. *American Journal of Human Genetics*, 70(2):461–471.

Emily, M., Mailund, T., Hein, J., Schauser, L., and Schierup, M.H. (2009). Using biological networks to search for interacting loci in genome-wide association studies. *European Journal of Human Genetics*, 17(10):1231–1240.

Eppstein, M.J., Payne, J.L., White, B.C., and Moore, J.H. (2007). Genomic mining for complex disease traits with random chemistry. *Genetic Programming and Evolvable Machines*, 8:395–411.

Greene, C.S., Hill, D.P., and Moore, J.H. (2009a). Environmental noise improves epistasis models of genetic data discovered using a computational evolution system. In *Proceedings of the Genetic and Evolutionary Computation Conference*, pages 1785–1786.

Greene, C.S., Hill, D.P., and Moore, J.H. (2009b). Environmental sensing of expert knowledge in a computational evolution system for complex problem solving in human genetics. In Riolo, R., O-Reilly, U.M., and McConaghy, T., editors, *Genetic Programming Theory and Practice VII*, pages 19–36. Springer.

Greene, C.S., White, B.C., and Moore, J.H. (2009c). An expert knowledge-guided mutation operator for genome-wide genetic analysis using genetic programming. In *Lecture Notes in Bioinformatics*, volume 4774, pages 30–40.

Greene, C.S., White, B.C., and Moore, J.H. (2009d). Sensible initialization using expert knowledge for genome-wide analysis of epistasis using genetic programming. In *Proceedings of the IEEE Congress on Evolutionary Computation*, pages 1289–1296.

Jenson, L.J., M.Kuhn, Stark, M., Chaffron, S., Creevey, C., Muller, J., Doerks, T., Julien, P., Roth, A., Simonovic, M., Bork, P., and von Mering, C. (2009). String 8 - a global view on proteins and their functional interactions in 630 organisms. *Nucleic Acids Research*, 37:D412–D416.

Jeong, H., Mason, S.P., Barabási, A.L., and Oltvai, Z.N. (2001). Lethality and centrality in protein networks. *Nature*, 411:41–42.

Kononenko, I. (1994). Estimating attributes: analysis and extensions of RELIEF. In *European Conference on Machine Learning*, pages 171–182.

Langdon, W.B. (1998). *Genetic Programming and Data Structures: Genetic Programming + Data Structures = Automatic Programming!* Kluwer Academic Publishers Group.

Moore, J.H. (2003). The ubiquitous nature of epistasis in determining susceptibility to common human diseases. *Human Heredity*, 56:73–82.

Moore, J.H., Andrews, P.C., Barney, N., and White, B.C. (2008). Development and evaluation of an open-ended computational evolution system for the genetic analysis of susceptibility to common human diseases. In *Lecture Notes in Computer Science*, volume 4973, pages 129–140.

Moore, J.H., Asselbergs, F.W., and Williams, S.M. (2010). Bioinformatics challenges for genome-wide association studies. *Bioinformatics*, 26(4):445–455.

Moore, J.H., Greene, C.S., Andrews, P.C., and White, B.C. (2009). Does complexity matter? artificial evolution, computational evolution, and the genetic analysis of epistasis in common human diseases. In Riolo, R., Soule, T., and Worzel, B., editors, *Genetic Programming Theory and Practice VI*. Springer.

Moore, J.H., Parker, J.S., Olsen, N.J., and Aune, T.M. (2002). Symbolic discriminant analysis of microarray data in autoimmune disease. *Genetic Epidemiology*, 23:57–69.

Moore, J.H. and White, B.C. (2006). Exploiting expert knowledge in genetic programming for genome-wide genetic analysis. In *Lecture Notes in Computer Science*, volume 4193, pages 969–977.

Moore, J.H. and White, B.C. (2007). Genome-wide genetic analysis using genetic programming: The critical need for expert knowledge. In Riolo, R., Soule, T., and Worzel, B., editors, *Genetic Programming Theory and Practice IV*, pages 11–28. Springer.

Moore, J.H. and Williams, S.M. (2009). Epistasis and its implications for personal genetics. *American Journal of Human Genetics*, 85:309–320.

Payne, J.L., Greene, C.S., Hill, D.P., and Moore, J.H. (2010). Sensible initialization of a computational evolution system using expert knowledge for epistasis analysis in human genetics. In Chen, Y.P., editor, *Exploitation of Linkage Learning in Evolutionary Algorithms*, pages 215–226. Springer.

Poli, R., Langdon, W.B., and McPhee, N.F. (2008). *A Field Guide to Genetic Programming*. Published via http://lulu.com and freely available at http://www.gp-field-guide.org.uk.

Ritchie, M.D., Hahn, L.W., Roodi, N., Bailey, L.R., Dupont, W.D., Parl, F.F., and Moore, J.H. (2001). Multifactor dimensionality reduction reveals high-order interactions among estrogen metabolism genes in sporadic breast cancer. *American Journal of Human Genetics*, 69:138–147.

von Mering, C., Jensen, L.J., Snel, B., Hooper, S.D., Krupp, M., Foglierini, M., Jouffre, N., Huynen, M.A., and Bork, P. (2005). String: known and predicted protein-protein associations, integrated and transferred across organisms. *Nucleic Acids Research*, 33:D433–D437.

Chapter 13

COMPOSITION OF MUSIC AND FINANCIAL STRATEGIES VIA GENETIC PROGRAMMING

Hitoshi Iba[1] and Claus Aranha[1]

[1] *The University of Tokyo, Department of Electrical Engineering.*

Abstract   We present two applications of genetic programming to real world problems: musical composition and financial portfolio optimization. In each of these applications, a specialized genome representation is used in order to break the problem down into smaller instances and put them back together. Results showing the applicability of the approaches are presented.

Keywords: portfolio optimization, music composition, memetic algorithms, interactive genetic programming

1.   Introduction

In this chapter, we will discuss the applications of genetic programming to two different real world applications: financial portfolio optimization, and music composition. While both domains use different algorithms to generate their solutions, the common ground between the two works is that it is a good strategy to generate simpler sub-solutions, and to put these solutions together to arrive at the desired goal. Both algorithms use genetic programming to generate these building blocks and assemble them into more complex solutions.

The first application is the optimization of financial portfolios. Portfolios are used by financial institutions in the management of long term funds, like savings accounts, retirement funds, etc. The idea behind a financial portfolio is that by investing in multiple assets with different characteristics, like, for example, stocks from competing companies, it is possible to mitigate the risk of the investment. The Markowitz Portfolio Model (Markowitz, 1987) describes how to minimize the risk of a financial portfolio, by distributing the capital into multiple, counter correlated assets. This model can be used to calculate the optimal distribution of capital in order to minimize the risk of an investment, for a given target return.

While the mathematical model proposed by Markowitz can be solved by simple programmatic methods, real world cases are much more complex. A large number of assets (multi-dimensional search space), restrictions on the maximum number of assets in a portfolio, or the maximum or minimum weights make the search for an optimal portfolio very hard. Meta-heuristic methods, including genetic programming and Genetic Algorithms, have been used with success in recent year to solve these harder cases.

We introduce an evolutionary approach for portfolio optimization based on our previous work with inductive genetic programming (IGP). Our approach is unique in that it uses the tree structure of IGP to generate a hierarchy of sub-portfolios tied together. The system works by learning good smaller portfolios (building blocks), tying them together in the hierarchy tree, and then using a local search operator to calculate the best weight between the sub portfolios. This allows the system to both select the best assets into the portfolio, and calculate optimal weights for them, while other methods have concentrated on only one of those.

The second application domain is music composition. By using stochastic techniques in musical composition, composers can obtain creative, unpredictable results. However, the disadvantage of those techniques is that composers must choose a good result from the large number produced by the computer program. Moreover, the composers need to correct and rearrange the produced results to actually incorporate them in their pieces. This selection and correction process becomes a huge burden. Taking this into consideration, we see that the application of Interactive Evolutionary Computation (IEC) has some advantages. In an IEC method, the initial population is generated randomly. Then the population converges by the interaction between the user, who gives fitness values to individuals, and the system which generate new candidates based on the user's evaluation. In this fashion, the user can get results that need no further correction. The use of genetic operations such as crossover and mutation, helps the generation of unexpected promising results. We introduce an IEC system named CACIE(Computer Aided Composition using Interactive Evolution). CACIE is aimed at aiding composers in the composition of traditional atonal pieces, e.g., modern-classic music. With our method, the user can interact with evolution process easily through the interface so as to generate long pieces without aggravation of convergence.

We will take a closer look at each of these applications, and their underlying problems, and discuss results that show how effective they can be in practice.

2.   Generating Portfolio Strategies

In financial terms, the portfolio optimization problem is an application of the strategy of diversification of investment. The many assets available for the investor are analyzed, and a strategy is chosen to distribute the investment in assets that are diverse to each other, in order to protect the portfolio as a whole from risk factors of the market.

In more mathematical terms, this is a parameter optimization problem, where the goal is to find out the best weights to a portfolio of investments, in order to minimize a risk measure, and to maximize a return measure. These measures are based on the weights of the parameters, the individual performance of each parameter, and the correlation between the performance of each pair of parameters.

The calculation of the above measures scales quickly in complexity with the number of assets (dimensionality) of the problem. Thus the search for efficient methods, including evolutionary approaches, to calculate optimum portfolios is a popular problem in the field of financial engineering.

However, to control the complexity of the problem, most of these approaches either concentrate only on the selection of the best assets to be added to a portfolio or on the calculation of the weight of a small number of pre-selected assets. Here we introduce an approach that performs both the asset selection and the weight optimization at the same time.

This approach, which mixes genetic programming and Memetic Algorithms, is based on the inductive GP algorithm introduced by Iba and Nicholaev (Nikolaev and Iba, 2001). Basically, small trees are used to find small, locally optimal portfolios using a local search operator, and then are put together through GP operators to form larger trees with full portfolios. The hierarchical structure allows this divide-and-conquer approach, which makes the selection and weighting of a much larger number of assets more feasible.

Problem Definition

The portfolio Optimization problem is commonly modelled as follows (Yuh-Dauh-Lyu, 2002): A portfolio P is defined as a set of N real valued weights $(w_0, w_1, ...w_N)$ which correspond to the N available assets in the market. These weights must obey two basic restrictions: the total sum of the weights must be equal to one; and all weights must be positive.

The utility of a portfolio is measured by its *estimated return* and its *risk*. The estimated return is calculated as:

$$R_P = \sum_{i=0}^{N} R_i w_i \qquad (13.1)$$

Where N is the total number of assets, R_i is the given estimated return of each asset, and w_i is the weight of each asset in the portfolio. In this work, the estimated return is calculated as the moving average of the past 12 months for each asset, but other estimation methods can be used instead.

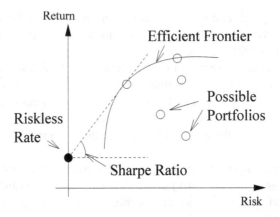

Figure 13-1. Risk-return projection of candidate portfolios. The search space is bounded by the Efficient Frontier. Sharpe ratio is the angle of the line between a portfolio and the risk-free rate.

The risk of an asset is given as the variance of its return over time. The risk of the whole portfolio is defined as:

$$\sigma_p = \sum_{i=0}^{N} \sum_{j=0}^{N} \sigma_{ij} w_i w_j \qquad (13.2)$$

Where $\sigma_{ij}, i \neq j$ is the covariance between i and j, and $\sigma_{ii} = \sigma_i^2$ is the deviation of the estimated return of asset i. While the risk is usually stated as the variance of the return of a given asset, there are other definitions of risk that can be used to bias the resulting portfolios towards certain kinds of investment strategies.

These two utility measures can be used separately to determine the optimal portfolio, or they can be combined. The *Sharpe Ratio* measures the trade off ratio between risk and return for a portfolio, and is defined as follows:

$$Sr = \frac{R_P - R_{riskless}}{\sigma_p} \qquad (13.3)$$

Where $R_{riskless}$ is the risk-free rate, an asset which has zero risk and a low return rate (for example, government bonds). The relationship between these three utility measures is illustrated in Figure 13-1.

Previous Approaches

Previous works using evolutionary approaches for the portfolio optimization problem have concentrated either in the optimization of weights of a set number of assets, or the selection of good assets without regard for their weights.

For the weight optimization strategy, the most common approach is the use of a Genetic Algorithm, where each element in the array genome is a real value representing the weight of one asset (Hochreiter, 2007). A limitation of this method is that the standard crossover and mutation operators of GA are ill-suited for the fine tuning and selection of real valued parameters (Ullah et al., 2007). Some attempts to address this limitation include the random selection of a subset of assets before optimization (Lipinski et al., 2007) or the use of a second binary genome for selection (Aranha and Iba, 2007; Streichert et al., 2003).

For asset selection strategy, the common approach is to assign a score to each asset available in the market, and use this score to rank the assets. Szeto (Jiang and Szeto, 2002) evolves rules based on the values of moving averages with different lengths to decided whether to add an asset on the portfolio. Wei and Clack (Yan and Clack, 2007) use genetic programming to evolve a decision system where a number of performance indicators from the asset are used as the input to calculate the rank for each asset.

The Memetic Tree Method

Our method for generating optimal portfolios consists of two main points: The tree representation of a portfolio, and the local search operator.

The portfolio tree representation is able to express and learn relationships between assets. Its recursive definition, which is based on the relationship between the terminal nodes as dictated by the intermediate nodes, also allows the algorithm to treat a sub tree as an entire individual, which allows a divide-and-conquer approach to local search, fine tuning of parameters, and crossover.

The optimization step uses a hill climbing algorithm on the local weights (intermediate nodes) of the tree, in a recursive bottom-up fashion, so that for each node only a simple two variable optimization needs to be done. Using a hybrid of local search and evolutionary methods (also called Memetic Algorithms) has been shown to yield good results for real valued problems (Ullah et al., 2007).

In total, the optimization becomes a two-stage process: In the first stage, the crossover and mutation operators select the assets, and establish relations between them using the tree structure. In the second stage, the local optimization directly modifies the weights of the intermediate nodes to establish the optimal weights for the assets given the tree structure of that individual.

Hierarchical Portfolio Representation.   Each individual encodes a candidate portfolio. An individual is a binary tree, with two different kind of nodes, the terminal nodes and intermediate nodes.

A terminal node holds an integer value, i, representing the index of an asset in the market. An intermediate node holds a real value w, between 0 and 1 inclusive. This value represents the relative weight between its two children sub trees. The left sub tree has weight w, and the right sub tree of has weight $1 - w$. Figure 13-2 shows a sample tree.

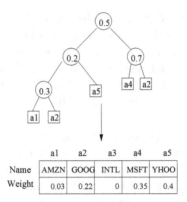

Figure 13-2. A tree genome and its corresponding portfolio. The values in the intermediate nodes indicate the weight of the left sub tree. The complement of that value is the weight of the right sub tree. The final weight of each asset (a_x) is given by the sum of the weights of all occurrences of that asset in the tree.

To extract the portfolio from this representation, we calculate the weight of each terminal node by multiplying the weights of all nodes that need to be visited to reach that terminal, starting from the root of the tree. After all terminal nodes are visited, the weights of those terminals that point to the same asset are added together. The assets which are not mentioned in the tree are assigned a weight of 0 (i.e. they have not been selected to the portfolio).

Crossover and mutation are the standard genetic programming operators. A random node is chosen in the tree, and the sub tree under this node is exchanged with another individual, in the case of Crossover, or replaced with a random tree, in case of mutation. The maximum tree depth is a fixed value that allows a full tree to potentially hold each asset in the market.

The Local Search Operator.   The crossover and mutation operators allow the algorithm to shuffle the asset indexes around, changing the tree structure. However, in our experience they are not sufficient to select the best weight values for the intermediate nodes. We use a simple hill climbing local search operator to improve these values.

At the start of every generation, we randomly select half of the individuals in the population to undergo the local search operation. We operate algorithms 2 and 3 on the selected individuals. The operation of these routines can be summed up as follows: starting from the bottom of the tree, for each intermediate node, the routine calculates the weight that offers the best risk and return values for that node as if it were the root node of the tree. This simplification is possible by treating the portfolio encoded by each sub-tree of the processed node as a single asset, using the return and risk values of the sub portfolio as the return and risk values of the fake asset.

Algorithm 2

---

if Child Nodes are not leaves or locally optimized **then**
    Recursive Tree Optimization(left child)
    Recursive Tree Optimization(right child)
end if
$weight$ = Local Search(this node)
Calculate Risk and Return ($weight$) **return** New Risk and Return Values

---

Algorithm 3 Local Search(tree node)

Require: Child nodes are leaves or locally optimized.
Ensure: Current node is locally optimized
  while ($|meme\_speed| > meme\_thresh$) AND
  ($0 < weight < 1$) **do**
    $old\_fitness = fitness$
    $weight = weight + meme\_speed$
    if $weight > 1$ **then**
      $weight = 1$
    end if
    if $weight < 0$ **then**
      $weight = 0$
    end if
    calculate_fitness($weight$)
    if $fitness < old\_fitness$ **then**
      $meme\_speed = meme\_speed * meme\_accel * -1$
    end if
  end while

In algorithm 3, *meme_speed, meme_accel and meme_thresh* are parameters. *meme_speed* is the value by which the weight changes every iteration; *meme_accel* must be < 1.0, and is the value by which *meme_speed* changes every time the weight crosses the optima point; and *meme_thresh* is the minimum value of *meme_speed* which signalizes the end of the search. The search also ends if the weight reaches 1.0 or 0.0.

Validation

To show the utility of the method presented here, we perform a comparison with other evolutionary algorithms in a trade simulation using historical price data.

We use two data sets in our simulations. The NASDAQ data set contains 100 assets from the NASDAQ index, which is composed mainly of technology related industry. The S&P data set contains 500 assets from the S&P index, which has a more varied composition, with assets from industry of many different fields.

For each data set, the log return of the monthly closing value is used as the monthly return value of each stock. The log return of an asset for time t is calculated as $r_t = ln(P_t/P_{t-1})$. We generate 36 monthly scenarios from January 2006 to December 2008, and evaluate a portfolio for each scenario.

We compare the results obtained by the discussed method with the Market Index, the Mixed Array GA implementation, and the DEahcSPX. The Market Index is a portfolio composed by all the assets in the market, weighted by their participation. This is a basic benchmark for portfolio optimization techniques. The Mixed Array GA is a representative of previous evolutionary approaches, discussed in section 2.0. The DEahcSPX is a differential method which has shown success in using a local search approach for solving real valued optimization problems (Noman and Iba, 2008).

We used the same parameters for all runs of evolutionary algorithms mentioned here. The number of generations was 500, with 200 individuals per generation. The crossover rate was 0.8 and the mutation rate was 0.03. The riskless asset's return was set at 3% (0.03). The parameter for the local optimization step are: 0.1 for $meme\_speed$, 0.333 for $meme\_delta$, and 0.003 for $meme\_thresh$. Other than $meme\_thresh$, which changes the precision of the search, changing these values does not seem to affect the quality of the local search.

We can see the performance of the different methods in table 13-1. By using the genetic programming to select assets to add in the portfolio, and using local search to fine tune the weight between those assets, the proposed method is able to outperform former GA-based methods (which use a binary array for asset selection but no mechanism for fine-tuning) and local search based methods (which are well suited for fine tuning of real parameter value but don't have a mechanism to select and establish relationships between different assets in the market).

3.   Evolutionary Music Composition

Here we detail the implementation of CACIE as an Interactive Evolutionary Computation system for musical composition. In any EC system care must be taken on the encoding scheme that represents the problem. However, in addition, the user interface and procedure for evaluation are also important in the case of Interactive Evolutionary Computation systems. The population size and the number of generations that IEC users can deal with are strictly limited as

Table 13-1. Sharpe Ratio value for some of the scenarios in the historical simulation. The results are the average of the best individual of 20 runs, and the values for the Memetic GP show a difference from the other values below the 0.05 level on a Student's T test.

NASDAQ data set

Scenario date	Memetic GP	Binary GA	DEahcSPX	Index
Feb. 2006	2.1142	1.0959	1.5667	-0.49
May. 2006	2.1485	1.3681	1.5733	-0.21
Aug. 2006	1.3522	0.5947	0.9662	-0.68
Nov. 2006	0.9035	0.5183	0.6963	-0.53
Feb. 2007	1.3606	0.4953	1.0521	-0.68
May. 2007	0.9339	0.5799	0.7969	-0.33
Aug. 2007	6.1738	0.8301	2.5784	-0.90
Nov. 2007	4.638	0.6612	1.8283	-0.30
Feb. 2008	0.5356	0.4038	0.4596	-0.49

SP data set

Scenario date	Memetic GP	Binary GA	DEahcSPX	Index
Feb. 2006	12.5015	1.2807	2.0617	-1.13
May. 2006	9.7257	1.4044	1.8598	-0.88
Aug. 2006	1.2239	0.5831	0.5196	-0.54
Nov. 2006	4.7003	0.5314	0.9648	-1.05
Feb. 2007	5.4636	0.5537	0.7403	-1.27
May. 2007	4.3045	0.7929	0.1383	-1.16
Aug. 2007	36.0465	3.1463	0.6763	-1.08
Nov. 2007	11.5642	1.7375	1.0450	-0.87
Feb. 2008	0.9033	0.7334	0.5680	-1.01

long evaluation periods can make the user tired and compromise their evaluation abilities or willingness. This problem is known as "user's burden". Several researchers have tried to solve the user's burden problem in different domains (Biles, 1994; Takagi and Ohya, 1996; Tokui and Iba, 2000; Unemi, 1998).

A wide variety of gene representation schemes and user interfaces have been tried in the development of IEC systems for music composition. A general review can be found in the survey by Burton (Burton and Vladimirova, 1999). In some cases, user operations and interface have been implemented as a "conversation" between the user and the system (Biles, 1994; Jacob, 1995). These results have shown some possibilities to reduce the user's burden.

Traditional composers often use tree topology to represent the analysis result for their own pieces. For this reason, the tree representation of a musical phrase seems to have advantages in the sense that it can easily be understood by those traditional composers. This has led to some works in IEC where the users refine or define a tree based genome directly. Another advantage of a tree

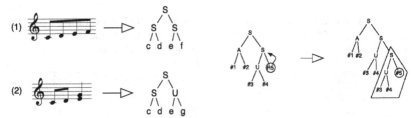

Figure 13-3. Tree representation of a musical phrase.

Figure 13-4. Developmental process of a Recursive terminal node.

representation is the ability to mask a part of genome manually. In addition, Palle (Dahlstedt and Nordahl, 2004) extended the tree representation so that it could represent musical repetition of typical classical pieces with a recursive tree topology.

However, representing a musical phrase with tree topology has some problems. For instance, the tree topology can easily becomes too complex when trying to represent a comparatively long piece. In systems where the user interacts directly with the genomic representation of individuals, this may lead to the user not being able to understand the tree easily. As a result, refining and defining the genome manually becomes more difficult. Also, dealing with complex and large trees degrades the performance of EC. For this reason, systems where the user interacts directly with the tree genome had little success in generating relatively longer pieces.

In developing CACIE, we have aimed to develop new evolutionary and interactive techniques aimed at avoiding these difficulties.

Gene Representation

A tree representation was adopted as the genome representation of a single musical phrase. The tree genome is based on a simplified version of traditional compositional expression. Figure 13-3 shows a simple example of converting a musical phrase into a tree-topology. Each terminal node of the tree contains a note or a musical motive. In the first example of figure 13-3, c, d, e and f are terminal nodes. A note contains four parameters: Note Number, Amplitude, Duration and Onset-Time. Zero amplitude represents a rest note. A non-terminal node represents a functions that merges or concatenates notes into a larger musical structure as a list of notes. In the second example of the figure, S and U are non-terminal nodes. The S function connects two nodes being as leaf, i.e., makes a list of notes. The U function merges two nodes that will be played simultaneously. The system provides many functions that operate on and enable a traditional musical structure. Table 13-2 summarizes a partial list

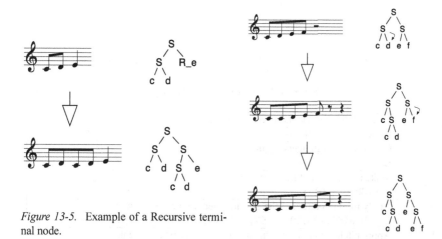

Figure 13-5. Example of a Recursive terminal node.

Figure 13-6. Increase mutation.

of functions that have been implemented in CACIE. These functions are also provided as libraries for the user to optionally edit the candidates directly.

To represent the repetition often found in classical music pieces, we use a special type of terminal node, named Recursive Terminal Node. A short genome with many notes of musical significance can be constructed using this node. Before the phenotype is decoded in the ontogeny phase, the recursive terminal node recursively expands the tree. Figure 13-5 gives a simple example of decoding a musical phrase with such a recursive terminal node.

Specialized Genetic Operators

The CACIE system employs two specialized genetic operations, named Increase and Decrease. The increase mutation is used to implement the above-mentioned recursive terminal node as a mutation. Figure 13-6 shows an example of the increase mutation. The decrease mutation has the reverse role of the increase mutation. The decrease mutation replaces a non-terminal node in a subtree with a terminal node.

User Interface and Composition Process

Figure 13-7 shows an overview of the CACIE interface. The window on the right side of the display is the population window, which presents the individuals to be evaluated. In the lower bar of the window, there exists a button to reproduce the population. The user can give fitness values to individuals in this window.

The top left window on the display allows users to edit chromosomes manually. The second window on the top left has buttons to start the manual editing

Table 13-2. List of part of functions

S	Connect two arguments successively. E.g.`(S a b) = (a b)`
U	Connect two arguments simultaneously. E.g.`(U a b) = (ab)`
SR	Make a repetition of two arguments. E.g.`(SR+5 a b) = (a b a b a)`
D	Apply rhythm pattern of the 2nd argument to the 1st argument. E.g.`(D a(60,100,10) b(62,120,20)) = a'(60,100,20)`
P	Apply pitch pattern of the 2nd argument to the 1st argument. E.g.`(P a(60,100,10) b(62,120,20)) = a'(62,100,10)`
A	Apply articulation pattern of the 2nd argument to the 1st argument. E.g.`(A a(60,100,10) b(62,120,20) = a'(60,120,10)`
RV	Reverse ordering. E.g.`(RV (a b)) = (b a)`
IV	Pitch inversion. E.g.`(IV a((60,100,10)(62,120,20)) =` `a'((62,100,10)(60,120,20))`
TP	Pitch transposing. E.g.`(TP+5  a((60,100,10)(62,120,20)) =` `a'((65,100,10)(67,120,20))`
MS	Return a sequence of arranged notes taken from two nodes alternately. E.g.`(MS (a b c) (d e)) = (a d b c e)`
MU	Return a sequence of arranged notes taken from two nodes simultaneously. E.g.`(MU (a b) (c d)) = ((U a c) (U b d))`
CAR	Return a sequence that contains the front X% of number of notes. E.g.`(CAR50% (a b c d)) = (a b)`
CDR	Return a sequence that contains the rear X% of number of notes. E.g.`(CDR50% (a b c d)) = (c d)`
ACML	Return an accumulated sequence. E.g.`(ACML (a b c)) = (a a b a b c)`

FILP	Return a sequence that contains a repetition with pitch transposing before the 2nd node pitch.
	E.g.`(FILP+2 (a(60,amp,dur) b(63,amp,dur)) c(65,amp,dur))`
	`    = (a(60,..) b(63,..)`
	`        a'(62,..) b'(65,..)`
	`        a''(64,..) b''(67,..) c(65,..))`

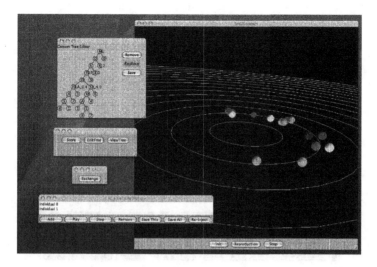

Figure 13-7. Overview of CACIE interface.

and to temporarily store an individual. The third window on the top left performs the manual crossover. The bottom left window shows the temporary storage.

In the population window, each individual is displayed as a 3D sphere icon. All individual icons are arranged along a circle. Each individual slowly flies around the circumference. Also, each individual is assigned a different color. The color is generated according to the chromosome's characteristics. In this way, genomes that are similar to each other, i.e., possess similar musical codes, will be similarly colored. Thus, the color can be used to identify the individual in the population. By double-clicking an individual icon, CACIE plays the music indicated by that individual. The playback continues until the end of the piece, or when another individual icon is double-clicked. The individual currently being played flashes on and off, and pulsates.

The position of an individual's icon, i.e., its distance from the center of the circle, determines the fitness value of that individual. Higher fitness degree is indicated by being nearer to the center of the circle, and lower fitness value is indicated by being away from the center. Each individual is placed at a position of neutral fitness value. By picking and dragging the chosen individual icon, users can give it a higher or lower fitness degree. When closer to the center, the individual's icon becomes bigger. Also, the fitness values of the whole population are arranged so that the icons of similar color have similar fitness values.

For the sake of validation, we have executed comparative experiments against a traditional IEC interface, and confirmed that CACIE motivates users better

Figure 13-8. An evolved piano miniature.

to utilize the composition aid system. The superiority of CACIE's interface is significantly shown by statistical tests with subjects' interview data (Ando et al., 2007).

Experiments and Discussion

For the sake of evaluating the system, we used CACIE to compose motif and musical variations (Ando and Iba, 2007). We also tried to compose a full piano miniature. Each of the melodies consisted of the repetition of notes or small array of notes. A part of the opening is given in Figure 13-8. In addition, we asked a professional classical pianist to play the generated piece for evaluation. The pianist generally had a good opinion of the IEC generated result. A SMF file with the MIDI piano performance as well as full musical score is available from the same web site[1]. The music pieces composed by CACIE have been selected for distinguished performance in some international computer music competitions. For instance, they were performed in ICMC2007 in Copenhagen by Jeanette Balland and in IC2007 in Tokyo by Yoko Shishido. We are currently collaborating with many professional musicians so as to further improve our approach.

---

[1] http://www.iba.k.u-tokyo.ac.jp/~dando/public/works/rattfylla.html

4.   Conclusion

In this chapter we have showed how Genetic Program mechanisms can be used to combine and assemble the building blocks in fields as diverse as music composition and financial investments in order to form complex and effective strategies/compositions. Both systems have seen deployment in practice; pieces composed by CACIE have been performed in international festivals, and the portfolio optimization is included in a investor support system, containing also a GP system for automated foreign exchange (Hirabayashi et al., 2009), developed by an industry partner.

References

Ando, D., Dahlsted, P., Nordahl, G. Nordahl, G., and Iba, H. (2007). Interactive gp with tree representation of classical music pieces. In *Proceedings of EvoWorkshops 2007*, pages 577–584.

Ando, D. and Iba, H. (2007). Interactive composition aid system by means of tree representation of musical phrase. In *Proceedings of the 2007 Congress on Evolutionary Computation (CEC2007), Singapore*.

Aranha, C. and Iba, H. (2007). Modelling cost into a genetic algorithm-based portfolio optimization system by seeding and objective sharing. In *Proc. of the Conference on Evolutionary Computation*, pages 196–203.

Biles, J. (1994). Genjam: A genetic algorithm for genrating jazz solos. In *Proceedings of 1994 International Computer Music Conference*, Arhus. ICMA.

Burton, A. R and Vladimirova, T. (1999). Generation of musical sequences with genetic techniques. *Computer Music Journal*, 24(4):59–73.

Dahlstedt, P. and Nordahl, M. G. (2004). Augumented creativity: Evolution of musical score material.

Hirabayashi, A., Aranha, C., and Iba, H. (2009). Optimization of the trading rule in foreign exchange using genetic algorithms. In *Proceedings of the 2009 Genetic and Evolutionary Computation Conference*, Montreal, Canada.

Hochreiter, R. (2007). An evolutionary computation approach to scenario-based risk-return portfolio optimization for general risk measures. In et al., M. Giacobini, editor, *EvoWorkshops 2007*, number 4448 in LNCS, pages 199–207. Springer-Verlag.

Jacob, B. L. (1995). Composing with genetic algorithms. In *Proceedings of 1995 International Computer Music Conference*, Alberta. ICMA.

Jiang, R. and Szeto, K. Y. (2002). Discovering investment strategies in portfolio management: A genetic algorithm approach. In *Proceedings of the 9th International Conference on Neural Information Processing*, volume 3, pages 1206–1210.

Lipinski, P., Winczura, K., and Wojcik, J. (2007). Building risk-optimal port-folio using evolutionary strategies. In et al., M. Giacobini, editor, *EvoWork-shops 2007*, number 4448 in LNCS, pages 208–217. Springer-Verlag.

Markowitz, H. (1987). *Mean-Variance analysis in Portfolio Choice and Capital Market*. Basil Blackwell, New York.

Nikolaev, N. Y. and Iba, H. (2001). Regularization approach to inductive genetic programming. *IEEE Transactions on evolutionary computation*, 5(4):359–375.

Noman, N. and Iba, H. (2008). Accelerating differential evolution using an adaptive local search. *IEEE Trans. Evolutionary Computation*, 12(1):107–125.

Streichert, F., Ulmer, H., and Zell, A. (2003). Evolutionary algorithms and the cardinality constrained portfolio optimization problem. In Ahr, D., Fahrion, R., Oswald, M., and Reinelt, G., editors, *Operations Research Proceedings*. Springer.

Takagi, H. and Ohya, K. (1996). Discrete fitness values for improving the human interface in an interactive ga. In *Proceedings of IEEE 3rd International Conference on Evolutionary Computation (ICEC'96)*, pages 109–112, Nagoya. IEEE.

Tokui, N. and Iba, H. (2000). Music composition with interactive evolutionary computation. In *Proceedings of 3rd International Conference on Generative Art (GA2000)*.

Ullah, B., Sarker, R., Cornforth, D., and Lokan, C. (2007). An agent-based memetic algorithm (ama) for solving constrained optimization problems. In *IEEE Congress on Evolutionary Computation (CEC)*, pages 999–1006, Singapore.

Unemi, T (1998). A design of multi-field user interface for simulated breeding. In *Proceedings of 3rd Asian Fuzzy System Symposium: The Korea Fuzzy Logic and Intelligent Systems*.

Yan, W. and Clack, C. D. (2007). Evolving robust gp solutions for hedge fund stock selection in emerging markets. In *GECCO 2007 - Genetic and Evolutionary Computation Conference*, London, England. ACM Press.

Yuh-Dauh-Lyu (2002). *Financial Engineering and Computation*. Cambridge Press.

Chapter 14

EVOLUTIONARY ART USING SUMMED MULTI-OBJECTIVE RANKS

Steven Bergen[1] and Brian J. Ross[1]

[1]*Brock University, Department of Computer Science, 500 Glenridge Ave., St. Catharines, Ontario, Canada L2S 3A1.*

Abstract   This paper shows how a sum of ranks approach to multi-objective evaluation is effective for some low-order search problems, as it discourages the generation of outlier solutions. Outliers, which often arise with the traditional Pareto ranking strategy, tend to exhibit good scores on a minority of feature tests, while having mediocre or poor scores on the rest. They arise from the definition of Pareto dominance, in which an individual can be superlative in as little as a single objective in order to be considered undominated. The application considered in this research is evolutionary art, in which images are synthesized that adhere to an aesthetic model based on color gradient distribution. The genetic programming system uses 4 different fitness measurements, that perform aesthetic and color palette analyses. Outliers are usually undesirable in this application, because the color gradient distribution measurements requires 3 features to be satisfactory simultaneously. Sum of ranks scoring typically results in images that score better on the majority of features, and are therefore arguably more visually pleasing. Although the ranked sum strategy was originally inspired by highly dimensional problems having perhaps 20 objectives or more, this research shows that it is likewise practical for low-dimensional problems.

Keywords: genetic programming, evolutionary art, multi-objective optimization

1.   Introduction

Evolutionary art is a well-established application area of evolutionary algorithms in the fine arts (Dorin, 2001; Whitelaw, 2002; Bentley and Corne, 2002). Dawkins first proposed the idea with his Biomorphs system, which generated 2-dimensional line drawings of figures (Dawkins, 1996). His intent was to show the variety of structures possible with evolution. Sims popularized the concept further, by evolving a number of highly complex and innovative images (Sims, 1993). Since that time, many others have explored the technology; some examples are (Bentley and Corne, 2002; Graf and Banzhaf, 1995; Lewis, 2000; Romero and Machado, 2008; Rooke, 2002; Todd and Latham, 1992).

Most evolutionary art applications have traditionally been interactive evolutionary algorithms, in which a user is the "fitness function", and manually assigns scores to images based on their suitability. The idea of automatic image generation has attracted interest. Earlier systems performed a suite of computer vision analyses on candidate images (Ibrahim, 1998; Wiens and Ross, 2002). The feature tests attempted to refine visual aspects of the images, such as color palette, luminosity ranges, or shapes.

Recently, the use of models of aesthetics have been considered, with the goal being the automatic generation of images that are visually appealing. Aesthetics is one of the most complex aspects of human cognition. Contemporary theories are pioneering explorations into the field, and they are necessarily rudimentary and superficial. No theory has been derived yet that encapsulates the substantial complexities contributing to notions of beauty. Therefore, as can be expected, the results of evolutionary art using aesthetic models are highly subjective. An image with good aesthetic scores may be unremarkable. Conversely, interesting images may have less-than-ideal scores. Hence, overall results are difficult to evaluate in empirically. Furthermore, artistic aesthetics relies upon complex cultural contexts and perspectives (Spector and Alpern, 1994), and a comprehensive, machine-interpretable theory of aesthetics still seems far from realization. Contemporary evolutionary art systems should be viewed as support tools for guiding and inspiring creativity, rather than autonomous systems that will replace human artists.

An early attempt at computationally encoding notions of visual aesthetics was in (Baluja et al., 1994), which attempted to train a neural network on aesthetically pleasing images. (Svangard and Nordin, 2004) reapproached the problem by using distance measurements against a library of images. Neither approach, however, was implemented within an evolutionary algorithm. The NEvAr system suggests a model of aesthetics that posits that pleasing images are both simple and repetitive, which can be measured by JPEG and fractal compression ratios (Machado and Cardoso, 1998; Machado and Cardoso, 2002). The model performed well on a standard art school test.

This paper uses Ralph's aesthetic model, which suggests that viewers are attracted to changes in color in an image (Ralph, 2006). The desired balance of color gradient change is based on the empirical analysis of many masterpieces, where it was discovered that many such paintings exhibit a bell curve distribution of color gradient. On the other hand, photographs, graphic design-oriented art, and images on a web site of "bad art" did not exhibit this distribution. This may be an unconscious goal of many artists.

Ralph's aesthetic model has been successfully used for image synthesis (Neufeld et al., 2008; Ross et al., 2006). Multi-objective Pareto ranking was used to evaluate the aesthetic and other feature test scores. This resulted in the synthesis of many intriguing images, with the benefit of producing a set of undominated solutions from which to choose. Unfortunately, a common result was the generation of outliers – images that score high in only one or two feature tests, and mediocre in the rest. Given that the aesthetic model uses 3 statistical measurements together (Bell curve fit, mean, standard deviation), it is unsuitable to have, for example, the standard deviation being a high matching feature, while the fit and mean are poor. With Pareto ranking, however, outliers are to be expected, due to the nature of dominance.

This paper shows how a summed rank scoring is beneficial in this problem domain. By considering the sum of ranks of the component dimensions of each individual, outliers are discouraged, and the generated results are better performers on the majority of feature tests. We show this by considering an analyses of fitness vectors obtained from both summed rank and Pareto ranking strategies. Although the scheme was originally proposed for use in high-dimensional multi-objective problems (Bentley and Wakefield, 1997), we show that it is also effective for low-dimensional problems. Note that our goal is not to evaluate the aesthetic merits of the images themselves. In fact, the central theme of this paper is not evolutionary art *per se*, but the comparison of summed rank and Pareto scoring strategies using an evolutionary art system as a test framework. The reader is referred to (Neufeld et al., 2008; Ross et al., 2006) for treatments of Ralphs's aesthetic model and evolutionary art.

Section 2 reviews the multi-objective strategies used in this research. The JNetic Textures system is described in Section 3. Experiment showing the benefits of our multi-objective approach are described in Section 4, and the results are shown in Section 5. Conclusions are given in Section 6.

2. Multi-objective Evaluation Strategies

A multi-objective optimization problem is one in which multiple features must be optimized together. The optimization may require features to be minimized, maximized, or made equivalent to some constraint value (which is equivalent to minimizing the error between the feature and the constraint). These features often affect each other in complex, nonlinear ways (Coello et al., 2007). Consider a feature vector $\vec{v} = (f_1, ..., f_k)$ for some $k > 1$, in which the f_i are to be minimized. The minimization problem can be cast into a single-objective optimization problem by defining a weighted sum of these objectives: $F = \sum_i w_i f_i$. Weights w_i are usually used to help flatten the search space, by rebalancing the feature scores with respect to each other. Of course, given the complexity of most problems, weights are necessarily *ad hoc* in nature. Unfortunately, ill-defined weights can severely handicap the performance of search algorithms.

Pareto ranking is the most common evaluation strategy in multi-objective search (Goldberg, 1989). Pareto ranking is a partial ordering, which uses the notion of *domination*. Individual a is said to dominate b if it is superior in at least one feature, and no worse in the remaining features. Letting a be denoted by feature vector $\vec{a} = (a_1, ..., a_k)$ (and similarly for b):

$$a \ \ dominates \ \ b \ \ iff \ \ \exists i : a_i < b_i \ \ \wedge \ \ \forall i : a_i \leq b_i.$$

Next, a Pareto ranking is defined. Given a population of individuals, those that are undominated are assigned a rank of 1. They are then marked as used, and the remaining individuals that are undominated are assigned a rank of 2. This continues until the entire population is ranked. These Pareto ranks become the fitness scores for evolutionary search, where lower ranks are preferable.

A solution is said to be *Pareto optimal* if there is no other vector in the search space that dominates it. Therefore, during a run of an evolutionary algorithm, the ideal is to discover a set of Pareto optimal solutions. Given the difficulty inherent many real-world problems, a more pragmatic goal is to produce an approximation of Pareto-optimal solutions, as far as can be determined by the evolutionary search.

Pareto ranking has been successfully applied to many multi-objective problems. Its main benefit is that heterogeneous objectives do not need to be explicitly reconciled during fitness evaluation, as is necessary in the weighted sum approach. Another benefit is the ability to have a set of undominated solutions produced during a run. Unfortunately, Pareto ranking has limitations. Premature convergence due to loss of genetic diversity in the population is common, and much effort has been undertaken to introduce diversity promotion stategies (Coello et al., 2007). Furthermore, Pareto ranking is usually practical up to a maximum of 3 or 4 objectives. Higher-dimensional problems typically result in highly undominated populations, because individuals will likely be undominated due to pure chance. Such situations result in a collapse of selective pressure, and evolution becomes ineffective.

Alternative multi-objective scoring strategies can be used for higher dimensional problems. This paper follows a basic approach in (Bentley and Wakefield, 1997), which works as follows. Consider a search problem with feature vectors $\vec{v} = (f_1, ..., f_k)$. First, the rank of each individual feature score f_i with respect to that feature within the entire population of vectors is determined: $\vec{v}_{rank} = (r_1, ..., r_k)$. Each r_i is the ordered rank of the corresponding f_i. For example, a rank of $r_i = 1$ is assigned to the feature value in the vector having the best (optimal) score in objective i. Once the rank vectors are obtained, a weighted summed rank score is derived for each individual: $Fit = \sum_i w_i r_i$. The weights w_i are problem specific, and by default are 1. This weighted sum of

Fitness vector	Pareto rank	Rank vector	Sum ranks
(10, 20, 20)	1	(1, 2, 2)	5
(20, 10, 10)	1	(2, 1, 1)	4
(20, 20, 30)	2	(2, 2, 3)	7
(30, 40, 30)	3	(3, 4, 3)	10
(500, 30, 500)	3	(4, 3, 4)	11

Table 14-1. Examples of Pareto rank and summed rank scores. Fitness values are being minimized.

ranks is functionally equivalent to the average r_i rank in a vector. By definition, ranks are relative, and are abstracted from the actual feature measurements. Hence the weight terms, if used, are insensitive to feature metric scales as with weighted sum scores at the beginning of this section.

The summed rank is more suitable for high-dimensional problems than Pareto ranking. It creates a more diverse, stratified fitness space than Pareto ranking in high-dimensional search problems, which in turn is better suited for fitness-driven evolution. It avoids the degenerate case seen in Pareto ranking, in which most of the population is undominated, and has the same fitness score.

Some example scores for fitness vectors are in Table 14-1. If a tournament selection scheme is used (as in this paper), the sum rank scores can be used directly as fitness values. Otherwise, it is possible to re-rank them again (the values then being 2, 1, 3, 4, 5 respectively). From the table, it is clear that Pareto ranks and summed ranks result in different overall score values and orderings. Summed ranks will usually create a higher diversity of score values than Pareto. The differences between them become even more pronounced for higher dimension problems.

3. The JNetic Textures System

JNetic Textures is an evolutionary art application for interactive and automatic image synthesis. At its core is a genetic programming kernel that uses the ECJ system (Luke, 2010). Like other evolutionary art systems, genetic programming constructs a texture formula (Ebert et al., 1998). An example of a procedural texture is the following:

```
Red:     (X+25) mod 60
Green:   cos(X*Y)-Y
Blue:    12
```

These three equations compute the values of the red, green, and blue channels, which together define the RGB color of a pixel. The equations are denoted

Mathematical operators	Texture/color mixing
+, -, *, /	Alpha blending
sine, cosine, power, log, mod	Mix 2 textures
	Mix texture and RGB

Texture terminals	
Random noise	Geometric shapes
Grass	Circles
Mandelbrot	Rectangles
Perlin Noise	Triangles
Marble	
Fireball	Misc terminals
Fur	pixel x, y
	ephem constant

Table 14-2. Language Primitives

by 3 branches near the root of the GP tree, and the mathematical expressions are composed in the usual way within a tree-based GP representation. Before interpreting these formulae to compute a color, the 2-D coordinate values of the current pixel to be rendered are set in the X and Y terminals. Subsequent execution of the formulae results in an RGB color value for that pixel.

Some example calculations using the above texture equations are now given. It is assumed that a 24-bit color space is being used, where each R, G, and B channel is denoted by an 8-bit integer, and hence ranges in value from 0 to 255. Since the primitives in the equations are floating point, the computed float values are converted to integers. Values that lay outside the range [0, 255] are "clamped" to these extrema. For example, negative values will be assigned zero. Using the above equations, a pixel with the XY-coordinate (0, 0) will have the RGB color (0, 1, 12) computed for it, which is very close to black. On the other hand, the coordinate (100, 100) will result in the RGB color (65, 0, 12), which is a dark scarlet. The expression is interpreted in this way over the pixel coordinate values for the entire bitmap. The equations define a color for any possible 2D coordinate value. Hence we say that the formulae define a "texture space", with a color defined at every position in the 2D coordinate system. Because changes in the coordinate values of the bitmap can result in different computed images, the coordinate range is user-specified. The end result of the texture-computation step is a mathematically-generated bitmap image, which will be analyzed during fitness evaluation (next section).

Formulae constructed by the GP kernel use a variety of primitives (Table 14-2). Basic mathematical operators such as arithmetic, trigonometric, log, and others, are common with other systems. Higher-level operators such as turbulence, Mandelbrot fractals, and fur are also available. Use of these primitives comes at a cost in performance, as they are extremely slow to render.

JNetic Textures has the ability to mix texture formulae with vector graphics-style geometric shapes, for example, circles, rectangles, and triangles. When used, the texture tree has two branches at the root: the usual RGB texture branch described above, and a branch with a chain of shapes. Each shape has information regarding its size and location, as well as a texture argument. For example, a circle object has a center coordinate (X,Y), a radius, and a texture expression. This texture expression is used to color the shape during scan conversion. When rendering an entire image, the main texture expression is used to completely render the background canvas. Then geometric shapes are rendered above it, using their own texture expressions.

Letting a user move back and forth between automatic and interactive evolution is a goal of JNetic Textures. Automatic evolution permits genetic programming to do what it does best – search for an image that satisfies challenging technical criteria. Automatic evolution lets the GP system use a selection of image analysis functions, based on aesthetics and color evaluation (described below). Interactive evolution relies on a user to inspect the population of candidate images, and then manually assign fitness scores. This allows the user to influence search directly, by applying his or her own criteria to the images being evolved. The user may switch between interactive or automatic processing at any time during a run. This lets JNetic Textures become an artistic tool, to be used in a manner the artist finds most helpful.

Fitness Evaluation

JNetic Textures uses Ralph's model of aesthetics (Ralph, 2006), which has been used in previous research in image and filter evolution (Neufeld et al., 2008; Ross et al., 2006). A brief overview of this model is now given. A color palette fitness test is also discussed.

Ralph's aesthetic model measures the color gradient distribution in an image, and then tests how well it fits a normal distribution. First, the color gradient is computed:

$$|\nabla r_{i,j}|^2 = \frac{(r_{i,j} - r_{i+1,j+1})^2 + (r_{i+1,j} - r_{i,j+1})^2}{d^2}$$

where $r_{i,j}$ is the red value at pixel (i,j), and d is a scaling factor. Green and blue are similarly processed. Then an overall gradient or *stimulus* S is calculated:

$$S_{i,j} = \sqrt{|\nabla r_{i,j}|^2 + |\nabla g_{i,j}|^2 + |\nabla b_{i,j}|^2}$$

Finally, the *response* R is computed:

$$R_{i,j} = log(S_{i,j}/S_0)$$

where S_0 is the threshold of detection, which is taken to be 2. A value of $S_{i,j} = 0$ (no change in color) is ignored.

The distribution of R is then estimated using a weighted normal distribution, defined by a mean (μ) and standard deviation (σ^2):

$$\mu = \frac{\sum_{i,j}(R_{i,j})^2}{\sum_{i,j}R_{i,j}} \qquad \sigma^2 = \frac{\sum_{i,j}R_{i,j}(R_{i,j}-\mu)^2}{\sum_{i,j}R_{i,j}}$$

Once μ and σ^2 are found for an image, the actual distribution of all $R_{i,j}$ for all pixels in the image is tabulated. Using a bin width of $\sigma/100$, a histogram is calculated, where each $R_{i,j}$ updates its bin using a weight of $R_{i,j}$.

Finally, the fit between the response actual distribution and the hypothesized bell distribution is determined. This is the *deviation from normality* or DFN:

$$DFN = 1000 \sum p_i log(\frac{p_i}{q_i})$$

where p_i is the observed probability in the ith bin of the histogram, and q_i is the expected probability assuming a normal distribution with the computed mean and standard deviation above. When $q_i = 0$, that bin is ignored. A DFN of 0 indicates a fit to a normal distribution.

In summary, the above computations result in 3 measurements that can be used as fitness measurements – μ, σ^2 and DFN. DFN is always minimized, while μ and σ^2 are given target values. For example, values of DFN=0, $\mu = 3.3$ and $\sigma^2 = 0.75$ were reported by Ralph in his studies of Impressionist masterpieces (Ralph, 2006). From one perspective, the precision of the aesthetic evaluation is not too critical. The main benefit of this model is that it permits image complexity to be controlled with three parameters. Its focus on image complexity puts it in the same category of aesthetic modeling as NEvAr (Machado and Cardoso, 2002).

Another automatic fitness test is color palette matching, which influences the color choices used in an image. A target image is read at the start of a run. A histogram of 512 quantized color frequencies is determined, and this is saved as a color target. Color quantization reduces the number of colors recorded in an image to the 512 most frequent ones. During evolution, a candidate image is likewise converted into a quantized 512-color histogram. The sum of errors between the histograms is determined. A value of zero is a perfect match – the evolved image uses the same quantized colors in the same proportions as the target image. Although it is relatively fast to do this calculation, it is a strict color matching scheme that is difficult to satisfy in the best of circumstances.

4.   Experiment Description

A set of genetic programming runs were performed, with the goal of illus-trating the quantitative differences between summed rank and Pareto evaluation

Parameter	Value
Color target images	5
Runs per target image	10 (5 summed rank + 5 Pareto)
Maximum generations	25 (summed rank), 25 & 100 (Pareto)
Population size	500
GP language	math, noise, circles, rects
Prob. crossover	90%
Max tree depth	17
Tournament size	4
Features	DFN, mean, std dev, CHIST

Table 14-3. GP Parameters

strategies. We will show quantitative differences in solution sets and their feature scores between the two techniques. These differences should indicate advantages and disadvantages of these approaches, for this and other similar low-order multi-objective problems. Our evolutionary art application can be considered to be a challenging low-order multi-objective problem in which outlier solutions are undesirable.

Table 14-3 shows various parameters used for the runs. Five different images were selected as color palette targets (CHIST feature), which can be viewed on the web site[1]. All these images were less than 200 by 200 pixels in resolution. To begin a run for a target image, a selection of texture language primitives were chosen. The full set of mathematical operators in Table 14-2 was used, as was the basic noise generator. More expensive functions such as Mandelbrot or Perlin were not used, due to their high computational cost. Various combinations and sizes of geometric primitives were selected. All runs use the following four feature tests and target values: (i) DFN=0.0; (ii) mean=3.75; (iii) standard deviation=0.75; (iv) color palette matching, CHIST=0.0. For ranked sums, all weights are set to 1.0. For each target image, 5 separate runs with fresh random number seeds were performed for each of ranked sum and Pareto fitness strategies. This results in 50 separate runs – 25 for each strategy.

Another set of 25 runs was done for the Pareto strategy, but with the maximum generations set to 100, and other parameters as above. These were done in case the Pareto runs are unable to adequately converge within 25 generations.

	Mean		Std dev		DFN		CHIST	
	μ	σ^2	μ	σ^2	μ	σ^2	μ	σ^2
(1)	3.84	0.19	0.77	0.14	1.11	2.05	30276.7	2859.4
(2)	3.61	1.16	1.20	0.91	14.93	37.06	38340.7	2441.0
(3)	3.09	1.15	1.47	1.09	15.96	40.12	38403.0	2542.3
target	3.75		0.75		0.0		0.0	

Table 14-4. Population statistics. Rows are (1) summed ranks, (2) Pareto 25 gens, and (3) Pareto 100 gens

5.   Results

Before presenting the main results, a few general observations should be given. A significant difference between the summed rank and Pareto runs is that the summed rank runs behave like single-objective genetic algorithms: runs converge to single small area of the search space. Such runs essentially generate a single solution image. The Pareto runs, on the other hand, converge to a set of solutions scattered throughout the Pareto front. A single Pareto run will produce a "family" of solutions, which are often quite diverse in appearance.

Another observation is that the color palette test (CHIST) is extremely challenging to satisfy, and especially in parallel with the other aesthetic tests. Consequently, performance differences between the summed rank and Pareto strategies on the color palette test is not pronounced. The CHIST test can be considered to be one that impacts the complexity of the search space for all runs.

The DFN score is also a difficult feature test to satisfy to a precise level. Although the DFN scores that follow are small in scale, the DFN formula is logarithmic. Very low DFN scores (less than 0.5) indicate a close fit to a normal distribution. Hence the scores we obtain are not necessarily representative of exceptional fits to normal distributions. Although quite low DFN scores are often seen in the population, they are usually accompanied by poor mean and standard deviation scores. Ralph's aesthetic model is not easy to satisfy.

Table 14-4 shows some population statistics for the runs. We use μ and σ^2 to denote mean and standard deviation, and these are distinguished from the feature tests of the same name. Standard deviations were calculated by finding the σ^2 for each separate GP run, and then averaging them across all runs and target images for each of the three experiment types. The main observation from this table is that the standard deviation for the Pareto runs are significantly

---

[1] http://www.cosc.brocku.ca/bross/JNeticTextures/paper_images/

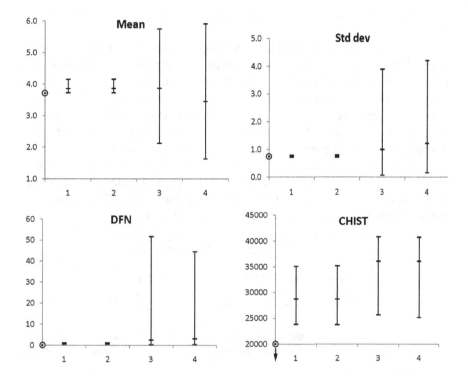

Figure 14-1. Solution feature score range bars – min, max, avg. Smaller bars are preferred. Columns represent (1) summed rank, (2) summed rank w/o duplicates, (3) Pareto (25 gen), and (4) Pareto (100 gen).

higher than for the summed rank. The Pareto populations have a more diverse range of values for each feature, since they reside throughout the Pareto front in the search space. The summed rank was also the best performer on all the features, and in particular, the DFN score.

It is sensible to consider the best performers in a population, since they are normally the only ones given consideration as potential solutions. Figure 14-1 shows the ranges of scores obtained for the elite scoring individuals in the runs. Column 1 in the charts are the ranges found for the top 50 solutions (50 lowest scores) for the summed rank runs. Since most summed rank runs produce many duplicate solutions, column 2 is a refinement of the ranked sum results, with duplicates removed as follows. The top 100 solutions were taken, and all duplicates were removed. Then the remaining top-scoring unique solutions were used, up to a maximum of 50. Column 3 is for the top 50 solutions from the 25-generation Pareto runs, selected from rank 1, and higher ranks if necessary. Column 4 is like column 3, but for the 100-generation Pareto runs. The bullseye on the vertical axis of each chart shows the target value for the feature. CHIST uses a target of 0.

Figure 14-1 shows that all the feature target values (other than CHIST) are adequately covered by the range of scores for the runs. The summed rank runs have honed in precisely to the target scores for each feature, while the Pareto solutions admit a wide range of scores beyond each target value. The removal of duplicates and expanding the solution set size of the summed rank runs (column 2) has negligible effect on the range of scores obtained. This suggests that a large portion of the summed rank population has converged. We also found that duplicate removal had a minor effect on standard deviation measurements (not shown) of summed rank solutions. Finally, running Pareto to 100 generations also has little impact on the range or quality of solutions obtained, which suggests that 25 generations is adequate.

	K= 0	1	2	3	4
Summed rank	99.5	0.5	0	0	0
Pareto	37.0	42.4	15.1	4.5	1.0

Table 14-5. Percentage of solutions having K outlying features. A feature is considered an outlier if it lays outside of one standard deviation (σ) from the population average. We use the Pareto run σ.

It is clear that the Pareto populations are more diverse than summed rank runs. To show the nature of this diversity, an analysis was performed in Table 14-5 to see how much of the population had features outside of a reasonable range. Such individuals are outliers, since they are diverging from the population norm on one or more feature values. Again, the top 50 solutions were considered from each run. We define the feature range to be the σ^2 for the feature score taken from the Pareto run for that target image. The Pareto σ^2 is used because we need a standard by which both summed rank and Pareto can be compared to each other. Table 14-5 shows that roughly 63% of the Pareto solutions have at least one feature that is outside the σ^2 range from the population average. This compares to only 0.5% of the summed rank solutions. Furthermore, Pareto solutions are often outliers on multiple features, and on occasion, all of them.

Figure 14-2 shows the performance curves for the summed rank and Pareto runs, for each of the feature test objectives. These are averaged over all runs for all target images, and plot the average raw feature scores over time, for the generation best and population average scores. A bullseye on the vertical axis indicates the target value. For the three tractable features (mean, standard deviation, DFN), there is always a best individual in the summed rank and Pareto runs that scores close to the target value for that feature. Both ranked sum and Pareto are equivalent in this regard. However, these graphs obscure the fact that

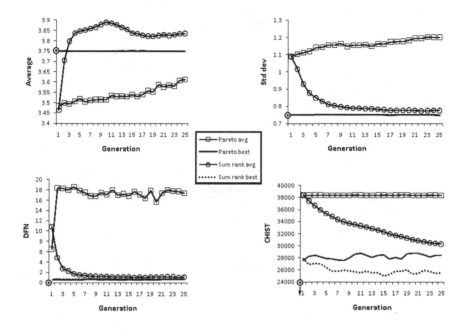

Figure 14-2. Performance curves for the 4 objectives.

such individuals are not necessarily scoring well in multiple features simultaneously. It has already been noted that there are a large number of outliers in the Pareto population. Looking at the population averages, both ranked sum and Pareto make progress with respect to the average score. The remaining features are also handled well by ranked sum, while they are problematic for the Pareto populations. Naturally, the diversity of the Pareto populations is a factor for these non-converging curves. Note that there were undefined average DFN scores in the Pareto populations, due to divide by zero computations for some degenerate cases; this contributes to the chaotic behaviour in the DFN plot for the Pareto population average curve.

Figure 14-3 are scatter plots of sum rank and Pareto solutions from one set of runs for a target image. We disregard CHIST here, due to its poor convergence for all runs. All the rank 1 solutions from the Pareto runs are plotted, and the sum rank are the top 50 solutions with duplicates removed (see the earlier description for Figure 14-1). The bullseye on the DFN plot denotes the exact spot on the XY plane for both the mean and DFN. Separate bullseyes are used on the mean vs standard deviation plot, so as to not obscure the plot of rank sum points. The Pareto solutions are indeed widely scattered, and it is clear how outliers will exist in this solution set. The rank sum solutions are converged to the target score location.

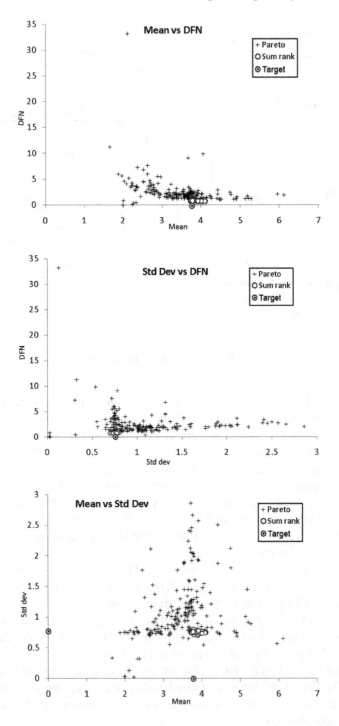

Figure 14-3. Solution scatter plots: sum rank and Pareto solutions from one run.

Two solution images can be found on the web site[2]. An image from a Pareto run is a typical outlier solution, with the following objective scores: mean=2.71, stdev=0.76, DFN=6.37, CHIST=23268. It is given rank 1 status entirely due to its standard deviation being close to the target value of 0.75. Its other scores are poor. The image from the summed rank run has these objective scores: mean=3.75, stdev=0.77, DFN=1.12, CHIST=15942. The summed rank image is superior on all scores, except its standard deviation is a bit weaker than that of the Pareto image. It has much more visual interest than the Pareto image, which is predicted by Ralph's aesthetic model. It is interesting to consider the situation that both images are in the same population under Pareto and sum of rank strategies. Neither image is superior in terms of Pareto dominance. However, either image could have a stronger Pareto rank than the other, as their Pareto rankings will also depend upon their relationships to other population members. In a sum of ranks run, although it is possible that the Pareto image could have a stronger sum of ranks score, it is probably unlikely to be the case, given that the right-side image is superior in 3 of the 4 objectives.

6.   Discussion and conclusion

The analysis in Section 5 is not intended to be a critique of Pareto ranking. Pareto ranking is popular precisely because it treats features independently, and permits the generation of solutions that adhere to the notion of Pareto dominance. For many application problems, this is a suitable characterization of solution quality. For applications such as JNetic Texture's aesthetic image evaluation, however, Pareto dominance is not so desirable. When evaluating color gradient distributions, having one of the distribution metrics score well, but the others score poorly, is normally unsatisfactory. This is especially problematic considering that there exist individuals in a random population will score fairly well on one of the objectives. The *best* curves in Figure 14-2 show that this is the case. Although the mean, standard deviation, and DFN features are intimately related, as they define the overall gradient distribution, it is still preferable to treat them as independent multiple objectives. This alleviates discovering a weighting relationship between them – which is difficult to do for the complex search space in this problem domain.

The most important result in this study is that summed rank performed so well in this problem domain. Although summed rank was originally intended for high-dimensional multi-objective problems, we have found it practical for low-dimensional problems such as our aesthetic image analysis. Runs usually converge on solutions that adhere to desired color distribution values. In fact, the 25 generations used in the runs is probably excessive, as populations usually

---

[2]http://www.cosc.brocku.ca/bross/JNeticTextures/paper_images/

converge by generation 15. Even though chromosomes in generation 0 may be high scorers on single objectives, the summed rank runs are searching for chromosomes that are strong in all objectives simultaneously. Pareto runs, however, are not focussed on this goal. Although strength in multiple objectives is always an advantage, it is not a necessary condition of Pareto dominance.

A minor enhancement that we have been exploring is the use of normalization during summed rank calculations. Referring to Table 14-1, by dividing each column in the rank vectors by the maximum rank, normalized values between 0 and 1 are obtained. The sum of these rescaled values is used as the fitness score. Normalizing the ranks tends to create an even fairer improvement of all objectives during evolution.

One advantage of Pareto ranking in evolutionary art is that it generates a diverse selection of images at the end of a run. Although many outlier images may be unsuitable, others may be of great interest. This is because most aesthetic models are at best heuristic measures of aesthetics, and feature scores should not be taken too literally. Interesting images reside in a large gradient space, which represents a wide latitude of acceptable scores. Therefore, although many solutions generated by Pareto ranking may not have exceptional feature scores, they can still be appealing. On the other hand, the convergence that arises with summed rank scoring means that only one solution arises at the end of the run. To obtain the same diversity of solutions as seen with Pareto, one will need to perform many more runs.

Other multi-objective scoring strategies for high-dimensional problems have been proposed (Corne and Knowles, 2007), and many of these could be used in place of summed rank. One contemporary approach called the average rank on undominated front (ARF) has been shown to be effective for high-dimensional problems (Corne and Knowles, 2007). To compute it, the undominated subset of the population is first determined. The weighted summed rank scores is found for this set, and it is then used for reproduction for the next generation. This works well for high-dimensional problems, because a large proportion of the population will be undominated (and hence the failure of pure Pareto ranking). For this reason, ARF is unsuitable for low-dimensional problems like ours. The pool of undominated individuals is relatively small. It is usually around 15 for generation 0 in our runs. Genetic diversity would be greatly handicapped if such a small set of individuals were used for subsequent reproduction.

We have not made any analytical or subjective arguments about the actual aesthetic quality of the images we obtained in the course of our experiments. Rather, we have made our case strictly using the score measurements obtained from our experiments. We have used summed rank scoring successfully in multi-objective applications in 2D floor plan design, 3D model synthesis, and bio-network modeling. Our results should be applicable to many other modest-sized multi-objective search problems, in which a consensus of high performance in many objectives is preferred, and in which outliers are undesirable.

Acknowledgements: Helpful suggestions by the reviewers is gratefully acknowledged. Research supported by an OGS award, and NSERC Operating Grant 138467.

References

Baluja, S., Pomerleau, D., and Jochem, T. (1994). Towards Automated Artificial Evolution for Computer-generated Images. *Connection Science*, 6(2/3):325–354.

Bentley, P. and Corne, D.W. (2002). *Creative Evolutionary Systems*. Morgan Kaufmann.

Bentley, P.J. and Wakefield, J.P. (1997). Finding acceptable solutions in the pareto-optimal range using multiobjective genetic algorithms. In *Soft Computing in Engineering Design and Manufacturing*. Springer Verlag.

Coello, C.A. Coello, Lamont, G.B., and Veldhuizen, D.A. Van (2007). *Evolutionary Algorithms for Solving Multi-Objective Problems*. Kluwer, 2 edition.

Corne, D. and Knowles, J. (2007). Techniques for highly multiobjective optimisation: Some nondominated points are better than others. In *Proceedings GECCO 2007*, pages 773–780. ACM Press.

Dawkins, R. (1996). *The Blind Watchmaker*. W.W Norton.

Dorin, A. (2001). Aesthetic Fitness and Artificial Evolution for the Selection of Imagery from the Mythical Infinite Library. In *Advances in Artificial Life – Proc. 6th European Conference on Artificial Life*, pages 659–668. Springer-Verlag.

Ebert, D.S., Musgrave, F.K., Peachey, D., Perlin, K., and Worley, S. (1998). *Texturing and Modeling: a Procedural Approach*. Academic Press, 2 edition.

Goldberg, D.E. (1989). *Genetic Algorithms in Search, Optimization, and Machine Learning*. Addison Wesley.

Graf, J. and Banzhaf, W. (1995). Interactive Evolution of Images. In *Proc. Intl. Conf. on Evolutionary Programming*, pages 53–65.

Ibrahim, A.E.M. (1998). *GenShade: an Evolutionary Approach to Automatic and Interactive Procedural Texture Generation*. PhD thesis, Texas A&M University.

Lewis, M. (2000). Aesthetic Evolutionary Design with Data Flow Networks. In *Proc. Generative Art 2000*.

Luke, S. (2010). Ecj. Last accessed Feb 24, 2010.

Machado, P. and Cardoso, A. (1998). Computing Aesthetics. In *Proc. XIVth Brazilian Symposium on AI*, pages 239–249. Springer-Verlag.

Machado, P. and Cardoso, A. (2002). All the Truth About NEvAr. *Applied Intelligence*, 16(2):101–118.

Neufeld, C., Ross, B., and Ralph, W. (2008). The Evolution of Artistic Filters. In Romero, J. and Machado, P., editors, *The Art of Artificial Evolution*. Springer.

Ralph, W. (2006). Painting the Bell Curve: The Occurrence of the Normal Distribution in Fine Art. *In preparation.*

Romero, J. and Machado, P. (2008). *The Art of Artificial Evolution.* Springer.

Rooke, S. (2002). Eons of Genetically Evolved Algorithmic Images. In Bentley, P.J. and Corne, D.W., editors, *Creative Evolutionary Systems*, pages 330–365. Morgan Kaufmann.

Ross, B.J., Ralph, W., and Zong, H. (2006). Evolutionary Image Synthesis Using a Model of Aesthetics. In *CEC 2006*.

Sims, K. (1993). Interactive evolution of equations for procedural models. *The Visual Computer*, 9:466–476.

Spector, L. and Alpern, A. (1994). Criticism, culture, and the automatic generation of artworks. In *Proc. AAAI-94*, pages 3–8. AAAI Press/MIT Press.

Svangard, N. and Nordin, P. (2004). Automated Aesthetic Selection of Evolutionary Art by Distance Based Classification of Genomes and Phenomes using the Universal Similarity Metric. In *Applications of Evolutionary Computing: EvoWorkshops 2004*, pages 447–456. Springer. LNCS 3005.

Todd, S. and Latham, W. (1992). *Evolutionary Art and Computers*. Academic Press.

Whitelaw, M. (2002). Breeding Aesthetic Objects: Art and Artificial Evolution. In Bentley, P. and Corne, D.W., editors, *Creative Evolutionary Systems*, pages 129–145. Morgan Kaufmann.

Wiens, A.L. and Ross, B.J. (2002). Gentropy: Evolutionary 2D Texture Generation. *Computers and Graphics Journal*, 26(1):75–88.

Index